"I can't think of anyone who knows more about, and has a deeper love for, the early days of NW R&B and rock 'n' roll than Peter Blecha. Lucky for us, he shares his love and knowledge in *Stomp and Shout*!"

Mark Arm, Mudhoney

"An impressive geo-musical chronicle of the pre-grunge Pacific Northwest music scene with an insightful and fresh approach that adds an essential layer of voices to this critical chorus of music writers, historians, and artists."

George Plasketes, author of *Warren Zevon: Desperado of Los Angeles*

"Grunge fans should check out *Stomp and Shout*, a meticulously detailed early history of Northwest R&B and rock and roll. Blecha presents a fascinating narrative of the globally influential garage bands that also inspired Sub Pop Records. Highly recommended!"

Bruce Pavitt, cofounder of Sub Pop Records

"*Stomp and Shout* extensively covers not only the broader history but also the intimate details of the journeys of Northwest musicians, including my grandfather Dave Lewis. A must-read for every musician in the greater Pacific Northwest."

D'Vonne Lewis, band leader/musician/drummer/poet

"*Stomp and Shout* succeeds in making the case for the Northwest Sound as a distinct musical genre and as a significant element of both Black culture and youth culture with a lasting impact on the regional psyche."

Kurt Armbruster, author of *Before Seattle Rocked: A City and Its Music*

STOMP
and
SHOUT

STOMP
and
SHOUT

R&B and the Origins of
Northwest Rock and Roll

PETER BLECHA

UNIVERSITY OF WASHINGTON PRESS   *Seattle*

A MICHAEL J. REPASS BOOK
Stomp and Shout was made possible in part by a grant from
the Michael J. Repass Fund for Northwest Writers.

CULTURE
This publication was also supported by a grant from
the 4Culture Heritage Special Projects program.

Additional support was provided by generous gifts from
Woods Fairbanks and Michael T. Wing.

Design by Thomas Eykemans
Composed in Source Serif, typeface
designed by Frank Grießhammer

28 27 26 25 24   5 4 3 2 1
Printed and bound in the United States
of America

UNIVERSITY OF WASHINGTON PRESS
uwapress.uw.edu

LIBRARY OF CONGRESS CATALOGING-
IN-PUBLICATION DATA
Names: Blecha, Peter, author.
Title: Stomp and shout : R&B and the origins
of Northwest rock and roll / Peter Blecha.
Description: Seattle : University of
Washington Press, 2023. | Includes
bibliographical references and index.
Identifiers: LCCN 2022039149 |
ISBN 9780295751252 (hardback) |
ISBN 9780295751269 (ebook)
Subjects: LCSH: Rock music—Northwest,
Pacific—To 1961—History and criticism. |
Rock music—Northwest, Pacific—
1961–1970—History and criticism. |
Rhythm and blues music—Northwest,
Pacific—History and criticism.
Classification: LCC ML3534.3 .B543 2023 |
DDC 781.6609795—dc23/eng/20220816
LC record available at https://lccn.loc
.gov/2022039149

ISBN 9780295753256 (paperback)

♾ This paper meets the requirements of
ANSI/NISO Z39.48-1992 (Permanence of
Paper).

CONTENTS

Illustrations follow pages 86 and 140

PREFACE

A quick note to the reader: this is a work of historical narrative. Though this book is the result of four-plus decades of research, it might never have been completed were it not for the COVID-19 lockdown of 2020–21. And that is because I had been assiduously avoiding the daunting task of writing it—a process that required digging back into the four hundred or so transcripts of interviews I had conducted with Northwest-based musicians, dance promoters, radio DJs, audio engineers, and record company operators. I'd known for years that it had to eventually be done—but *how* to ever find the time? But then I received a furlough notice from my job, so the time had arrived

After I cleaned up my garage, reorganized my record collection, and did everything else I could to distract myself, by April 2020 I was ready to buckle down. It had been a dozen years since my last book—*Sonic Boom: The History of Northwest Rock, from "Louie Louie" to "Smells like Teen Spirit"*—which admittedly covered *some* of the same history. And those years were not idle ones. So, *Stomp and Shout* benefits greatly from all the additional research invested in its development, which revealed plenty of new stories and unearthed previously unpublished photographs along the way.

The first big difference between the two books is that the former covered twice the time span (1957–1990s) in fewer words, while *Stomp and Shout* digs into the details of how rhythm and blues arose locally and morphed into the "Northwest rock" sound between about 1958 and 1965. The second is that *Stomp and Shout* is built on the direct quotes from the players themselves. Indeed, this book is only possible thanks to the cooperative spirit that those many interviewees brought to the table. My goal has been to capture their stories accurately, by faithfully presenting each person's unique way of expressing themselves. While those folks are generally quoted verbatim, in various cases some editing of their statements was done for concision or clarity.

ACKNOWLEDGMENTS

The creation of this book was only possible due to the contributions made by several hundred members of our music community who enthusiastically participated in interview sessions over the past five decades. Many of those individuals are no longer with us. But they told their stories, and we get to savor hearing from them.

A sincere note of gratitude must go out to a number of individuals who generously made available to this project quotes from their previously published books or interview notes: Mary Willix, author of *Jimi Hendrix, Voices from Home*; Paul de Barros, author of *Jackson Street after Hours: The Roots of Jazz in Seattle*; Claudia Doege, author of *Paul Revere and the Raiders: History ReBeats Itself*; and Little Bill Engelhart, musician and author of two published memoirs. Various musician interviews were also provided by Mike Feeney (who conducted them in the 1970s while a radio DJ at KUID) and Bruce Smith, the publisher-editor of the *Northwest Disc-Coveries and Sound Report* magazine and cofounder of the Northwest Music Archives website.

Special thanks are also due to a few folks who lent critical support along the way, including Little Bill Engelhart, Merrilee Rush, Peter Riches, Gino Rossi, Shelley Taylor, Linda Holden Givens, Pat Lee, Roger Wheeling, Jeff Miller, Eric Predoehl, Brenda Johnson Ford, Judy Shelman, the Museum of Pop Culture's Jacob McMurray and Stefanie Terasaki, the Museum of History & Industry's Aurora San Miguel, the Seattle Municipal Archives' Julie Irick, the Puget Sound Regional Archives' Midori Okazaki, and the Tacoma Public Library.

In addition, I wish to salute Andrew Berzanskis, senior acquisitions editor at the University of Washington Press, who instantly saw the value in having so many varied voices telling their own stories within these pages. Indeed, the entire UW Press team—including Nicole F. Mitchell, Caroline Hall, Kait Heacock, Laura K. Fish, David G. Schlangen, Molly Woolbright, and Mike Baccam—plus *Stomp and Shout*'s two extraordinarily skilled editors, Joeth Zucco and Nicholas Taylor—who all helped make the creation of this book a most enjoyable adventure.

Thanks once again to all!

INTRODUCTION
The Sea-Port Beat

Once upon a time—decades prior to "grunge" rock being even a gleam in Sub Pop's eye—the Pacific Northwest was the birthing ground to a rockin' R&B scene that created its own unique strain of rock 'n' roll. This was a distinctive "rude-jazz"–tinged mutation that erupted in the sea-port towns of Seattle, Tacoma, and Portland between the approximate years of 1958 and 1965 and would come to be called the original "Northwest Sound"—or in some circles the "Sea-Port Beat" or "Sea-Port Sound."

Music critics, historians, and even a few ivory-tower academics have explored the saga of the scene that produced this energetic music. But the deep backstory has never been told by the musicians who created the sounds, as well as key local music industry figures who pushed a remarkable number of their recordings into genuine radio-hit status. Now those luminaries finally get a chance to have the story presented in their own words.

One of the Seattle scene's most consequential music-biz cats of the 1940s and 1950s, Robert "Bumps" Blackwell, was well known for wielding a quiver of clever hipster sayings. Among them was one intended to encourage people around him to step up and speak what was on their mind: "Say the word, and you'll be heard." Interviews with over three hundred relevant individuals conducted between 1970 and 2021 provided the quoted recollections that make up the heart of this telling of their story.

The Northwest Sound's origins trace back to a small circle of budding young players who had initially been inspired by the '50s rhythm and blues hits they'd heard on records. Then, at mid-decade, a few promoters began bringing some of those very same hitmakers on tours through this region, so the locals got to witness genuine gutbucket R&B stars live and in person. By that point, a few leading local bands—in particular, Seattle's Dave Lewis Combo and Tacoma's Wailers—were carving out their own distinctive modes of rocking, and scores of subsequent bands copied their sounds. The eventual result was that a new mode of driving rock 'n' roll emerged—one that was particularly beholden to rude jazz, with all the blatting saxophones and rumbling organs that label implies.

Forged in the high school gyms, skating rinks, community halls, National Guard armories, and rowdy dance halls of the region, the Northwest Sound evolved incrementally, by trial and error. Local bands employed a process of experimentation, gauging the audience response to their song selections and noting what tunes were most effective in rousing their dance crowds. Along the way, astute bands copped certain musical elements from the vocabulary used by various R&B stars, and then used those as building blocks to create their own musical language. The result was a slew of hit records that went from regional radio novelties to national and international hits. Local fans loved that their own town's bands were successful, but outsiders also found these sounds impossible to resist.

So, while there are plenty of northwesterners who share a provincial pride in our region's musical arts, there's really no need to go too far out on a limb arguing that something unique and precious had occurred here. And that's because experts from *outside* the region have already made that case for us.

As early 1968, Barret Hansen—the California-based ethnomusicologist (and future radio host known as "Dr. Demento")—recognized that the Northwest had created something unique. He wrote that "there was, and perhaps still is, a very lively rock scene going on there, with a distinctive sound that has spread far and wide from the teen palaces of Portland, Tacoma and Seattle."

In 1973, Mark Shipper, founder and editor of California's *Flash* fanzine, wrote:

> The story of rock 'n' roll has been in large part the story of local sounds coming to national prominence—Liverpool, San Francisco, Detroit, to name a few. The distinctive "sound" of any given region usually came as a result of hordes of area bands that would attempt to imitate the local kingpins, thereby stamping their particular region with an instantly identifiable and recognizable music of its own. One very important but often overlooked sound was the one emanating from the Northwest USA. . . . These gritty bands were a far cry from what the rest of the country was listening to in the early 60s, and were, without realizing it, conditioning their audience to a taste and acceptance of music that those outside the Northwest simply would not be able to relate to. For this reason, major labels

avoided the area and, as a result, the Northwest Sound to this day remains an obscurity.

That same year, Ken Barnes wrote in the Boston-based *Fusion* magazine, "All over the country during the mid-Sixties, local band scenes sprang up with groups playing a crude and derivative, exuberant and energetic brand of rock 'n' roll for the home crowds. Great music came out of all these scenes, but unquestionably the raunchiest sounds emanated from the Pacific Northwest."

Then, in 1976, the New York City–based founder of *Kicks* magazine and Norton Records, Billy Miller, confessed, "As a tried and true East Coaster I can't tell downtown Seattle from uptown Tacoma—drop me off a bus in Portland and I may as well be on Mars. Despite my geographical shortcomings, however, I can spot a vintage Northwest disc at a hundred paces in a blizzard. It ain't all that hard mind you. There's a feel about the way they tend to pound a little harder and blast off faster than most rock & roll records." What made the Northwest Sound stand out was that "in an era of especially thin sounding dance records, these bands unleashed conspicuously explosive vehicles of thunder."

Echoing those thoughts, Greg Shaw, garage-rock historian and founder of California's *Bomp!* magazine, wrote, "Not every region of the United States had its own distinctive sound in the Garage Band Era (prolific as they were, places like Florida, Pennsylvania, Wisconsin, New England and Ohio certainly didn't)—but everybody knows instantly what is meant by The Northwest Sound."

Concurring with that observation, the British A&R agent Alec Palao once noted, "In regions as disparate as Texas, the Bay Area and the Southeast, white kids were playing black-styled R&B, but it would be safe to say that when it came to an unbridled fervor for rootsy rock and an accomplished reinterpretation of the same, the Pacific Northwest had everywhere else beat."

Another Brit, music historian Vernon Joynson, once observed, "The Pacific Northwest, from the late fifties onwards, had been the home of some of the finest instrumental combos in the land, bands like The Wailers, The Ventures, and The Frantics. What characterized them from the 'also rans' of the era was their very strong, powerful, upfront rhythm section. The music of the Northwest was raw, aggressive, and powerful."

The *Los Angeles Reader* once published an overview essay about our rock history that stated, "The *thang* in the Northwest was bruising, loud, and thoroughly unstudied bands that played primarily instrumental sets at local armories. Though the bands were white, they played gutbucket numbers, usually embellished with stomping horn lines and seesawing keyboard riffs, which bore a strong resemblance to instro R&B numbers of the day."

In 1984, Greg Shaw weighed in on this topic once again, offering this not-so-secret recipe behind the Northwest's magic music:

> Take a loud, sloppy, grungy band, give 'em an old R&B riff like "Louie Louie" or any Little Richard song, add a vocalist who has mastered the blood-curdling visceral scream and a guitarist conditioned to spring into action at the words "Let's give it to 'em!," and record the whole thing live in some teenage nightclub in suburban Oregon or Washington, and you've got a prototypical Northwest disc. It became a matter of pride for the bands to outdo one another in greasy crudeness. The 'frat bands' so common around the country would wither like pale slugs in the noonday sun before the onslaught of the least memorable band at any Northwest high school. Maybe it was the presence since the late '50s of such regional instrumental giants as the Raiders, Wailers, Ventures and others that taught area kids respect for the raunchy sax and powerhouse rhythm; whatever the sociological explanation, the Northwest had a standard of sonic integrity dimensions beyond that which prevailed elsewhere. The best Northwest bands, like the Sonics, hit realms of intensity unmatched by anybody, anywhere, anytime.

Grunge chronicler Brad Morrell noted, "There's a tradition of hard-edged, raw, unsophisticated rock music from Washington State. . . . Part rock 'n' roll instrumentals, part fierce rhythm and blues, their sound was blacker and heavier than anything from California or New York. As a result they were usually restricted to regional hits."

That fact was certainly one of the reasons that even *more* records didn't break out and decades later someone like Mark Shipper could fairly refer to Northwest rock as an "often overlooked sound" or the music critic Dave Marsh could reasonably describe all the local action as "a great lost rock 'n' roll scene." And he elaborated, "The biggest reason Seattle rock wasn't mass merchandised stemmed from its content.

Listening to the Wailers, the Sonics, the Frantics, and the rest involved direct and dangerous encounters with madness, poison, the edge of criminal lunacy. The best Seattle records sound like they were made by people involved in an occult ritual—in short, they appear as a prophecy of nineties grunge."

But it was the late Simon Fraser University professor of urban geography Warren Gill who put it best, when in 1993 he posited that "the rhythm-and-blues-based music of the dance halls of the region was, in its own way, as fresh an interpretation of the African-American roots of rock 'n' roll as that of the pioneers of the genre in the mid-1950s and the revival to come from the United Kingdom in the 1960s. In a period bereft of these elemental aspects of rock 'n' roll, the Northwest Sound was not simply a return to a previously successful formula, but a different evolutionary direction in response to local conditions."

Stomp and Shout is all about those "local conditions."

CHAPTER 1

ALONE IN THIS CITY

It was at around five o'clock on a brisk March morning back in 1948 that a grimy transcontinental Trailways bus coughed its way into Seattle's bleak, old downtown depot at 308 Virginia Street. Among the road-weary folks disembarking there was a skinny Black teenager from the Deep South who'd been stuck riding in that bus's back seats all the way across America. He arrived with only a chipboard suitcase and his dreams of starting a better life.

Ray Charles Robinson was a blind, seventeen-year-old music prodigy from Florida who had *zero* connections in this strange new town. But the kid harbored a burning desire to make his mark in the wide world of music. Back home, he'd already been a gigging member of Jacksonville's musicians' union but felt stifled there and chose to get far, far away by relocating to the opposite corner of the country. Stepping off that bus with no plans, the shy guy began asking strangers where he might get a room. Checking into one nearby and crashing for nearly twenty-four hours straight, he then asked the hotelkeeper where he could grab some grub.

She informed him that just about every restaurant was already closed—except for an after-hours nightclub called the Old Rocking Chair at 1301 East Yesler Way over in the Central District, where Seattle's Black community mainly lived. And thusly did this hungry musician (who called himself "R.C." but would soon start working simply as "Ray Charles") bravely took the next steps on an unknowable path to his future.

"I thought that I had gone as far as I could go in Florida," Charles would recall decades later while gigging in Seattle. "This is the real *truth* of the matter: I was too scared. Not afraid, *scared*. You have to understand there's a big difference. See, I didn't want to go to Chicago or New York, or places like that, that I'd heard about. 'Cause I just thought that I would be smothered. Plus, I guess I didn't have the self-confidence one needs. But, on the other hand, I thought if I could go to a medium-sized town and start to do my own little thing, maybe I could make it. And so, I selected Seattle."

Charles was far from the only southern newcomer to discover that the Northwest could make for an attractive home base. And what they also discovered was that it was already home to vibrant underground jazz scenes that had fermented in a few specific areas: Seattle's notorious red-light district around South Jackson Street and the Black-oriented business strip along East Madison Street; downtown Tacoma's Broadway Street; and the "Little Harlem" section along Williams Avenue in Northeast Portland's Albina neighborhood.

All this setting-the-scene is directly relevant to a recounting of the rise of R&B and rock 'n' roll music in the Northwest, because the particular musical vocabulary that would mark this region's early rockin' R&B traditions was inherited via the lingering local nightlife culture dating back to the Prohibition era (1916–33). Even though liquor sales had been made legal again via Repeal in late 1933, there remained an "underground" speakeasy world of illicit booze sales at various after-hours dance halls, reefer dens, and gambling joints. Partying hardy 'til the wee small hours while dancing to honking saxophones and bluesy keyboards—that's a formula for fun that worked well way back when, and continued to fuel the action right up into the rock 'n' roll age.

Seattle's early jazz scene was energized by a few key players who are particularly relevant to this story—Black musicians like Oscar Holden, Frank Waldron, Robert Alexander "Bumps" Blackwell, Alexander "Frank" Roberts, and Billy Tolles—each of whom were active back in the day when working musicians all across America were artificially divided into racially segregated musicians' unions. In Seattle those were the American Federation of Musicians Local 76 (for white folk) and Local 493 (for most everyone else).

This arrangement mainly benefitted the white players (who'd formed their union back in 1890) because it effectively divvied up the town into turf zones—and they got to dominate all the lucrative downtown gigs at the major theaters, hotel ballrooms, restaurant lounges, fancy nightclubs, and radio stations.

Overlapping with these circumstances were other factors—including the passing of laws intended to restrict both public dancing and alcohol consumption. As far back as 1881 Washington Territory legislators had—with obvious deference to the religious preferences of some citizens—passed a law intended to prohibit fighting, horse-racing and dancing on Sundays. More social-control measures would be introduced over time. In 1902, the Seattle City Council passed another anti-dance ordinance that forbade youths under the age of eighteen from attending a public dance unless accompanied by a parental chaperone. Then, 1909 brought the "Sabbath breaking" law, which expanded the 1881 ban to many other business activities as well.

In 1923, the council passed a new ordinance that defined offences and penalties related to public dancing, and established that the chief of police would appoint a "Supervisor of Dances" who would "investigate all complaints of public dance halls and dances" and see to it "that standards of decency and good taste are maintained, and that disorderly, familiar or objectionable conduct is not tolerated." That same ordinance had also—quite conveniently for certain mainstream organizations—provided some slack for a select few. Example: while dance promoters would generally be required to hire a "matron" who would monitor their dance floor's action and report directly to the new supervisor, an explicit exception was carved out for "dances given by responsible fraternal or labor organizations, charitable or philanthropic agencies, schools, churches, bona fide community or patriotic societies" who would, instead, just need a chaperone on site.

Even after the repeal of Prohibition in late 1933, new regulations—commonly called blue laws—still prohibited the sale of alcohol on Sundays. Further ordinances also outlawed businesses from selling mixed cocktails; forbade single women from even sitting at a bar; and restricted any customer from moving around a bar with drink in hand. In later years, additional laws would be passed in an effort to control nightlife activities—especially those of youths.

By the late 1930s, big band dance orchestras were a popular attraction, and there were numerous ballrooms where adults could attend weekly events. For the high school crowd, the options were far more limited, yet eventually "all-city" dances sponsored by various youth-oriented organizations (like the Ambassadors, Mutineers, or Phi Chi) came along featuring the sounds of white bands led by Archie Kyle, Gay Jones, Charles Center Case, Archie Nutt, and Homer Sweetman.

Meanwhile, the members of the so-called Negro's Musicians' Union, AFM Local 493, made do with the leftovers. Those dive taverns, restaurants, and community halls were mainly strung along two particular streets—South Jackson and East Madison—which marked the southern and northern borders of Seattle's Central District (known locally as the CD) and had developed business strips that served the African American community.

It was along Jackson Street that a vibrant jazz scene had been fermenting since the earliest years of the twentieth century. By 1919, the jazz scene was already robust enough to attract traveling professional musicians—in particular, a band led by a Black clarinetist, Oscar Holden, who had grown up in the South playing on Nashville-based Mississippi paddle wheel riverboats with his lifelong trumpeter buddy Louis Armstrong. Backed on piano by the fabled New Orleans Creole ragtime legend Ferdinand "Jelly Roll" Morton, the combo took on a gig at the Entertainers Cabaret. Legend holds that Morton—a genuine diamond-toothed, pistol-packin' pimp—sunk into some serious gambling debt in one of Seattle's illicit speakeasies and hightailed it out of town. Morton wrote a jaunty rag—"Seattle Hunch"—that marked his correct instinct to flee the area, which he later recorded for Victor Records.

Oscar Holden, on the other hand, settled here and eventually joined AFM Local 493, formed his own band, and made a good living gigging at numerous venues, including Russell "Noodles" Smith's Black and Tan club and the nearby Old Rocking Chair. In 1929, Holden, who also played piano, married a piano-playing Yakima girl, Leala Carr, and they founded a musical dynasty by bearing five children (Oscar Jr., Grace, Dave, Ron, and Jimmy)—who would each go on to contribute to Seattle's jazz and rockin' R&B scenes.

Initially the Holden family lived at Twenty-Sixth Avenue and East Madison Street, then at Twenty-Fourth and East Madison, and finally in a large house at 1409 East Fir Street, which over the decades would become a genuine center of musical activity in the 'hood. It was also conveniently located directly across the street from the Washington Hall, a hub of Seattle's growing Black community, where the Oscar Holden Quintet opened shows for the likes of Louis Armstrong, Cab Calloway, Ella Fitzgerald, Lena Horne, and Duke Ellington.

By the 1930s and '40s, South Jackson Street was the home to dozens of jazzy taverns and nightclubs, while up on East Madison Street additional taverns, pool halls, and dance halls also became particularly important to Seattle's nightlife scene. One of the key characters on East

Madison was an ambitious and winsome Black businessman named Robert "Bumps" Blackwell, a Seattle-born, Garfield High School grad who also studied at both the University of Washington and Cornish School of the Arts.

Blackwell first gained local notoriety while leading Bumps' Rhythm Maniacs back in 1935. Blackwell—who played a bit of piano, trumpet, and vibraphone—later led his own popular society dance "orchestra," an ensemble that sometimes included Oscar or Leala Holden or both— and that got so popular they became the first Black band to start getting hired to play for various white, elite organizations like the Seattle Yacht Club and the Seattle Tennis Club.

Blackwell also always had endless side hustles: in addition to working as a draftsman at the Boeing Company on his off nights, he also ran, at various times, a taxicab company, a jewelry business, plus, with his brother Charlie Blackwell, a butcher shop at 2302 East Madison Street. Directly upstairs from the butcher shop was the Washington Social and Educational Club and across the street were the Mardi Gras Grill at 2047 East Madison—a restaurant-lounge that had been in business since the 1930s—and the legendary Savoy Ballroom. ★

CHAPTER 2

STOMPIN' AT THE SAVOY

The Savoy Ballroom at 2203 East Madison Street held its grand opening on December 27, 1942. It was launched by a Black businessman named Lemuel Honeysuckle, who ran a popular café–card room–pool hall also on East Madison. Noting a pent-up demand for more nightlife action in the 'hood, Honeysuckle acquired the old 1930s Gala Theater building, leveled the floor, renamed it the Savoy, and hired a hot young swing band he'd seen playing a few youth-oriented shows across the street at the Washington Social and Educational Club.

Once ensconced as the house band, they were dubbed the "Savoy Boys"—an eleven-piece band that featured a hotshot teen sax player, Billy Tolles, who'd moved to town from Illinois at age five, way back in 1929. Tolles's mother played organ at the Mount Zion Baptist Church, where he joined the junior choir. But Tolles soon discovered Seattle's seedy underside as a young paperboy delivering copies of Black-oriented newspapers like the *Chicago Defender* and the *Pittsburgh Courier* to his customers, who hung around the brothels and gambling dens all along Jackson Street.

Tolles was ten when he began studying the piano under Professor Magruder; later, while attending Garfield High, he played trumpet in the marching band. Then, when the annual Garfield Funfest talent show came along, he was recruited by Blackwell's younger, guitar-playing brother, Charlie Blackwell, to perform a Mills Brothers' pop song with his quartet, the Four Sharps. Then, at sixteen, Tolles was exposed to a whole 'nother form of music that blew his mind: wild jazz.

"I sneaked off with my little girlfriend one Sunday to a music concert—at the Moore Theatre, down on 2nd Avenue—and it happened to be Lionel Hampton, with Illinois Jacquet and a rhythm section from Seattle," Tolles would recall. "Illinois Jacquet almost made me jump out of the balcony, man! I've *never* been so roused up in all my life! . . . I saw how he could contort and really, really swing this horn around, and be active, and that just wiped me away, man. . . . From that day on, I started listening to the saxophone."

Within days Tolles happened upon a moldy old saxophone, took it home, fixed it up, and began learning to play. It was in 1941 that he—along with two fellow members of the Four Sharps: Quentin "Sonny" Booker (trumpet) and Gerald Brashear (sax)—helped form the combo that became the Savoy Boys. Honeysuckle soon had them playing Saturday-afternoon dances for the younger set, a popular attraction that lasted for many months.

Along the way, Tolles developed into an excellent tenor sax player—albeit one who, amazingly enough, was entirely self-taught. Even when he had the opportunity to receive some instruction, he was confident to the point of sheer arrogance and opted not to. So, when Seattle's fabled Black jazzman Frank Waldron—a player, composer, and proprietor of the Waldron School of Trumpet and Saxophone at 1242 Jackson Street—approached him, Tolles passed on the opportunity.

"Frank Waldron would come around and listen to me play and he would say, 'Man, you are really *playing* that saxophone. There's a couple of things I can teach you if you want to come by.' But I never did go. I always, secretly, wanted to get with him. . . . He would come around quite a bit. . . . He'd say, 'I can't believe that you just taught yourself.'"

It was in 1943 that Tolles split to start college down in Greensboro, North Carolina. While there, he picked up some gigs playing with the proto-R&B pioneer bandleader Louis Jordan. From there he went on to study music at the Schillinger House in Boston, where he gigged with Billy Eckstine's band (which included such greats as Sarah Vaughan, Miles Davis, Dizzy Gillespie, Gene Ammons, Sonny Stitt, and Charlie "Bird" Parker). In 1945, Tolles returned home and gigged throughout that summer before moving to Virginia where he played with jazz and R&B stars including Jack McDuff, "Little" Jimmy Scott, and Ruth Brown.

In 1947, a significant new teen band formed in Seattle when tenor saxophonist Charlie Taylor—a son of the pianist Evelyn Bundy, who'd formed the pioneering Garfield Ramblers jazz combo here back in the

1920s—met a fast-learning, young trumpeter named Quincy "Quick" Jones in the band room at Garfield High School. Jones's family had moved from Bremerton to Seattle in 1944. Taylor, too, had been a quick study: "I got a saxophone for Christmas when I was eighteen. I took lessons from Frank Waldron. He was *really*, really good. For six months I practiced about six hours a day. . . . At the end of six months . . . I quit lessons and started a band."

The Charlie Taylor Band came together when he and Jones recruited, among others, two of Oscar Holden's kids—Oscar Holden Jr. (sax) and Grace Holden (piano)—and Jones's brother Waymond Jones (drums). (Meanwhile, the Joneses' other brother, Lloyd, got a job working at Blackwell's butcher shop.) The band first played a lunch break at Garfield High, then the spring season's Garfield Funfest talent show. Following that came their first paid gig: a teen dance at the East Madison YMCA. It was while playing a show out at Vasa Park on Lake Sammamish that Blackwell popped up and offered to manage them under a new name: the Bumps Blackwell Junior Band.

The kids agreed, and thus began intensive months of training and rehearsals at Blackwell's Central District bungalow at 217 Fourteenth Avenue North. It was here where Blackwell nurtured numerous budding jazz talents, including future stars like Ray Charles, Quincy Jones, Patti Bown, Floyd Standifer, and Ernestine Anderson. In 1983, while visiting his former home in Seattle, Blackwell reminisced about the old days: "So, the music scene . . . *this* is actually where it started. We used to rehearse—I'd have them in the bathroom, in the dining room, the kitchen, the upstairs bedroom, downstairs bedroom, in the front room and the den. All playing on their instruments. *Learning.*"

And Blackwell did his best to teach the kids about the entertainment business's wild ways. "Bumps acted like a father to us," Taylor would later recall. "He gave us lectures on dope and drinking—don't do this, don't do that." But such temptations would always be present.

When Blackwell figured all these kids were polished enough, he scored them a regular Sunday gig at the Savoy, and then began booking them into the now-legendary Washington Social and Educational Club that yet another Black businessman, "Reverend" Sirless F. "Sy" Groves, had founded back in 1944.

Among the blue laws still on the books was the one that forbade nightclubs from serving mixed cocktails; instead, there would be BYOB venues called "bottle clubs," where patrons arrived with their own booze (which was expected to be discreetly kept in a bag and on the floor under each patron's table), and the house made its profit by selling "setups" (ice and glasses). Exempt from such rules were various private "social" or "educational" clubs—a legal wrinkle that allowed mainstream organizations like the Eagles, Elks, and Moose lodges, and tennis and yachting clubs, to freely get their party on. In addition, there were still (until 1966) no liquor sales allowed on Sundays—except at the numerous local officers and enlisted men's clubs on local military bases.

This was the legalistic backdrop Sy Groves faced when he'd wanted to run his own nightspot. His clever solution was to incorporate a business as a "private," members-only organization. Indeed, he seized the opportunity with gusto, choosing to bestow it with an absurdly exacting name: it would be both a social and educational club that would happily sell a "membership" to any fun-seeking Jack or Jill who showed up.

"I never *did* figure out where the Reverend Groves' church was," Jones would later joke:

> Nor did I know how his club got the "education" part of that title, unless you consider the act of lifting a peach jar full of VAT 69 whiskey to your lips and sliding it down your throat educational, but the Reverend's club was definitely social. People brought bottles of whiskey and wine in paper bags, paid a dollar or two for a "setup" from the club—a bucket of ice, four water glasses, and maybe some soda pop—and then partied all night long drinking whiskey and eating home-cooked barbeque while watching us play. . . . Occasionally there were police busts, fistfights, even gunfire and we'd have to haul ass out the back door.

Among the stars that Groves booked were Cab Calloway, Charlie Parker, Lester Young, Dexter Gordon, T-Bone Walker, Jack McVea, and B.B. King—in other words, some of the finest musicians alive. It was a room players loved to play, and where partiers loved to party. The popular—and sometimes *way* over legal capacity—venue would see many a wild night and more than one news-making police raid. In 1947, the Seattle Police Department started to crack down on after-hours venues. That year alone, they raided ninety-some nightclubs including jazz and R&B rooms like the Black and Tan as well as the Rocking Chair, which was shuttered the following year. Between 1948 and 1950, the Washington Social and Educational Club was raided on several occasions, with Groves himself being arrested a couple times before he grew tired and quit the biz.

Meanwhile, Bumps Blackwell had continued making professional connections all around the region and was able to book his Junior Band into a wide variety of shows—all the while making serious inroads on Seattle's segregated scene. In time, they began getting better and better gigs—even some in downtown venues that AFM Local 76 had traditionally controlled. Somehow Blackwell was able to get his band into the Metropolitan Theatre at Fourth Avenue and University Street, at Club Encore student events up on the University of Washington campus, and then some shows supporting touring stars like "The Hi De Ho Man" himself, Cab Calloway, at the Civic Auditorium at 225 Mercer Street, and the jazz world's reigning diva, Billie Holiday, at the Senator Ballroom in the Eagles Building at 700 Union Street.

And then, as if they weren't already plenty busy, in October 1947 Blackwell, Charlie Taylor, and Quincy Jones all joined the military, with Blackwell becoming the first Black officer in the Washington National Guard and leader of the 41st Infantry Division Band based out of Fort Lewis. Yet, they still had time to keep up their gigging.

"On the first of the week we would be in the National Guard Band," Blackwell recalled:

> I was playing military music—then on Tuesday or Wednesday we'd be at the Workman's Circle playing for a bar mitzvah. Then on the early part of Friday or Saturday night we'd be playing for the ski clubs where we'd be playing schottisches, mazurkas, hambones, things like that. Then after we finished that, down at Broadmoor or Madison Park, or wherever we were, we'd end up at the Washington Social and Educational Club at 2:30 or 3:00 in the morning and play until about 6:30 or 7:00 the next morning. That's where they'd sell a gallon of wine for about thirty-five cents. [*laughter*]

"We'd play five nightclubs a night," Jones confirmed. "First we played pop for the white kids at the Seattle Tennis Club. We'd have our little cardigans on and ties. Then we'd change into our suits and go over to the Washington Social and Educational Club. . . . We played everything: rock 'n' roll, rhythm and blues. Then we'd go down to the red-light district and have bebop jam sessions."

Blackwell also played a role in pushing Seattle's popular Trianon Ballroom at 218 Wall Street to finally allow Black patrons to attend dances—albeit only on Mondays, the hall's new "Colored Folks" night. Nothing came easy in those days, but Blackwell took things in stride, accepted these small steps toward social progress, and always moved forward with positivity. "With all the good, the bad, and the ugly in the industry," Blackwell later reflected, "music is still like a religion to me."

The personnel roster of Blackwell's Junior Band evolved—seemingly only getting better over their three-year run. When their drummer split, Blackwell came up with a killer replacement, Tommy Adams, who is considered the father of Northwest funk. Blackwell also discovered another newcomer to town, the teenage Texan singer Ernestine Anderson. Though her parents had hoped that moving to Seattle would keep their daughter away from a raucous music scene like Houston's, that plan didn't really work and Anderson fell right in with Blackwell's outfit. Then, in 1947, a visiting star, Oakland's R&B pioneer Johnny "Hand Jive" Otis, heard Anderson sing and immediately recruited her to join his traveling revue. In 1948, she scored a contract and cut her first R&B record, "Good Lovin' Babe" backed with "K.C. Lover," for the Black & White label. Soon after, she joined Lionel Hampton's band, and from there Anderson was well on her way to jazz stardom.

This, then, was the current state of Seattle's hip music scene that Ray Charles had stumbled into upon his arrival back in 1948. Based on the tip he'd lucked into at the bus station—that it was "Talent Night" over at Old Rocking Chair club—Charles somehow made his way across this strange new town and over to Thirteenth Avenue and Yesler Way in the CD, where he instantly heard the strains of a jam wafting out the jazz room's door. Charles tried to enter, but the doorman blocked his path and denied him entry due to his obvious youthfulness. But Charles pleaded that he was new in town, was starved, and was a pianist and singer who just wanted to play a few songs for the crowd.

Showing mercy, the doorman let the kid slip in, and Seattle would never be the same. Because *Ray Charles* was in-the-house—and he came bringin' the blues. When his turn came to mount the modest stage, Charles sat at the house piano and proceeded to play and sing two mellow West Coast hits by the Los Angeles singer Charles Brown: "Traveling Blues" and "Drifting Blues."

"I must tell you, I really sang my ass off," Charles remembered. "I mean, I'm singing the *blues*! I know that song as well as my own mother, and when I'm through, I can tell that the folks dig it: The place rings with applause."

That's about when Charles was approached by a man who complimented his playing and asked if he might be able to pull a trio together. Charles's answer was an enthusiastic yes, and with that he was offered a prime gig at the Black community's beloved Elks Club on South Jackson Street. After recruiting a couple of players at the AFM Local 493 union hall—which happened to be just upstairs from the Elks—his new trio played the gig and Charles was instantly welcomed into the Seattle jazz community. Indeed, Georgia Kemp, a cook at the Elks Club, invited him to move into her rooming house at Twentieth Avenue and East Madison.

Settled in, Charles was able to eke out a living by gigging long nights in various after-hours clubs. But one night, he crossed paths with a young fellow who would soon steer him to an opportunity to scrape up a few extra bucks by performing with, and then penning arrangements for, Bumps Blackwell.

"I had my little trio at the Black and Tan club one night," Charles fondly reminisced, "and this fourteen-year-old cat comes up to me talking about music, about jazz, about Dizzy Gillespie and Charlie Parker. He said, 'I'm Quincy Jones and I play trumpet and I want to write music.'"

Thus began a lifelong friendship between the two player's players. They started hanging out at Charles's apartment, where he shared some advanced music theory lessons, and they began gigging together with Blackwell's Junior Band.

During this postwar period, popular music was evolving quickly and swing jazz, jump blues, bebop, and early R&B were all advancing. Given Seattle's growing Black population and ever more venues popping up where all this beat-driven music could be performed, more stars from outside the region began touring here. Among them were the red-hot bands led by Louis Jordan, Lionel Hampton, T-Bone Walker, Big Jay McNeely, Bill Doggett, Hank Ballard and the Midnighters, Little Willie John, and the tenor sax honker Jack McVea.

It was the latter's combo who came through Seattle in '48 to play the Washington Social and Entertainment Club, and Charles's trio happened to get hired to open. So, McVea and Charles got to talking: "One evening, he asked McVea if he could try his sax. Ray had learned how to play the instrument, along with trumpet and clarinet, in school. McVea agreed and was stunned at how well Ray played. The audience went wild over Ray's solo." Upon his return home to Los Angeles, McVea passed the word to a Black executive named Jack Lauderdale, president of Down Beat Records (which was one of the very first Black-owned, independent labels). Meanwhile, Charles was winning fans with his soulful singing and stunning musical chops; after recruiting Garcia D. "Gossie" McKee (guitar) and Milton S. Garred (bass), they formed a more permanent unit—the McSon Trio. They then scored a regular gig at the Rocking Chair as well as their very own show on KRSC, Seattle's first TV station.

It was in November 1948 when Lauderdale followed up on McVea's hot tip and made his way up to Seattle. The story goes that one night while shootin' dice upstairs at the Rocking Chair, Lauderdale began diggin' the tunes that were echoing up from downstairs and searched out Charles: "One night he approached me and told me that he had a record label. Wow! Just the *thought* of getting the chance to *record* was a thrill—A record! Man, that was the ultimate! I had been listening to records my whole life . . . and here I was actually about to make one. Yes, we'll cut a record, Mr. Lauderdale. *Good God Almighty!* Just show us the way, Papa."

Lauderdale showed the trio the way downtown—most likely to the KOL radio–associated Western Recording Studios facility—where they recorded two songs, "Confession Blues" and "I Love You, I Love You." That night they cut the very first R&B record ever produced in the Pacific Northwest. Released nationally by Down Beat in February 1949, the record—as credited to the Maxin Trio—sold well in Seattle, and in April "Confession Blues" entered *Billboard* magazine's "Race Records" charts at number 11, lingered for a good three months, and peaked at number 5. Lauderdale was pleased, and he had Charles cut a few more songs including the originals "Alone in the City" and "The Snow Is Falling" (a song Charles wrote during his Seattle days), as well as McKee's "Rockin' Chair Blues."

The latter was a sweet tribute to the barfly regulars at that friendly venue. Released in November 1949, the latter tune's guitar work hinted at the future arrival of rock 'n' roll. As one writer later noted, "Ray's tone is straight out of the cocktail blues playbook. . . . As soft and dreamy as Ray's part had been, the over-amped bridge sounds as if it was packed with dynamite. . . . The eventual shift in rock 'n' roll's most dominant lead instrument that would occur a decade down the road was just starting to take shape. . . . They're only two instances, coming back to back, but they snap you out of the dreamy lull you were in and push you to the edge of your seat."

In June 1950, Lauderdale sent Charles out on a long tour with the bluesman Lowell Fulson. When they came to Seattle on October 16, 1951, the advertising for their show at the Eagles Auditorium noted that Fulson was bringing his orchestra along with "Seattle's own blind sensational singing star! Ray Charles."

In time he would, of course, become a worldwide star who earned—based on his immortal rockin' R&B hits like 1954's "I Got a Woman," 1956's "Mary Ann," and 1959's "What'd I Say"—the moniker the "Genius of Soul." But back in Seattle, the jazznik crowd had already seen that Ray Charles's impact was utterly profound. His rootsy sound and indelibly blue influence played a key role in the eventual rise of an original school of rockin' R&B that would come to be known as the Northwest Sound. ★

CHAPTER *3*

BILLY'S BUCKET OF BLUES

The year 1948 saw Billy Tolles graduating from college and returning home to Seattle only to discover that the entire musical landscape had changed while he'd been away. He found that Bumps Blackwell had successfully carved out, and was carefully managing, a lucrative circuit of dance gigs for his bands. By this time, Blackwell was playing the vibraphone in his own namesake dance orchestra while also mentoring the Junior Band and managing another young Black group, the Homer Carter Quintet. He effectively had the town wired—which frustrated Tolles. "When I got home from college, he had *all* the music corralled. If you wanted to work, you were working in one of his bands. And he would come and collect the money off of each gig, and pay you what he wanted you to have. He had the thing locked up. If you wanted to work, you worked for him."

So, Tolles fell in and began gigging with the Junior Band—but before long, he scored a steadier gig playing nightclubs in a combo led by an AFM Local 493 officer, bassist Bob Marshall. But then the US Army drafted Tolles and he split the scene for a while. Upon his return, he picked right up where he'd left off.

In May 1951, AFM Local 493 held a benefit concert at the Senator Ballroom to help raise funds for the building of a new headquarters. Among the acts lined up were Bumps Blackwell's Orchestra, Cecil Young's Combo, and Seattle's first swing band: Billy Tolles and His Men of Jive. Tolles, having recently been discharged from the military, had designed his new group to grab some of the high-society dance gigs that Blackwell had nearly cornered.

15

Among the new talents in Tolles's band were two genuine Black blues singers, the electric guitar–wielding Clarence Williams and Bea Smith. Williams had originally arrived in town with New York's Blackberries of 1946 traveling troupe and was promoted as the "Prince of the Blues." By 1948, Williams was gigging with the Leon Vaughn Band in the Basin Street Club at 411 Maynard Street; and by 1950, he was with Al Hickey's Band gigging at the Washington Social and Educational Club. Now Williams's electric guitar was attracting crowds who had rarely, if ever, seen or heard one before.

And that's when Tolles first connected with a towering legend in the Northwest radio biz. Wally Nelskog had started out in the '40s as a DJ at Seattle's tiny KRSC station with a dance music show, *Wally's Music Makers*, which gained such popularity that KJR hired him to move it to their broadcast studios. Before long, he proceeded to cultivate a youth audience and began promoting public dances for the teen set at various high schools and area towns. But his most successful events were the dances held at Seattle's Eagles Auditorium, where by 1950 he was attracting as many as three thousand kids on Friday nights.

Nelskog would recall decades later:

> The first band I used was Quincy Jones's—but he was a little too *jazz*-oriented and refined for the young people. From my position in radio I could see that music was going through a transition. Kids didn't like the big band sound of fifteen pieces—or the complicated arrangements bands had gotten into after the war. They were looking for smaller groups who could put out a strong, basic, instrumental beat. So, after Jones, I started using another group: Billy Tolles's—an eight-piece, predominantly Black group. At first they were just sitting down reading charts. I told them to animate their act as much as possible. So, they got into gymnastics and ad-libbing on their instruments, which the kids really went wild over.

Even though Nelskog was running a clean operation—he'd hired adult, paid-staff chaperones to help keep order in the Eagles Auditorium—the very sight of a few thousand kids coming and going from the hall on those nights, alas, caught the unwanted attention of City Hall. It was in 1953 that trouble arose when an envious crosstown competitor in the dance business—the Trianon Ballroom—raised a stink, and the city responded by using a 1902 anti-dance ordinance that forbade public dancing by minors unless a parent accompanied them. But Nelskog was too wily to go down without a fight:

> That came about when [the bandleader] Ralph Flanagan appeared at the Trianon Ballroom and drew 500 people—while I was drawing 3,000. So the manager of the Trianon Ballroom went to the police and said, "Hey, this guy's running an illegal dance." They shut me down right in the middle of an evening, which dumped 3,000 kids out onto the streets all at once. That night those kids created a lot of havoc. They stole cars, broke windows, and such, all because they were mad at the City. In a way it was kind of humorous. Later on I said, "Well, what's good for the goose is good for the gander." And so, on another night I went to the City and said, "You'd better check his attendance too!" Which they did. So, he had to close down too.

After those incidents, Nelskog knew that to carry on with his lucrative dance business he would have to move outside Seattle's city limits. But to do that he wouldn't need to reinvent the wheel. Back in the 1920s and '30s, numerous Prohibition era–entertainment entrepreneurs had constructed roadhouses and ballrooms along various highways in spots purposefully selected because they were located in unincorporated county areas close to cities. Most notable among them were the Evergreen Ballroom (outside of Olympia at 9121 Pacific Avenue SE), the Spanish Castle Ballroom (midway between Tacoma and Seattle, at 23003 Pacific Highway South), and Parker's Ballroom at 17001 Aurora Avenue North on the old Seattle-Everett Highway.

Nelskog initially chose yet another venue, moving his dance activity north of the city limits, up to the Palladium Ballroom at 12500 Aurora Avenue North—until, that is, the City of Seattle adjusted its border northward to include that area. After that, he moved his operation farther north to Parker's, a dance hall where much history would be made.

Meanwhile, the outbreak of the Korean War caused the army to recall Billy Tolles for a second stint. But after serving for only eight months he was discharged in Southern California, where he immediately scored a couple of weeks' work backing Billie Holiday at LA's Tippin' Inn. Then Tolles headed back home, where his new awareness of the cutting-edge music being created out on the East Coast and in South Central Los Angeles had caused his own personal sound to evolve toward a bold R&B style. And that new energy would prove to have a major impact here.

"I was already into rhythm and blues," Tolles would brag, "playing the style that I learned with Louis Jordan. He just made everything just happy, you know, just playing those little shuffle rhythms and the blues and keeping it comedic and high octane."

Directly inspired by the wild bands led by Louis Jordan and Lionel Hampton, Tolles set out to form what he would later describe as the "first rock 'n' roll band in Seattle." Billy Tolles's Four Question Marks was a combo that included Roy Moore (piano), Floyd Standifer (trumpet and sax), and Tommy Adams (drums).

"We kicked ass right from the beginning," Tolles gleefully recalled, "because we were playing those *heavy* shuffles. And that Tommy Adams had such a raw sense of rhythm, boy. He'd be chopping wood, and there'd be wood all down up under the snare drum, where he'd been hitting that rim stick. Boy, we'd be roughin' it up."

The Four Question Marks wowed local audiences from day one. In no time, they were invited to compete in a Battle of the Bands event where their high-energy music set them apart from the town's top jazz groups, including the Elmer Gill Trio and the Cecil Young Quartet.

Elmer Gill's group played a polite form of jazz, while Cecil Young's biracial group offered a more energetic, early take on bebop. Indeed, the latter ensemble is remembered as the first since Ray Charles to cut jazzy recordings here that had an impact *outside* the region. That occurred when tapes of their June 10, 1951, show at the swanky Metropolitan Theatre were issued as the *Concert of Cool Jazz* album by Cincinnati's successful independent label King Records. The disc included "Who Parked the Car" featuring Gerald Brashear's vocals—a tune that America's premier jazz critic, Ralph Gleason, rated as "the best scat solo ever recorded."

But neither Gill's nor Young's band was fully prepared to compete against the wailing sounds and hipster stage moves of Tolles's crew. Like so many hep players, Tolles and company had been bowled over by the 1942 jump blues hit "Flying Home" by Lionel Hampton and His Orchestra. The tune—which is considered a direct precursor to rock 'n' roll—featured screaming sax work by Illinois Jacquet. Even *Billboard* had noted the song as "a jumper that defies standing still." No wonder Tolles had buckled down and learned the tune note for note:

We played riff things, and played a lot of Illinois Jacquet's things—Lionel Hampton's things. I was a master of [their hit] "Flyin' Home." And we were the only ones doing that forceful, ruckus, *hard-driving* [sound]. That's what [promoters] always would put in my little resume when they were going to have a little concert: the "hard-driving Billy Tolles Band." There was a couple of jazz Battle-of-Bands in the '50s. We won our first battle of bands. We played "Flyin' Home" at the Eagles Auditorium and walked off with the prize, man! We were all raggedy-looking and the rest of the bands were all dressed up and Cecil Young and Elmer Gill—they were so sophisticated, and intellectual, and so on, and we came on there with that blues and that "Flyin' Home" and just walked off with that $150 prize. I said, "To hell with that *being nice*, man." Forever, it was "the hard-driving" Billy Tolles Band.

Around 1956, Tolles's trio—with Tommy Adams and Mike Taylor (piano)—had a steady gig at Ayers Café at 1311 East Yesler Way, where their funky music and kickin' beats were so novel that even white University of Washington students showed up in droves. The overflow crowds were there to hear the wild sounds as well as witness Tolles's over-the-top showmanship:

For a long time, I was a honker like Illinois Jacquet and Big Jay McNeely, because that's what they wanted at that time. That's what got us over in those jam sessions. Tommy could get that beat going and I could just honk, and walk through the joint, jump from table-top to tabletop, honking on my Bb [tenor sax], walk the bar, and all that, go outside and come back in the back door, and all that kind of stuff. That really got us over, during those '50s jam sessions. Those white kids, they'd be in there clamoring for that.

No doubt Tommy Adams's drumming was certainly a big part of the draw—and drummers from far and wide came by regularly for some serious schoolin'. And Tolles was happy to claim some of the glory:

When I got back to Seattle, nobody was popping the sock cymbal two-four. They were all just kinda leading their sock cymbal, hitting it a lick or two. Back East, boy, they were popping that sock cym-bal—and I got him doing that, and that brought a whole new thing of drums to Seattle, because nobody was popping. I brought that from back East, and later on some drummers came through and they were doing it, but Seattle drummers was kind of "rat-a-tat-tat." I got Tommy doin' that right away, boy, and that's what set everything on fire! That tight *backbeat*, man. We were playing those heavy shuffles.

In time, Tolles hooked up with keyboardist Dave Holden, another of Oscar Holden Sr.'s progeny. All the Holden kids grew up watching their father rehearsing in their living room with AFM Local 493 players like Frank Waldron. In addition, when Dave's brother Oscar Jr. played with Bumps Blackwell's Junior Band, they sometimes rehearsed there as well. When Dave Holden joined the Garfield High School band, his father gave him the treasured silver clarinet he'd played decades prior with Louis Armstrong.

Holden also picked up a bit of piano, and one day he crossed paths with Billy Tolles when he walked by Ayers Café, around the corner from the Holden house. Tolles's band was playing, and when he saw the underage Holden peeking in the door he invited him inside to join the jam on piano. Holden only knew three songs, so the band played them each twice. Then Tolles asked if Holden wanted to join the combo. After a couple of afternoon sessions to learn more songs, Holden gigged with the trio at the café every Thursday, Friday, and Saturday night for about six weeks. That's about when Holden got a phone call from Ben Beasley, owner of the Mardi Gras Grill, who asked if wanted to join his club's trio, which included a couple heavyweight jazz cats: Pony Poindexter (alto sax) and Vernon Brown (drums).

Meanwhile, back around July of 1951, Bumps Blackwell had moved to California, where he took a job as an engineer and draftsman for the City of Los Angeles. But his failing eyesight led him back to the music biz, where Art Rupe, owner of Specialty Records, hired him as an A&R agent—a key record industry role that boils down to matching the right singers with the right songs. His first assignment was to work as arranger and studio bandleader for the R&B singer Jesse Belvin. Then, in 1955, Blackwell became intrigued by a demo tape mailed in by a maniacal singer named Little Richard. Traveling down to New Orleans, Blackwell took on producing sessions and would be credited as a cowriter on some of Richard's biggest hits including "Long Tall Sally," "Rip It Up," "Reddy Teddy," and "Good Golly Miss Molly."

It was in 1957 that Blackwell produced a session for Sam Cooke, star vocalist in the popular Soul Stirrers gospel group. They cut two songs: a soulful rendition of George Gershwin's "Summertime" and a promising original, "You Send Me." Art Rupe, however, was displeased that his gospel star had cut these secular tunes and Blackwell was fired. The consolation prize was that Blackwell was allowed to keep Cooke's contract—as well as the master tapes. He took those across town to Bob Keane, a former big band leader turned Hollywood-based record mogul wannabe. Keane saw the promise of Cooke's songs and at once offered to form a new label, Keen Records, and issue a single. Soon after, record in hand, Blackwell and Cooke set out on a promotional tour. They arrived in Seattle and headed over to a few radio stations to see if they could charm any DJs or program managers into supporting the new disc with some airplay.

It was November 1957 when "You Send Me" broke out on KOL, and within weeks the song had become a national number 1 hit—the first ever by a solo Black artist; an international smash; one of the biggest sellers of the year; and an all-time classic. While visiting, Cooke happened into the Mardi Gras Grill seeking a bit of fun, and he ended up thrilling the crowd by sitting in with Dave Holden's trio. Later, in 1958, Billy Tolles recruited Holden to join him for a new a gig at Dave Levy's hot venue, Dave's Fifth Avenue—a downtown room whose convenient location ensured the overflow crowds of fanatical dance enthusiasts who wanted to both swing and rock out.

The Billy Tolles trio created a whole new level of nightlife excitement downtown, but the action on East Madison was picking up as well, and it had a new energy that was about to really launch Seattle's nascent R&B scene. ★

CHAPTER 4

ROCK 'N' ROLL PARTY

Mardi Gras was the name of Seattle's new annual six-day celebration of Black culture launched on August 4, 1952. The festival was dubbed in a nod to the centuries-old New Orleans–based event of the same name; in Seattle, it would feature a parade, a public barbeque highlighting southern cookin', carnival activities, a costume contest, and ballroom dancing. But for neighborhood kids, the best part may have been the free Saturday-night street dance held at Twenty-First Avenue and East Madison.

As it happened, Billy Tolles had just begun a new side career—that of concert and dance promotion, which would benefit from the myriad connections he'd made over time within the wider jazz and R&B worlds. Initially, he began working in collaboration with a local Black real estate man named Leonard Russell who happened to be serving on the Mardi Gras organizing committee. And, for that debut year's festival, Tolles didn't disappoint: he hired the hot Los Angeles–based blues band led by electric guitar ace T-Bone Walker, who rocked the whole 'hood.

From there, Tolles started renting a couple old downtown halls— the Eagles Auditorium and the Palomar Theatre at 1300 Third Avenue— and producing concerts and dances that would feature all sorts of major stars. Over the next few years, Tolles also made money by booking bands into a new nightspot in the Madison neighborhood.

Meanwhile, another of Seattle's great early R&B honkers, Frank Roberts, had returned to town from serving in the US Air Force, and his background is worthy of review. New Orleans–born, Roberts and his family moved here when he was a third grader. And although sports were his first interest, Roberts studied clarinet under Frank Waldron and also learned the violin. It was at the age of twelve that he took on a job peddling copies of the *Chicago Defender* newspaper around town, which was how he first saw Ray Charles singing at the Tuxedo Club (just off South Jackson Street). He also witnessed some exceptional live music at his school's dance parties. "The music scene at that time," Roberts would reflect many years later, "it was kind of like . . . you know, I *remember* Ray Charles and Quincy goin' in and playin' my grade school dances!"

Roberts's paper route brought other eye-opening experiences: one night, Roberts sold a paper to the famed bandleader Count Basie, and on another he met up with Billy Eckstine outside the Paramount Theatre. Asking for any advice he could offer a young musician, Eckstine's words of wisdom to the lad were, "When you get through playin', *always* put your coat on." Indeed, being prepared to skedaddle on a moment's notice from rough nightspots was a lesson hard-learned by many an experienced player. Another time, Roberts and some pals went down to the Evergreen Ballroom where he met his hero, the jazz giant Charlie Parker, who was watching Dave Brubeck play before his own set began. After Roberts gushed to Parker that he thought he was a "genius," Bird sagely replied, "There's no genius. There's just *practice*."

And so, practice he did. After buying a sax in a pawn shop, Roberts formed his first combo with fellow Cleveland (and Garfield) High kids, and they played their first couple shows at the Neighborhood House, a youth-guidance and recreational center where a Black teacher named Louis L. Wilcox led a community youth band. Meanwhile, when the Savoy Boys foundered after Billy Tolles had split, Lemuel Honeysuckle hired the Frank Roberts's Combo to gig at the Savoy. From there they moved up to gigging at the Washington Social and Educational Club. That's where Bumps Blackwell noticed them one night and mentioned he would be willing to be their manager. The guys were all excited, but then Blackwell seemed to disappear and Roberts's combo took over the Savoy gig for a couple years before he headed off to serve in the air force.

During his three years of service he was stationed in England, where he paid his own tuition to attend the London Conservatory of Music. "I went in," he recalled, "because I wanted to be a big band leader like Count Basie." Roberts also played sax in a sizeable military band. But later, after he was discharged in 1955, Roberts landed in San Francisco and had to adjust; "I remember going from a 16-piece band, where I could just kind of play along, to a much smaller band, where I had to really get out there and solo. It was uncomfortable at first—you know, walking up to the microphone, letting it out. But I learned a lot. It forced me to become good." Indeed, Roberts became a very good player and quite the showman, one who would walk the bar top while blasting out the blues or jump down to the dance floor and do the splits. That's how he came to be known as the "Incredible Wildman on Saxophone." After getting his act together in California, he decided to return home to Seattle and form a new band, which would feature himself on bari sax, Wayne Perkins (guitar), Donny Osias (organ), and Dickie Enfield (drums).

"That's when my career really started to take off," Roberts acknowledged. "I was playing rock." Oh, yes he *was*. Just a few years later Frank Roberts and the Soul Brothers would begin recording R&B gems like "Blue Groove" and "Miss Ann" and also make local history as the first Black R&B band to hold down a steady gig at a central downtown joint, the Roll Inn Tavern at 1526 Eighth Avenue.

Meanwhile, it had been on the evening of August 15, 1955, that yet another local Black entrepreneur, named Wilmer Morgan, threw a grand opening show at the Birdland Supper Club—his newly revamped venue situated in the old Savoy Ballroom building. Renamed in honor of "Bird" Parker, the room debuted with a show booked by Billy Tolles that featured the longtime Dizzy Gillespie's big band sax man James Moody, who now had his own group, the Bop Men. The turnout was encouraging and the show a great success.

It seems the locals had been starving for a human-scale room—rather than those huge rooms, the Eagles or Palomar—that could regularly present major R&B and jazz stars. Morgan set out to remedy that situation by hiring Tolles to book the top touring acts—many of whom would appreciate this new chance to get a multi-night gig in Seattle. Among those who would play the Birdland were such icons as: T-Bone Walker, Ruth Brown, Big Jay McNeely, Bill Doggett, Little Willie John, Dexter Gordon, Cal Tjader, Percy Mayfield, Amos Milburn, Lowell Fulson, Pee Wee Crayton, B.B. King, Lloyd Price, Guitar Slim, Clyde McPhatter, Johnny "Guitar" Watson, Solomon Burke, James Brown, and Hank Ballard and the Midnighters.

The Birdland joined a small but growing string of rooms that began serving as the Pacific Northwest's version of the South's "chitlin' circuit." Word spread quickly and the joint became a hot after-hours spot for touring players like organ master Jimmy Smith and trumpet god Miles

Davis to jam after their gigs elsewhere in town. In no time, even the kids in the 'hood figured out that this new East Madison hotspot was jumpin'.

Among them was Dave Lewis, whose family had moved from Texas during World War II to the shipyard neighborhoods of Bremerton, where Quincy Jones was one of his boyhood pals. His father, David Lewis Sr., was an accomplished amateur guitarist who attempted to get his son interested in playing the guitar, but it was his mother's piano that intrigued him. Eventually both the Lewis and Jones families moved across the Puget Sound and began settling into their new city life in Seattle's CD. One of Lewis's first neighborhood pals was Barney Hilliard, who would soon also be his bandmate. It was 1950 when the boys entered Meany Junior High School. Before long Lewis and Hilliard, who was studying under Frank Waldron, joined with another Black student, John Johnston (drums), and this trio played a few school events.

As Hilliard would remember those early times:

> In 1950, Dave and I were starting to listen to rhythm and blues songs on records. It was difficult to find music by Black artists. We had to buy 78 rpm records from the Little Record Mart on 22nd and East Madison, or the Bob Summerrise record store on South Jackson Street. We often huddled around the radio to hear DJ Bob Summerrise play records made by black artists on a Tacoma radio station, for one hour in the evening. But it was always more enjoyable to hear R&B records at house parties, where students with gathering space in the home would invite school friends to meet, mingle, and dance with other boys and girls. We did not know in those days that music created by black artists was banned from mainstream radio and television stations as "race music."

In the fall of 1953, the boys entered Garfield High School, and Lewis (baritone) and a few fellow students—Ronnie Height (lead tenor), Larry Lombard (second alto and baritone), Henry Rollins (bass), and George Griffin (second lead), a kid fresh from New Orleans—formed the Five Checks, an a cappella, doo-wop quintet. They formed after hearing about the upcoming Garfield Funfest talent show. According to Lewis, they did the natural thing: "We put together this group just to get out of class."

Then they began rehearsing at Lewis's house with Lewis Sr. guiding them and teaching them chords. The group's singing—not to mention their eye-popping matching threads: boldly checkered dress shirts—evidently made a big impression. After that first show, they were invited to perform at pep rallies and assemblies, first at Meany and then at other public schools all across Seattle, in the process giving a lot of Seattle kids their very first exposure to live doo-wop singing.

Meanwhile, all the musical action on East Madison was providing the neighborhood kids with a sense of the nightlife. Moreover, the music that seeped out of the nightclubs served as a siren song that drew them in.

Thinking back to his boyhood days, George Griffin said, "Madison Street was very interesting to me because when you get on the top, there was nice restaurants and people—it was like a little small Harlem. People were nice. There was Birdland. Honeysuckle's. Jack's Pool Hall. We was watching everybody. What was happenin'. And the Mardi Gras: I went in there a few times—like just boys. And taverns, we weren't supposed to really be that place but everybody knew us on Madison Street."

Years later, when the guys in the Five Checks graduated from Meany and moved up to Garfield High, Lewis got serious about forming his own working R&B combo. Initially the Dave Lewis Combo comprised Lewis on piano, Hilliard on sax, Griffin—a New Orleans–raised drummer—and another kid fresh from Louisiana, John Gray, as their bassist. A bit later, the Combo added another hot sax player, J. B. Allen, solidifying their sound. As they built up their repertoire, they got their first few modest gigs playing for teenage sock hops at the East Madison YMCA. And the neighborhood's young folks loved them—Seattle now had its very own young rockin' R&B band!

"Because R&B music was so scarce, and here we were learning these R&B songs—and playing them live—we were filling a *void*," said Barney Hilliard. "When these top R&B bands would come to town, like the Eagles Auditorium, we would all be able to go see them. But when they weren't here, there was no music around. There were musicians around, but they weren't teenagers. So, that's kinda how we got our following. Because we were the young guys playing young music for the young people."

One evening in 1954, while the Combo was performing at the Washington Social and Educational Club, AFM Local 493 president Emmett Lewis took note of this up-and-coming young band. And thusly the Dave Lewis Combo was about to get schooled on union issues in general—and in particular, the simmering issue over whether the two segregated AFM locals would, or should, ever merge.

"The Combo had played all these high school dances and YMCA and all 'round and no one said a thing," Barney Hilliard recalled:

> But the moment we started playing these cabaret dances—Washington Social Club, Washington Hall, Chamber of Commerce, Casa Italiana, Polish Hall—that's when Emmett Lewis came from 493. He says, "If you guys are gonna do cabaret dances you gotta join the union." We said, "Yes, sir." So, we went down and signed up. *That's* when we learned the musicians' unions in Seattle were segregated. Of course we learned later that musicians' unions were segregated nationwide. I'll never forget this as long as I live. It's almost like it was yesterday: after we joined and started going down there on occasion to the union meetings, we found that there was a great big discussion going on within 493 about the upcoming merger with 76. And there was questions like about: "Do we *really* want to do it? Is *now* the time? Are we gonna get more jobs—or is it gonna be *fewer* jobs?" That was the mood at the meeting.

The mood within musicians' circles citywide was increasingly one of frustration. Some, of course, were satisfied with the segregated status quo—but plenty of others realized that both unions boasted fantastic players as members. As time went on, rules were being bent and norms challenged: AFM Local 493 had welcomed a few white players to join their ranks, and now a few interracial combos began popping up.

Seattle's popular Black pianist and vibraphonist Elmer Gill had formed a trio with Al Larkins (bass) and a white player, Al Turay (guitar). In August 1956, he "decided to challenge the whole rotten system of union segregation. The climate was ripe. Two years earlier, the US Supreme Court had forcibly integrated schools in Little Rock, Arkansas." People had watched televised reports of fire hoses beating back demonstrators; with a good portion of the public repulsed, it seemed like it was finally time for change.

Gill's trio made their move: they approached the management of Seattle's New Washington Hotel with an offer to play its Brigadier Room—a prime downtown gig traditionally controlled by AFM Local 76. The hotel's manager, however, balked at hiring an AFM Local 493–associated band that might attract a Black clientele. Nervous about the proposal, he asked the hotel chain's LA-based board of directors to weigh in on the matter. To everyone's surprise, they voted in the affirmative; as simple as that, the Elmer Gill Trio had caused the walls of segregation to crack just a bit.

Another historical breakthrough was about to occur at that venerable North End venue Parker's Ballroom, which had been hosting white bands and audiences at dances since its opening back in the Prohibition era. The catalyst for this change was none other than Billy Tolles, who'd been promoting his own teen dances every Sunday at the Washington Social Club for years. But by 1953—after playing at a couple of Wally Nelskog's Music Makers Dances down at the Eagles Auditorium—Tolles began competing with Nelskog by buying radio ads on KJR to promote his own Bop City dances up north. "He was pissed off about it, but I was *serious*," Tolles maintained. "I had been doing it in the Black neighborhood for a long time, and I'd have three or four hundred kids up there, for a dollar. . . . He was on the radio all the time. So . . . he stopped hiring me. But he would accept my money to advertise my own. I said, 'Well, I'll fix him.' And I went out to Parker's Ballroom and talked to them."

It was the spring of 1956 and Vern Amundsen, the manager at Parker's, was evidently not quite ready to upset the applecart and let Tolles rent the ballroom—which had been the exclusive turf for AFM Local 76 since day one back in 1930. But then, within months, a different boundary-pushing opportunity arose. As events unfolded, a popular local dance band, the Ted Simon Octet, comprising young but still old-school white guys who sat while playing tunes from charts set on music stands, were booked at Parker's for a dance. But Simon had come to be quite impressed by the Dave Lewis Combo and wanted to have them serve as the opening act.

He arranged to meet Lewis at the ballroom so he could introduce him to the manager and ask if his request would be granted. Presumably tired by now of all this segregation crap, Vern Amundsen got on the telephone right then and there with AFM Local 76 headquarters to seek approval. As Dave Lewis would recall many years later, the union balked at the request and pointedly reminded Amundsen that the North End was still their turf; if Parker's went ahead, the union would mount a picket line boycott of the ballroom.

The hall's manager's brave reply was nonnegotiable: either the union would overlook his booking of the Dave Lewis Combo or he would never hire local white musicians to perform there again. To Lewis's astonishment, accommodations were suddenly made and a new era began. It was on May 11, 1956, that the Ted Simon Octet was allowed to have the Dave Lewis Combo—along with the Five Checks—perform at Parker's for a Dance and Jam Session gig. The show was a complete success, with hordes of white and Black kids intermingling without incident.

With another crack splitting the segregation wall, Tolles made his next move. He went back to Parker's management and negotiated the rental of the hall on Friday nights that summer of '56. Tolles had ambitious plans. He'd already been supplying KCPQ-TV with various local teenaged bands and doo-wop groups who performed for free at their Tacoma studios, but now Tolles raised the stakes by suggesting to management that he could produce and emcee a new teen dance show, *Rock 'n' Roll Party*, which would feature his new band, the Vibrators, and other musical guests—including Seattle's first white rock band, the Four Frantics—all to be broadcast live from Parker's. Tolles's TV show made its debut on July 13, 1956:

> I said, "I've been doing *this* for *you*, so why don't you just put *me* on the TV?" I became the emcee. We did that for a whole summer. We had twelve Friday nights. They put it on TV, live, for an hour, and then I got a couple of sponsors. Boy, it had built up to about three, four, or five thousand kids that were coming out there. That was a big thing. I had two or three white groups, and I had five or six black groups, vocal groups, bands—Dave Lewis was one of my little teenage bands."

Still, the powers that be were not yet as willing as Parker's to be in the vanguard of all this societal change. So, even though Tolles made every effort to run respectable dances—he always hired two off-duty female and three male sheriff's deputies for security—some young attendees still created havoc drinking, puffing pot, necking, and brawling in the parking lot. Another issue was that both white and Black kids were coming out.

"The police didn't like *that* part," Tolles gravely recalled:

> So one day, the big sheriff came and I saw the way he was looking at me that he didn't appreciate me even *being* there, so we

stood outside and watched all these kids file out—and they were all mixed up, having fun—and that cracker stood right there with that cigar and said to the lady (I guess she was Dick Parker's wife or something, but she had charge of Parker's Pavilion), and he said, "There's just too goddam much mixing here!" She'd been running a cabaret on Saturday night, which was her mainstay—a very profitable thing for her. All she needed was that one night, and she could live like a queen, so something went down where he intimidated her: "If you continue on with this, we're going to have to take this other thing away from you." And they broke that up, man. So I started taking the Rock 'n' Roll Party to Everett. Bellingham. Tried it in Puyallup, but they ran me out of there. Tacoma. And around different places, but it never did get to be that big anymore. That one at Parker's was a hell of a thing.

The battle against racist practices in the music biz, and the wider world, would of course continue for years. But credit must be given to folks like Elmer Gill, Ted Simon, Dave Lewis, Billy Tolles, and Parker's management, who each contributed in significant ways to the eventual collapse of the old order. It was on December 11, 1956—mere months after these incidents—that the members of AFM Local 76 voted to approve a merger between the two musicians' unions, and AFM Local 493 members followed suit on the fifteenth. But significant changes take time, and the actual melding still did not occur for another couple of years. ★

CHAPTER 5

DAVID'S MOOD

The Eagles Auditorium's weekend R&B shows were becoming a happening thread in Seattle's cultural fabric by the mid-1950s. Their producers—Leonard Russell and Billy Tolles—had realized that lots of touring bands booked for Saturday night adult dances were happy to lay over and do Sunday afternoon shows for the town's younger set. This was how local teens were able to attend incredible shows by such seminal artists as T-Bone Walker, Muddy Waters, Howlin' Wolf, Fats Domino, Bobby "Blue" Bland, Little Milton, Bo Diddley, James Brown, Earl Bostic, Pee Wee Crayton, Bill Doggett, the Five Royales, Roy Milton and His Solid Senders, Roy Brown and His Mighty Mighty Men, Hank Ballard and the Midnighters, and even those pioneering rockers Little Richard and the Upsetters.

Seattle's Dave Lewis Combo scored the opening slot for many Eagles shows. The guys in the Combo had graduated from Garfield High School in 1956 and added their first guitarist, Al Aquino, a talented Inuit who'd just arrived in town from Alaska. At that point, no other local band had a rockin' guitarist of his skill level. That same summer, an Oregon-based, veteran dance promoter, Pat Mason, gave the Combo their biggest break yet: he hired them to fill the opening slot on the Northwest leg of a tour by the Pennsylvania-based, white rock 'n' roll pioneers Bill Haley and His Comets, who'd scored a breakthrough hit back in 1955 with "Rock around the Clock," which featured in the epic juvenile delinquent film *Blackboard Jungle*.

Rock 'n' roll was new and Haley was leading the pack, heading out on a nationwide concert tour in theaters, ballrooms, and country grange halls. Mason promoted the tour, touting the Dave Lewis Combo as the "Northwest's Greatest Rock 'n' Roll Band." The tour kicked off in Seattle with a show at the Eagles Auditorium on June 30 and it was a doozy. The

Seattle Times reported that the audience "acted in a disorderly manner." "The kids ran up and down the aisles, congregated around the stage, broke up some seats, tore down some decorations, and got out of hand generally," complained the hall's assistant manager to the city council. From there the Comets and the Combo were off to other dates, bringing their big-beat music to sleepy towns across the region.

For their part, the Combo created such a stir at those Haley gigs that Mason hired them to headline the Big Jamboree show at Oregon's Jantzen Beach Ballroom on September 29, 1956. Russell also continued booking shows into the Palomar Theatre as well as the Trianon Ballroom. And it was the Dave Lewis Combo (along with the Five Checks) whom he preferred to hire as the opening act for stars like Sugar Chile Robinson, Nellie Lutcher, and the R&B organist "Wild" Bill Davis.

In addition to booking the Combo to play on an outdoor stage built right in the middle of Twenty-First Avenue for an exciting street dance associated with the East Madison Mardi Gras festival, Russell also booked them for their biggest gig yet: opening a show down in Portland for B.B. King. They also opened the show by the Platters at Olympia's Evergreen Ballroom. And then came a long series of gigs at the Eagles Auditorium.

As 1957 dawned, the Combo had quite a few achievements under their belt, and their notoriety had reached such a level that Wilmer Morgan hired them in May as his house band at the Birdland. Scoring this gig was very important to Lewis, as he'd been intrigued by the joint ever since he was a kid. Years later, Lewis was sittin' on top of the world—at least the rockin' R&B world in central Seattle. They began by playing after hours on Fridays and Saturdays, from 11:30 p.m. until 3:30 a.m.

As Barney Hilliard recalled:

So, all the other musicians around town that played from eight to twelve or nine to one—they would get off work and come to the Birdland to either sit in or just be there because it was like *the* place to be. It was like high-energy because we played high-energy rhythm and blues music. I mean, athletes playing football out at the University of Washington—they would be there. Military servicemen that came to town—they'd ask a cabdriver "Where's the best action in town?" They'd say, "Birdland." People that lived in the Yesler Terrace projects, they would be there. So it was always exciting.

As the months went by and the Combo built up their following, Morgan grew fond of the boys and worked to help them succeed. Once, when he heard that Bumps Blackwell was back visiting Seattle, he invited him over to audition the Combo at the Birdland and determine whether they might merit a record deal. The Combo knocked out eight or ten tunes before Blackwell and Morgan stepped out of the room to huddle and discuss. Hilliard remembered that he and the other guys were jacked with excitement when Morgan came back alone: "'Well, guess what he said, guys.' We said, 'What? What? *What?*' Bumps said, 'You are very, very good at what you are doin' but all the music you play is cover music. You don't have any original songs. That if you want to be successful, you'd have to start writing songs and do some *original* music.' Wow. That hit us like a ton of bricks. That brought us back to Earth. All we were doing was covering other bands."

The truth hurts. But Blackwell, a music-biz veteran now, was a straight shooter who always said what he thought. Years later, he would explain that he always tried to teach his artists "the business side of music, because I don't want my pupils to be unprepared like I was, like [Little] Richard was, like we *all* were." And thus, in this instance, it was Lewis and his band that benefited from hearing the plain truth.

The Combo rebounded from the disappointment and took action. Lewis proceeded to write a couple of *extremely* catchy, unnamed instrumentals that the Combo began performing. One that Hilliard came up with, titled "Barney's Tune," became the Combo's debut single, released by Northgate Records. Other tunes, like "David's Mood"—which shared rhythmic DNA with "Louie Louie"—"Candido," and "Little Green Thing" were instantly popular with the fans; years later, when he finally got around to recording them, the tunes became established as regional standards.

Although the Combo was now starting to focus on writing originals, they were about to stumble across yet another "cover" song—one that would have a lasting impact on the Northwest teen scene. It was on the evening of September 21, 1957, when an R&B revue that was touring their way up the West Coast made a stop at the Eagles Auditorium. Headlining the show that night—which was promoted as a Battle of the Blues—were a couple of famous hitmakers: Little Junior Parker and Bobby "Blue" Bland. But *opening* the show was Richard Berry, a fairly obscure Los Angeles singer who was promoting his new single, which had just been released in April.

"Louie Louie" was a magnificently simple song—a cha-cha-driven three-chord ditty, built on a killer riff with a skip-beat feel and loaded with memorable hooks. The Dave Lewis Combo heard it, bought the record, and quickly adopted it into their set list. The popularity of the song grew and grew as the Combo continued to perform it at the Birdland. Eventually it entered the canon of "standards" that countless teen-R&B and garage-rock bands would enshrine.

It was from his perch at Birdland that Dave Lewis was fast becoming the most influential figure on the budding local scene. He would go on to shape the aural esthetics behind Seattle's teen-R&B sound more than any other single individual. His Combo was so good—especially by 1958, when Chuck Whittaker (with his Fender electric bass guitar) and Bud Brown (an experienced nightclub guitarist) replaced Jack Gray and Al Aquino—that for the next few years they were the town's top dance attraction. The band began drawing a racially diverse crowd, and the Birdland soon earned its reputation as the hottest after-hours dance hall in all Seattle. And there was a good reason the place became so popular: big-beat music.

"What was playing on the radio," Lewis winced as he remembered, "was Les Paul. Mary Ford, Kay Starr. *That* was the Top 10 on regular AM radio. But I wanted to do something. . . . I wanted to play for *dancing*. And we tried to find the records that were, I guess, Black-oriented. And then try to introduce them to a lot of people. I think that's what got us over. Because, here in Washington, there wasn't a big opening for underground R&B music. And that's what really got us into having something to offer everybody."

Yet looking back, it was, beyond the great musical grooves, likely the specific location of the Birdland—situated as it was on the "border" between the CD and Seattle's rather more affluent, homogenous (i.e., white) North End neighborhoods—that would make the place so significant to Seattle's musical richness.

"To me Birdland was a *Black* club," George Griffin has stated. "But I really liked that it was racially mixed. We had high school friends—white kids coming from different parts of the city to Birdland at night. That's why Morgan put that balcony up there—'cause most of the kids when they came in there they mostly went up to the balcony and let the bottom part be for grownups. But everybody mixed. It was very well integrated, I thought. People got along."

Although Seattle's Black population had created their own cultural universe here—right under the previously oblivious noses of most of their white neighbors—white music fans eventually found their way to the Birdland. And it would prove to be one of the places where, with all this ethnic intermingling—a new sense of racial tolerance began to take hold. That is not to say that it was a utopian oasis. "As I recall," Hilliard said, "at one point we said that the Dave Lewis Combo is 'music to fight to.' Because there was a fight *every* weekend."

The late 1950s was a time of rapid social change and conflict, but also one when people were looking to connect. At the Birdland, folks of varying means and circumstances could find common ground while dancing until the wee hours to performances by some of the greatest musicians around.

A night out at the Birdland would typically feature the Dave Lewis Combo playing instrumentals along with plenty of vocal numbers featuring either Lewis or George Griffin singing lead. In addition, there might be a few songs that spotlighted an exotic dancer or two onstage. But then there would be the surprise guest artists who would show up, either big-time stars sitting in or local talents—including doo-wop groups like the Barons and Joe Boot and the Fabulous Winds who would sing a cappella or with the Combo's backing.

The Barons were the very first teenage R&B group from the Northwest to have any impact in the record biz. Formed in 1954 by four Black Tacoma kids—William Gold (lead), Carl Charles (baritone), Stokey Wilford (tenor), and Malcolm Parks (bass)—the Barons had all come up in the town's Eastside housing projects, singing together in the Bethlehem Baptist Church choir, discovering R&B music via Bob Summerrise's show on KTAC, and hanging out at Eager Beaver's Broadway Record Shop.

The neighborhood offered—if not much else—a chaperoned youth club called Club 24, where every Friday night kids gathered and danced, played ping-pong, and clowned around. But on occasion they were allowed to see R&B shows in local halls. As Wilford would recall, "At that time, the Century Ballroom and the Evergreen Ballroom was the only thing goin' here. Of course, there was the Oddfellows Hall—they used to have dances down there. But that was mostly for the *white* kids. So for our little group, Club 24 was the only place for us to go. But then once a month or two, somebody would come to town, and even the kids could go out to the Evergreen: we seen the Clovers and James Brown out there."

Luckily, Club 24 also provided a tape recorder (and some reels of magnetic tape) that the kids occasionally messed around with. The Barons used that opportunity to cut a few songs and then mailed that self-recorded demo tape off to a few of the top R&B record labels in California. To their great surprise, they soon heard back from Modern Records, which invited them to come and lay down some tunes. Long story short: on Christmas break from Stadium and Lincoln High Schools in 1955, the Barons hitchhiked to Los Angeles, only to be stalled, and refused entry to the busy studio upon arrival. Frustrated, they went across town and knocked on the door of Imperial Records, the home for great artists including Fats Domino, T-Bone Walker, and Big Jay McNeely. Several discs were eventually released, with "I Know I Was Wrong" becoming the Barons' commercial zenith by hitting number 14 on *Billboard* magazine's "R&B Jockey" chart in 1956.

While in Los Angeles, the Barons did score a few gigs, including one thrilling night at the legendary 5/4 Ballroom, where they got the chance to sing with Fats Domino and his band. Although the Barons did enjoy some publicity in publications like *Jet*, they were underpromoted and returned home, where they gigged at various high school dances in Seattle, Everett, and Tacoma as well as at Seattle's Spanish Castle Ballroom and the Birdland.

The backstory of Joe Boot and the Fabulous Winds—which included singers Robert Ayers, Charles Thompson, Rogers Wright, and Deacon Brown with Jim Foster (electric guitar)—traces back to a gospel group, the Southwinds. But then they met and added a fireball of an R&B shouter from Louisiana named Joe Thomas, who boasted a gravelly voice that was inspired a bit by his old friend from down south, Little Richard. Thomas—who later owned the Music Menu record shop—earned his nickname of "Joe Boot" due to a bulky orthopedic heel on one shoe.

In the fall of 1957, Boot and the Winds entered another of Seattle's very first recording studios, Chet Noland's Dimensional Sound, which was also the home for his jazz- and pop-oriented Celestial Records label. As it turned out, Boot had been around and seemed to know someone in every R&B or jazz band coming through town. Thus, one night Little Richard stopped in to check out the studio action, and another time

Bumps Blackwell and Sam Cooke dropped by. It is fun to think that Richard's or Cooke's presence is what fired up the Winds—and their backing band, local jazzman Floyd Standifer and his combo—while recording their most rockin' two tunes, "Rock and Roll Radio" and "That's Tough." A few months later, Celestial issued the single; however, the Northwest radio industry was still generally avoiding rock music and Celestial had no luck promoting the record. Nevertheless, the disc still holds the distinction of being the first rock 'n' roll single ever produced in Seattle.

That such good music could not make headway locally was a given that local music-biz entrepreneurs had to deal with. Consider what occurred during one of the many times Big Jay McNeely had come to town since the late 1940s. He was a Watts-based R&B sax honker who'd been inspired by Illinois Jacquet but turned from jazz to proto–rock 'n' roll. McNeely's riveting sax work screeched and squalled like nobody's business, and he became famous for launching storming solos that often built up to his signature of holding onto one final, climactic note for a marathon length of time. Looking back on his beginnings, McNeely recalled, "I was very poor and I needed to make some money . . . so I just started playing one note, and screamin' and hollering, and playing soul. And it had such an effect on the people, and I just kept on doing it."

McNeely had been recording hits on seminal Black-oriented labels (including Imperial, Savoy, Federal, and Aladdin Records) for a full decade. And he was already very popular in Seattle, where more than once his band had played extended engagements at the Birdland and Dave's Fifth Avenue. In 1957, McNeely was between recording contracts, but he had this new song that his singer, Little Sonny Warner, had penned. "There Is Something on Your Mind" was fated to become a big hit and a core tune on the nascent teen-R&B scene in the Northwest. The song was blessed with a wonderfully lazy blues riff played hypnotically by the combo's sax choir, and featured a sweet melody sung soulfully by Warner.

In Seattle, McNeely was anxious to finally get his combo into a studio and cut Warner's promising song. Asking around where they might be able to record, McNeely was advised—quite probably by either Bumps Blackwell or Wilmer Morgan—to talk to Tom Ogilvy, who had recently scored a local pop hit on his and his wife Ellen's Seafair Records label. They (with Chet Noland engineering) had recorded a novelty record—"Old Rooster Tail"—in tribute to a spectacular hydroplane crash on Lake Washington during the 1955 Seafair Gold Cup competition. The disc garnered prominent local news coverage, captured the public's imagination, and became the talk of the town for weeks. And with that success, Ogilvy suddenly became known as Seattle's "record man."

And so, McNeely called the Ogilvys saying that his recording contract had expired, he was a free agent, he had a song, and he wanted to try recording in Seattle. Could Ogilvy help out? By now there were a couple of studios in town, so it certainly *could* be done. But as far as ever issuing anything by McNeely on Seafair Records, well, they'd just have to talk about that matter later.

It was right around New Year's Day 1958, and McNeely's combo came through on a tour headlining Chuck Berry and Bobby Darin and then settled into their own extended-length gig at the Birdland. Then Tom Ogilvy made arrangements to get McNeely over to the home basement studio run by Joe Boles. Boles was a successful businessman who had taken up recording mainly as a hobby, but his skills had become so good that word about his work had spread far and wide within the biz. Already all sorts of industry folks—including the Four Freshmen, Moses Asch, Wally Heider, Gus Mancuso, Jack Jones, Buddy Greco, the Martin Denny group, and Buck Owens—had stopped by to check out the sounds. Now it was McNeely's turn, and he was about to cut the best-known song of his long career.

"We recorded our biggest hit in Seattle: 'Something on Your Mind.' Joe Boles was a really great guy. He came and recorded live at the club, you know, and then we got off from work and went over to his home basement and recorded all night. He had a 2-track. Great sound. Great balance, you know—stereo. And so, we really had a lot of fun doing recording. It was really tremendous."

After the session, McNeely, Ogilvy, and Boles huddled to discuss next steps. They all agreed that "There Is Something on Your Mind" was a ready-made hit. McNeely was willing to let Ogilvy release it as a single on his Seafair label, but both Boles and Ogilvy realized that would be futile given the unsupportive stance of local radio regarding R&B. So, they considered other options while the master tapes rested on Boles's shelves. Meanwhile, upon the completion of their Birdland gig, McNeely's combo packed up and headed back home.

Then, nearly a year later, the combo returned to Seattle, and this time Ogilvy and Boles encouraged McNeely to take the tapes elsewhere.

When back in Los Angeles, he contacted the city's top R&B radio DJ, Hunter Hancock, who upon hearing the tape immediately offered to form his own label to issue it.

And thus, in mid-February 1959, Swingin' Records' inaugural release, "There Is Something on Your Mind," made its KGFJ radio debut when Hancock spun the record on his popular afternoon show *Harlematinee*. The song shot up to the number 5 slot on *Billboard*'s R&B charts and crossed over to the pop charts, peaking at number 44 (and number 41 in *Cash Box*) in sixteen weeks of action, becoming one of the top-selling R&B songs of the year. Swingin' then released a second single from the Seattle sessions, Ogilvy's "I Got the Message."

This success was bittersweet for Boles and Ogilvy as they formed a partnership label, Bolo Records, but must have always looked back at "the one that got away." Everyone could hear what a great tune it was, but no one could have guessed back in the day that it was destined to become a standard in the Northwest teen-R&B canon and a cornerstone in the creation of the Northwest Sound.

Decades later, a tape recording of Big Jay McNeely's band cut back in 1957 by the Seattle audio engineer Fred Rasmussen surfaced and resulted in the commercial release of the *Live at Birdland* album in 1992. An amazing aural document of nighttime action at the fabled club, the disc reveals a happy crowd reveling in the sounds of a masterful R&B combo playing, among other tunes, "There Is Something on Your Mind," Bill Doggett's "Honky Tonk," and Ray Charles's "I Got a Woman." ★

CHAPTER *6*

TEENAGE HOP

Vibrant local music scenes are typically built on cornerstones that include musical talent, supportive radio, accessible performance venues, and good record shops. Neighborhood platter shacks have long served as social hubs where musicians and music fans can hang out, hear new tunes, and make connections. Such shops are often where young players cross paths and go on to form bands.

Throughout the 1950s, Bop City Records served that purpose down in Portland, in Tacoma the action was at Eager Beaver's Broadway Record Shop, and in Seattle the town's Black citizens—and a few hip, young white kids—discovered all the latest R&B sounds at the Little Record Mart on East Madison and the Groove Record Shop on South Jackson, which Seattle's Black DJ Bob Summerrise bought and later recast as the World of Music.

At the same time, Seattle's teen-R&B scene was steadily growing with an increasing number of new bands emerging from various neighborhoods. By 1958, the best of these combos were the Playboys from the CD and the Frantics from the North End. The Playboys were a rare, racially integrated ensemble that emerged from an earlier group, the Doug Robinson Combo, based out of Garfield High School. Formed in the spring of 1956, it was led by their drummer and included the Filipino sax player Johnny O'Francia, Jimmy Pipkin (piano), and two of Seattle jazzman Floyd Standifer's brothers: Alonzo (vocals) and Jim (sax).

O'Francia once recalled, "I started out with the Doug Robinson Combo. They were all colored kids except for myself, and it was strictly rhythm & blues oriented. More and more high school dances were starting to hire young groups. All of a sudden there was a bigger demand for bands. There was a shortage of bands, actually."

Then, as the year ended, O'Francia decided to form a new band and hooked up with Bob Risley (piano), Andy Duvall (drums), Roland Green (guitar), and Carlos Ward, who had been playing both baritone and alto sax for Garfield's pep band. One day, Ward struck up a conversation with a Garfield football star named Rolen "Ron" Holden, yet another of Oscar Holden Sr.'s musical offspring, and invited him to audition as their singer. Having come up in Seattle's CD, the Playboys were all directly inspired by the Dave Lewis Combo.

"When I first started getting into the musical scene, we had to sneak into places like Birdland," Holden remembered. "*That's* where the music was happening. They would let me in the backdoor. The main opening act that I knew of was the Dave Lewis Combo. He was the hottest thing happening. He was it. He played all of those gigs. They had a saxophone duo. It seemed like it was the hottest sax duo anywhere in the world! Yeah—those twin horns they were just monsters. That combo *owned* this city. They were the hottest rhythm and blues band. Well, it was rhythm and blues—but they called it 'rock 'n' roll'! [*laughter*]."

While providing a model of success to emulate for younger musicians, the Dave Lewis Combo's dominance of the scene also made it necessary for newbies to lower their sights a bit and take whatever modest gigs they could rustle up.

As the Playboys refined their sound and stage act—which included a ton of Ray Charles tunes—and began building up their own following, they started earning a reputation as the CD's baddest up-and-coming teen-R&B combo. But then, at about that same time, another promising band began making waves. As Ron Holden put it, "The Playboys' first recognizable competition came from the Frantics." Indeed, this new Frantics band would soon be "borrowing" songs straight from their set list, including, as the Playboys' drummer Andy Duvall would recall, "Louie Louie": "We were getting most of our tunes off records that Ron Holden was bringing over. He was getting them from his older brother Dave. For instance, we were the first that played 'Louie Louie' in town. Because Dave had just come back from LA with the record by Richard Berry and the Pharaohs. The Frantics caught it the first time we played it and started doing it too. . . . Pissed us off when everybody else recorded it!"

The Frantics traced their beginnings back to a duo called the Hi-Fi's that was formed in 1953 by two Jane Addams Junior High School kids:

Ron Peterson (guitar) and Chuck Schoning (accordion and sax). In '54, they added Dean Tonkin (bass) and Joel Goodman (drums) and became the plaid-jacket-clad Four Frantics.

The band's secret weapons were that each member could read music and play charts, and thus the band could whip off any old pop standard you requested; and that Peterson was an electric guitar whiz who had initially been attracted to the instrument by the playing featured on KING-TV's early local kiddie show *Sheriff Tex's Safety Junction*, which starred the nationally famed country music veteran Texas Jim Lewis. By age thirteen, Peterson had become so skilled that Seattle's Celestial Records began using him on various pop sessions. With that background, Peterson created a unique, signature lead guitar style—a sort of proto–spaghetti western thing—that largely defined the Frantics' early sound.

With a few other Talent Fest performances under their belts, the Frantics were now ready to play for larger crowds. In 1956, they won first prize at West Seattle's annual Hi-Yu summer fair talent show and progressed to playing at a PTA-sponsored All-City Dance at the old Civic Auditorium. These dances typically featured a big band orchestra that played mainstream swing and pop for ballroom-style dancing. But the Four Frantics volunteered to play a few rockin' numbers during the headliner's intermission breaks.

This approach went well at first—but it also put them in the cross-hairs of the AFM Local 76's union boss, Chet Ramage. One night, Ramage took note of the Four Frantics and without warning yanked the power supply to their amps, barking in their faces, "You guys aren't gonna play another job in this town until you join the union." Still reluctant to join, the Four Frantics needed to learn their lesson the hard way. At that time, the popular *Ted Mack Amateur Hour* TV show was holding its annual nationwide talent search, and the band progressed to the local runoffs at KING-TV's studios before it was discovered they were not union members and they were then disqualified—thus clearing the path for the Five Checks to win.

That summer of '56, both the Four Frantics and the Dave Lewis Combo made multiple appearances on Billy Tolles's *Rock 'n' Roll Party* on KCPQ-TV, broadcast live from Parker's Ballroom. But as the teen scene continued developing and resistance to teenagers dancing began to ease up, such ballrooms were not the only large venues where such events could take place. The whole range of opportunities for independent dance promoters came to include various National Guard armories, community halls, and roller-skating rinks.

In the fall of '57—and after shortening their name to the Frantics—they added Jim Manolides (electric bass), and Bob Hosko (sax). By this point, they were the most prominent pure rock 'n' roll band in Seattle, and great gigs were coming their way: from shows at the Eagles Auditorium, to the Trianon Ballroom—where they once opened for Hank Ballard and the Midnighters—and back to the Civic Auditorium, where they were included on the fabled Jazz at the Philharmonic concert roster with the likes of Stan Getz, Gene Krupa, and Ray Brown. The band also opened for Johnny and the Hurricanes at the Spanish Castle and backed Gene Vincent there and at Portland's D Street Corral at 17119 SE Division Street.

"We leaned more towards Dave Lewis than the Frantics did," Johnny O'Francia noted:

> We were more rhythm and blues—colored-oriented—they were more like Bill Haley and some of the other white artists around. Even when we played the same songs there was a distinct difference. They had their sound and we had our sound. They were working a lot more than we were. They were all white. That was *part* of it, I know. There were places we couldn't play because of having colored guys in the group. I can remember a couple of instances where we really had trouble, but we went ahead and did it anyhow. We all kept the attitude: if people didn't want us—we sure didn't want to play for them! There was discrimination, but we were considered an "entertainer"—you were there for a job and then left. No problem.

One factor that did help the Playboys secure more gigs was the addition of their first electric guitarist. "Right after we started playing 'Louie Louie' we knew we needed a guitar," Andy Duvall recollected, "so we found Roland Green. He's just come up from Louisiana—really an 'Under the Apple Tree'–type colored player. He'd taught himself how to play and never tuned his guitar like anybody else. But he could sure play. It was like a magic-sounding guitar. He played the style of the day: bass, solo, and really not too much rhythm. The piano carried a lot of the rhythm." ("Under the Apple Tree" is a reference to the 1942 Glenn Miller Orchestra–Andrews Sisters pop hit "Don't Sit under the Apple Tree [with Anyone Else but Me].")

Then, just like the Dave Lewis Combo and the Frantics before them, the Playboys were also "invited" to join AFM Local 76. Duvall explained the lay of the land back then:

> The Frantics joined the white local. We went down to join that one and they said, "You can't join because you've got colored people in your band." We really started to get pissed about that, but then went down and joined Local 493 in the Central District. It was a lot cheaper. Bob Risley and I were the *only* white guys in the Black union at that time. Ray Charles belonged to that union. There were a lot of heavyweights in the Black union, so we used to go down and sit in at the union hall just to see if we could meet all these guys that were happening! ★

CHAPTER 7

"LOUIE LOUIE" ARRIVES

In Tacoma, the earliest R&B music was being played by a handful of Black bands including the Blue Notes, Swingin' Esquires, Ivories, Launchers—and the Dukes of Rhythm and the King's Men, two bands founded in sequence by sax man Johnny Moorehead, who allegedly settled in town after being fired on the spot by Chuck Berry one night for overdrinking at a gig up in Seattle.

A locus of the action in town was Eager Beaver's Broadway Record Shop, which was situated in the middle of Lower Broadway, Tacoma's Black business district. The joint was a combination barber shop–record store; until it was eventually raided by lawmen, it was *the* place where trusted customers could come away with a new hairdo, a couple new jazz or R&B platters, as well as a matchbox of reefer or a handful of pills. But for some young R&B buffs—including a few in-the-know white teenagers—the biggest attraction was just that the shop's racks were well stocked with a great selection of records that weren't available at the Upper Broadway shops that catered to the town's white majority.

Tacoma was a tough place in the mid-'50s, with various white hotrod clubs throwing dances that often descended into brutal parking lot brawls, while Black gangs conducted turf wars against forays by invaders from Seattle and Bremerton. Yet the Broadway Record Shop stood as one place that welcomed anybody's business—including that of white outsider misfits like Little Bill Engelhart.

Little Bill was a soulful teenage guitarist and budding hipster who would go on to found the Northwest's first all-white, purely R&B-focused combo, the Blue Notes. But as a candidate for pop stardom, he was an unlikely choice. The son of Montana chicken ranchers who had relocated to Chelan, Washington, Little Bill contracted polio, which resulted in his need for a wheelchair and then crutches, and his enrollment in the cruelly named Crippled Children's School. Luckily, after showing an interest in music and getting a cheap guitar, his father's country guitarist friend began to teach a few chords to the kid (whose grandmother called him "Little Bill" to differentiate him from his namesake grandfather).

Later, after the family moved to Tacoma, his father bought him a better guitar at Bark's Music Shop, and at age twelve he was paired up with a talented fiddle-playing peer named Donny Ulrich. This duo played country tunes for patients at the nearby Puyallup Indian Hospital and at the enlisted men's club at Fort Lewis.

Little Bill soon entertained dreams of forming his own band. But *not* a country and western outfit. Instead, Little Bill's far-fetched idea was to lead an R&B group, even though the odds against ever finding other young white R&B fans in Tacoma in the mid-'50s were steep. But one day in early 1955 he got a break. Little Bill was about fifteen and attending a vocational school, where one day he spotted a note pinned to a bulletin board. It said that the school was organizing a lunchroom dance and anyone with a musical instrument was welcome to audition. So, he brought his guitar, but only two other guys showed up: a trumpeter and a Black drummer named Jimmy Green. Don't worry, Green said, he would round up some additional musician pals to help with the upcoming dance.

The good news was that Green's friends—Marion Jenkins (piano), Theotis (alto sax), and Willie Pierre (tenor sax)—happened to be some of the skilled Black musicians who usually picked up work playing the dives on Lower Broadway. The school dance went fine, and afterward the guys invited Little Bill over to a Black after-hours bottle club, the George Washington Carver Legion Hall, where he sat in with the band playing there. Those cats dug the skinny white kid's guitar skills and hired him on the spot. Just like that, Little Bill was suddenly a member of a band—a shambolic band, sure—but still: the Blue Notes, a genuine R&B outfit.

"It was a Black and white group playing pretty much all shuffles and blues," Little Bill recalled. "Almost everything was in B-flat. There was no bass. Just an old rhythm-heavy piano player. We weren't doing anything creative. Maybe at the time I thought we were, but as I look back now, it was the blues and shuffles. Shuffles and blues. It really didn't amount to much musically—and we really had a hard time finding places to play."

Still, they did get an opportunity or two to gig at Tacoma's El Paso Tavern, the Friendly Tavern, and the Fort Lewis Officers Club. But mainly it was those Friday or Saturday night gigs at the Hilltop neighborhood Legion Hall. And the action there could get plenty wild. Just ask Little Bill: "Theo's sister (and Jimmy's girlfriend) was Inez, and from where I sat, it looked like she was dead-set on driving Jimmy nuts. Whenever we would play a slow blues, which was about every other song, she would grab onto somebody and start with the bump and grind on the dance floor. Well, Jimmy would take it for as long as he could, and then he would stand up and start yellin', '*INEZ: Set your ass down, NOW!*' This would, of course, have zero effect on her, and she would just continue with the rub a dub dub. Finally unable to contain himself any longer, Jimmy would fly off the stand, razor in hand, and scare the crap out of the guy she was dancing with. On a good night Jim would chase Inez's bump partners around the room half a dozen times! I loved it!"

Over the next few months, a few different players drifted in and out—a young white kid named Frank Dutra had shed his accordion, taken up the tenor sax, and replaced Willie Pierre. Not long after the Blue Notes decided to try something new: playing a dance for a teenage crowd. That hadn't been done before in Tacoma, but in the fall of '55 they got an invitation to play a teen dance up in Port Townsend. The event was well attended and the guys made some coin, but the hassle of driving eighty miles each way to only pocket a few bucks broke up the Blue Notes. But along the way Little Bill and Dutra had struck up a friendship, and they immediately began trying to scope out potential players at Stadium High School to reconstitute the band.

They had no luck until one early summer evening in '57, when they went to the Sunset Theater to attend a screening of *Blackboard Jungle*. The movie featured a prototypical juvenile delinquent teen-gang plot set in the heart of New York City, so the involvement of Bill Haley's twangy rock sound was a bit of miscasting: "By all logic, the theme song of the film should have been something more R&B or doo-wop in its sound. Haley's spit curl rockabilly/C&W was about the farthest thing from the Bronx it was possible to get, but very close to a sound the rest of the country was tuned into."

But nitpicking aside, anyone interested in rock 'n' roll or rhythm and blues was in attendance that Friday night. And so it was that, hanging out in the lobby, Little Bill and Dutra happened to strike up a conversation with a couple younger guys: John "Buck" Ormsby and Lasse Aanes, mere eighth graders at Jason Lee Junior High, as well as another kid, Paul Cassidy, who mentioned that he owned a guitar. Ormsby, who had been studying Hawaiian steel guitar, told the guys he had a Fender electric steel guitar on which he could play bass lines, and Aanes explained that he had a drum set and that they'd already been jamming a bit. The five agreed to meet the next day at Little Bill's parents' garage at 840 South Prospect Street.

After just a couple jam sessions, the boys decided they should choose a name and become a real band. Since the Blue Notes had broken up and Little Bill had a large stash of preprinted Blue Notes dance poster blanks they could use, the boys agreed to adopt the name for their new R&B band. They practiced, learned more songs together—including an original instrumental, "The Boogie"—and then this new Blue Notes made their modest debut at a house party. A few more such private party gigs followed, and then the band got the opportunity to play a dance held at the Manito Hall. Capacity for the venue was limited to seventy-five attendees, so when 150 teens packed themselves in—and alcohol imbibed on both sides of the bandstand fueled the excitement—a brawl broke out among some local toughs.

The Blue Notes' drummer Lassie Aanes remembered the night: "That was where the cop got his uniform ripped up and they stole his gun, his handcuffs and everything. Terrible." Beyond that, the ruffians also kicked in Aanes's bass drumhead, and their guitarist Paul Cassidy got punched out. Having seen enough of this rock 'n' roll realm, Cassidy dropped out of the Blue Notes. Meanwhile, the Blue Notes added a second sax player, Aanes's old friend Marvin "Buck" Mann, which enriched their overall sound. But then, in September 1956, the guys stumbled on a kid who would soon become their new singer and, in time, a genuine Northwest teen-R&B legend: Robin Roberts.

Robin Roberts had been raised in Queens, New York, as the only child of an acclaimed architect, but he and his mother moved to an affluent neighborhood on the north side of Tacoma to start anew after Mr. Roberts's early death. Robin initially came off as a charismatic oddball. He was an ultra-brainy nerd type: Science Club secretary, German

Club vice president, Honor Roll, PTA representative, Red Cross representative. But as his new bandmates would soon discover, he was a rock 'n' roll Clark Kent: unassuming in appearance, but onstage a maniacal, high-voltage, rockin' R&B singer. It didn't take long for the kid to pick up his new nickname: "Rockin' Robin."

One day while the band was rehearsing after school in Little Bill's garage, Rockin' Robin stepped outside for a minute, only to rush back in and tell his bandmates that they needed to come out and have a look. The scene they beheld was about forty fellow teens dancing in the alley. Little Bill would never forget what happened next: "So Robin—being real shrewd—said, 'Let's rent a hall.' [*laughter*] So, that's how we got started."

That's how the Blue Notes came to be the Northwest's original independent, white, DIY rockin' R&B band. Over the following months, the Blue Notes began throwing their own dances at spots including at a pavilion up on Angle Lake about twenty miles north of Tacoma. From there, the band expanded to a few more out-of-town shows at halls in the nearby burgs of Auburn, Enumclaw, Sumner, and Puyallup. For each they would have posters printed, rent a Coke machine, and hire ticket takers. Then there was the matter of getting a city or county dance event permit and hiring an off-duty police officer for security. With all those preparations handled, Little Bill figured they'd done everything to ensure safe and successful gigs:

> Normally everything went fine. The kids had a great time at the dances, nobody tore the place up, and we made some pretty good money. Then we rented the Old Mill, a community hall on the Puyallup Indian Reservation. The county was very reluctant to issue us a permit and said we would need at least six policemen. Seems the Old Mill had a rep for hell-raising. *Hell-raising* was putting it mildly. At the first dance a group of Native Americans turned a patrol car over with two sheriff's deputies inside! There were several fights between the "cowboys" and the "Indians," and a number of arrests were made and we were closed down about an hour into the dance. We were told not to even try and hire police for any upcoming dances at the Mill.

Word quickly spread about the band, and in no time they—cruising to their gigs in Little Bill's sharp '48 Oldsmobile—became a bit of a sensation. "We were green. But we were the only ones around. If you're the only one, then you're the best."

Then came the day in January 1957 when the Blue Notes signed up to compete in an amateur talent show at a major downtown hall, the Crescent Ballroom. That show was produced by Bill Griffith and Grover Jackson, whose country band had long been ruling the roost there on most Friday and Saturday nights. At the show, the Blue Notes faced the expected amateur competition: screechy violin players, warbly singers, and a couple of tap-dancing kids. Worthy foes no doubt—and, to Little Bill, the whole event seemed like a huge deal:

> We beat the tap dancer! Which is *unheard* of! The worst thing in an amateur contest is to come up against a six-year-old tap dancer. A girl. But we had enough of our followers there, so we won the night—the Trials—so we got to come back [in March 1957] for the Finals. . . . And we won the contest so they gave us a clock radio [*laughter*] and a trophy. And then, the guy who was running the dance hall said, "Well, these guys have actually won something that they don't know about: They'll be playing the first half of the dances every Saturday night here."

Bill Griffith and Grover Jackson also mentioned that they were inviting the Blue Notes to guest on their radio show, and after that the two old cowboys wasted no time having the band appear on their other program, KTNT-TV's *Bill and Grover's Variety Show*. It was at this point that the Blue Notes came to the attention of the Tacoma musicians' union, AFM Local 117. One day the phone rang ominously at the Engelhart's home. "'Hello, this is Bill,' I say with all confidence I can muster at seventeen," recounted Little Bill. "On the other end of the line a very gruff voice lays out the plan. 'You boys get down here and sign up, or I'll blackball the whole bunch of ya.' Now there's something we hadn't thought of. In the beginning, this was just for fun. A way to be popular at school. A way to pick up girls . . . and now this. BLACKBALLED!"

As none of the boys had the required, and daunting, fifty-dollar union membership fee on hand, union head Grady Morehead signed them up. Assuring them they "had done the right thing" and were now professional musicians, he also informed them they would be allowed to make installment payments to be added to their monthly dues.

In fairness, Tacoma's Local 117 was not all that different from plenty of other musicians' unions in that regard—they were typically led by establishment players who harbored little empathy for either R&B or rock 'n' roll music. Nonetheless, they had the power to force individuals to pay up even if the organization couldn't provide any income-generating work.

Meanwhile, Rockin' Robin—as a certified R&B fiend who favored Ray Charles, Little Richard, Hank Ballard, and all the rest of the good stuff—had already discovered the Broadway Record Shop. He began buying records there, and then hung out so regularly that the charmed owner soon had him working part-time. Meanwhile, the town's pioneering Black DJ over at KTAC, Bob Summerrise, began airing that new single by Richard Berry, "Louie Louie." From there, the single began getting tons of plays on the jukeboxes in the taverns scattered along the perimeters of Fort Lewis and the McChord Air Force Base, and also selling like crazy out of Summerrise's World of Music shop up in Seattle.

The three-chord ditty was as basic—and therefore unforgettable—as can be, while the lyrics tell the tale of a sailor who is pouring his lonely heart out to his patient bartender named Louie. In a mildly clipped patois he repeats how "me gotta go" and set sail for Jamaica to reunite with his island girl. Musically "Louie Louie" employed elements of the island music craze that included the Tarriers' "The Banana Boat Song," Harry Belafonte's "Jamaica Farewell," and Chuck Berry's calypso-tinged "Havana Moon."

Rockin' Robin was instantly attracted to the record. Then, because he became thoroughly obsessed by the song, the Blue Notes added it to their repertoire, albeit in an arrangement that dropped the exotic Caribbean aspects—a process that later teen bands continued until "Louie Louie" was transformed into a straight-forward garage-rock pounder. Eventually it was established as the signature rock song of the whole region. ★

CHAPTER 8

THE EVERGREEN

The Evergreen Ballroom—that fabled musical outpost in the woods on the outskirts of Olympia—had been presenting dance music regularly since its founding back in 1931. Due to the hall's existence, locals had once-in-a-lifetime opportunities to see live music performed by all the big-name orchestras as led by Louis Armstrong, Duke Ellington, Count Basie, Benny Goodman, Harry James, Lionel Hampton, Tommy Dorsey, and Woody Herman. Similarly, country music fans were able to witness performances by the likes of Hank Williams, Roy Acuff, T. Texas Tyler, Ray Price, Hank Thompson, Ferlin Husky, Marty Robbins, Faron Young, Johnny Cash, and Buck Owens.

But it was an entirely different audience that was attracted to another set of touring acts booked here—those that played blues, R&B, and rock 'n' roll. Among the former were Ray Charles, Lowell Fulson, Roy Brown, Earl Bostic, Jimmy Reed, Bill Doggett, Etta James, B.B. King, Little Willie John, Hank Ballard and the Midnighters, Lloyd Price, Fats Domino, Lavern Baker, Jackie Wilson, James Brown and His Famous Flames, Ike and Tina Turner, the Platters, Richard Berry, Bobby "Blue" Bland, Little Junior Parker, the Drifters, Rufus Thomas, Freddie King, Marvin Gaye, and Junior Walker and the All Stars. Some of the pioneering rockers who played the "Green" were Little Richard, Chuck Berry, Gene Vincent, Jerry Lee Lewis, Buddy Knox, Wanda Jackson, and the Coasters.

The Evergreen's management had done what they could to increase opportunities for the disadvantaged and young to attend shows. First, they arranged to have a dedicated bus circulate a circuit of stops around Tacoma offering free transportation to and from the hall (naturally the Broadway Record Shop served as one of these spots). They had also purposefully built the hall's beverage bar in an area physically separate from the dancefloor so that minors could watch the bands. And that hip teenager from Tacoma, Little Bill, became a ringleader who guided his buddies out to witness all this action. The first show he attended there was the James Brown Revue in 1956. He would later enthuse, "It was the greatest school there was for young musicians."

The act of witnessing a gut-bucket rhythm and blues revue was an experience no Eisenhower-era teenager was likely to forget as innumerable surprises awaited the uninitiated: from the smoky payday party atmosphere where the audiences were as loose as the music was tight, to a dance floor as sweaty and packed with fun lovers as any delta juke joint or ghetto jazz dive.

The Blue Notes were among the first local white kids to brave the trip out to attend these R&B shows at the Evergreen—and Little Bill took every opportunity to meet his idols:

> Those Sunday nights at the Evergreen were always a big event. We would show up early either to watch the bus pull in, or in most cases the station wagons pulling trailers, or we would be waiting inside positioned to watch them all walk in the door. I remember they all looked real serious. Some wore head rags to keep the process in place (the hair straight). They all looked plenty road weary as they filed back into the dressing rooms. We, in turn, made our way to the bandstand and took our regular spot up in front; we didn't want to miss anything. They would all be dressed up in suits and ties. Back in those days, bands dressed up and looked real sharp.

The Blue Notes' Buck Ormsby recalled the excitement they felt: "We'd go out there go right up to the stage, and they'd have this railing, and we'd grab onto that and we wouldn't let go of it all night. Ray Charles would be there and we could reach out and touch him."

On one particularly memorable night, Little Bill made his way backstage to meet Charles. The resulting conversation was as brief as it was lastingly inspirational. Charles asked the kid something like "So, are you a musician?" Little Bill replied, "Yes." "Oh, well, what kind of music do you play?" "The blues." And then, after a significant pause, Charles inquired, "You're white, aren't you?" "Yes." "Well, it doesn't matter if you *feel* it—but don't sing 'em if you don't *feel* 'em." Truer words have never been spoken, and the young singer took that sage advice to heart. On another night not long after—February 2, 1958—Little Bill worked up the courage to get up on the Evergreen's stage:

> I was so nervy when I was nineteen years old that I walked up to
> B.B. King and asked him if I could sing with his band. And he said,
> "Sure! Whudya wanna do?" And I said, "Well, mostly I just do
> some of the stuff you do." He said, "Well, go on up and do it."
> I mean, this was a really an *unbelievable* thing. But it really hap-
> pened and Buck was in the audience. So, I got up there and it was
> great. He had like this big fifteen-piece band then and I was just
> in seventh heaven. So, I sang a couple songs and into the second
> one I heard a guitar behind me and I turned around and it was B.B.
> King—and he had this big smile on his face!

The guys in the Blue Notes—like other young local players—relished their opportunities to see the hottest bands in America make a stop at the Evergreen. Drummer Lassie Aanes described one memorable night there:

> The place'd be full of people, but we'd just mow our way right
> up in front of the bandstand and hang on and watch. I remember
> one night, catching B.B. King—for about the tenth time. After B.B.
> got through playin', Bill was talking to him, and he said, "This is
> a group, isn't it?" Bill says, "Yeah." B.B. says, "I know that." He
> says, "You play sax. You play sax. You're a guitar player. You're
> a drummer." We're goin' "*Wow*! How does this guy know about
> *us*?" B.B. says, "Well, hell, every time you guys come out, you're
> always watching that guy, and *you're* always watching the drummer.
> *You're* sitting there staring. I *know* what you guys play." He had us
> pegged.

By this point, the hard-core R&B music the boys were reveling in began to have a major impact on them. It was providing the musi-cal vocabulary that was shaping their own band's sounds. And the thing that truly made a lasting impression was that many of the acts they saw at the Evergreen—in particular, the rockin' R&B bands led by Big Jay McNeely, Bill Doggett, Bobby "Blue" Bland, Hank Ballard, Ike Turner, Little Richard, James Brown, and Ray Charles—included fab-ulous horn sections. Just consider: McNeely, Doggett, and Bland each often sported a tenor and bari sax combination to great effect; Ballard's

Midnighters utilized a sax and trumpet; Turner employed a tenor sax, bari sax, and trombone; Little Richard's Upsetters at times featured five sax players; Brown's Famous Flames raised the stakes with three saxes and four trumpets—but Charles reigned supreme by occasionally performing with *ten* saxes!

Proof that all this had a keen impact in the Northwest is the sheer number of important early bands that would adopt the multiple-horn blueprint: the Savoy Boys, Bumps Blackwell's Junior Band, Billy Tolles's Octet, the Frank Roberts Combo, the Dave Lewis Combo, the Blue Notes, Clayton Watson and His Silhouettes, the Playboys, the Thunderbirds, the Velvetones, the Dynamics, and the Counts.

The Blue Notes were committed to always improving their show and their sound—and when Buck Ormsby finally dumped his steel guitar and acquired a booming, newly marketed Fender electric bass guitar, the band was fully state of the art. And the resultant new whomp and oomph in the Blue Notes' music was impossible to ignore. This upgrade, and ongoing efforts—inspired by the Upsetters show at the Evergreen—drove the boys to create their own version of a choreographed R&B stage show.

"One of the groups we were *all* fascinated with," admitted Little Bill, "were the Upsetters. They did a lot of choreography that the guys wanted to do. In fact, they taught the fellows choreography. We had three men, and Robin, out front doing steps. We were the first band in the Northwest that ever did any choreography."

These slick stage moves not only won them fans but also caught the attention of media members, who were clearly befuddled by the specter of a white teenage R&B band doing such wild steps. This disconnect was perfectly expressed in a newspaper article bearing an inflammatory headline—"Thrill Jive Addicts"—which went on to misidentify them as "Pierce County's candidates for the hall of fame in the field of modern jazz." Though hardly a jazz band, the Blue Notes were extremely novel.

"The Blue Notes," Little Bill proudly stated, "were the only band around that area for at least a year that actually played that kind of music. There were other young bands but they were all sitting down with their dinner jackets and reading sheet music from the '40s. So we were kind of an oddity. Later we heard about this group out in Lakewood, a Tacoma suburb."

A new group. One that the Blue Notes would initially assist by giving them opening slots at their dances. A group that would later poach a couple of Blue Notes into their own lineup. A group that would eventually overtake the Blue Notes in prominence and become Northwest rock's top dogs for the next decade. ★

CHAPTER 9

WAILERS HOUSE PARTY

Youth fads come and go, pop culture evolves, and the music always rolls on ahead. So, by the late 1950s, a fresh wave of teenage rock 'n' roll bands emerged in the wake of the original rockabilly pioneers. Among the first of these to score hits nationally were South Carolina's Joe Bennett and the Sparkletones, Ohio's Johnny and the Hurricanes, Pennsylvania's Freddie Bell and the Bellboys—and from Tacoma, the Wailers. It was the latter whom historians have credited with taking things a big step toward the future by embodying the concept of a teenage rock 'n' roll *band*. They accomplished this feat simply by not highlighting some bandleader's name and instead presenting themselves as coequals: the Wailers. It was a move that advanced the concept of distinct group identities over the typical model of a backing ensemble supporting the big-name star out front.

The band's origins trace back to a Dixieland outfit—the Knightcaps—founded at Tacoma's Clover Park High School by an acoustic bassist named Woody Mortenson and a trumpeter named John Greek. They began by casually hiring a varying cast of supporting players and booking themselves around as either the M-G Trio, the M-G Quartet, the M-G Quintet, or the M-G Octet, depending on a particular gig's musical requirements—and budgetary limits.

The personnel varied according to who was willing and able to do one-nighters on short notice, and thus a bunch of different guys passed through the ranks. But one keeper was Rich Dangel, a kid from a military family who lived on the McChord Air Force Base near Tacoma and whose father had taught him a few Hawaiian songs on his guitar.

Initially Dangel had hooked up with a couple other kids and they'd played a couple of talent shows and other minor gigs on the base. But one day when he was fourteen, he was approached at school by John

Greek, who explained that his Dixieland band was getting more frequent requests for rock 'n' roll songs. Would Dangel like to make some money by playing a few songs each night with them? "I just had a teeny, little amplifier and a Supro guitar that my dad found in a pawnshop. But the piano player and bass player in the Dixieland band, they quit, 'cause they couldn't hear themselves anymore [*laughter*], *see*? Anyway, we had to find another keyboard player—and in the process of doing that we somehow found Kent Morrill—and he could sing some rock 'n' roll music." Not only could Morrill pound out some mean rock 'n' roll piano, he sang—inspired, as he recalled, by Ray Charles and Little Richard—with a mercurial, high tenor, and even brought along an original full-tilt "Tutti Frutti"–styled song called "Dirty Robber" in his bag of tricks.

As the lineup began to stabilize, they added a couple of guys from Stadium High School—a sax player named Mark Marush and a lanky badass drummer named Mike Burk. Another sax player named Tom Geving also showed up and began jamming. This revamped musical aggregation, dubbed the Knightcaps, went on to perform their debut gig at McChord Field's teen club in June 1958. Word of that dance got around, and soon the band was hired to play at the base's enlisted men's nightclub, the Snakepit. After that Wednesday night show, the band played a Friday night dance in the Grange Hall at Clear Lake out in Eatonville, plus other occasional early shows at the local Frisko Freeze where they were compensated with free ice cream.

It was at about this point when the Blue Notes began to catch wind of the Knightcaps' emergence, and Little Bill magnanimously invited them to play the intermission at a Blue Notes dance scheduled for the next weekend in the Lake City Community Center at American Lake just outside Tacoma. And it was on that very night that John Greek suggested his band adopt a permanent new name, inspired by a piece of old sheet music titled "Chant of the Whalers"—and thus emerged the Wailers.

The Blue Notes also invited the Wailers to join them for a couple more gigs up at the pavilion at Angle Lake. But this interaction would soon prove to have repercussions: the Wailers were about to lose one of their sax players to the more established band. In August 1958, Tom Geving—who discerned the differences between the two rival groups—made his choice to jump ship, joining the Blue Notes as their *third* sax man. "The Blue Notes were a lot more well known, and pretty much into shuffles and rhythm and blues," he remembered. "The Wailers were

much more original—a guitar band with a little horn. They were playing a much more commercially acceptable beat: this new syncopated
rock 'n' roll. When I left, the guitar became really dominant. I wasn't
crazy about playing in the keys that guitar players [preferred], especially
learning guitar players—which seems to be E and A. I couldn't really do
all the things I wanted to do. Whereas, in the Blue Notes, I could. I liked
the music better."

The Blue Notes had been reaching for an ultimate sound, and now
with Geving on board—and Buck Mann switching from tenor to baritone
sax—the band boasted a truly rich "sax choir." "The three saxes sounded
sweet together," Buck Ormsby recalled, "allowing us to create more
diversity. We styled it after seeing Little Richard and the Upsetters who
had the same horn configuration. It sounded real *ballsy*, and the band
had quite an advanced and tight show for a bunch of young guys . . . a
classic R&B sound that worked perfectly."

Perfectly, that is, until it became clear to local teens that the Wailers
were developing a more rock 'n' roll sound that seemed, admitted Little
Bill, more *modern* than the Blue Notes' classic R&B mode: "The Blue
Notes played a more sophisticated rhythm and blues sound with horns.
Patterning ourselves after Little Richard and the Upsetters, B.B. King,
Bobby 'Blue' Bland, et cetera. We were a white, Black-sounding group.
When the Wailers came along they were playing Duane Eddy and more
teenage-type things so they caught on with the younger kids. We were
rivals for quite a long time, but then they surpassed us as far as crowds."

It was in October 1958 that the Wailers played what would be a
breakthrough gig at a post-ballgame dance at Bellarmine High School.
They bowled the crowd over, after which word about the Wailers spread
citywide. Soon thereafter, when they played the Tacoma Armory's All-
City Halloween Dance, a huge crowd of 1,800 teens showed up. It was
notable, however, that those attendees were uniformly *white*.

Perhaps still a bit irked decades after the fact, Little Bill remembered:

> The Wailers were giving us a rough time as far as competition,
> because [now] there was a choice. It was a bitter moment. They
> were smart, because here we were playing R&B but there were no
> Black kids at the dances—I don't remember any Black kids ever
> coming to any of our dances. I don't know where they went. Maybe

they had their own dances. Hopefully they did. Tacoma has *always* had a problem. Tacoma was very segregated in those days: the Blacks lived in one part of town and the whites another. That might have been one of the reasons the popularity of the Blue Notes wasn't as big as it could have been: 'cause we were playing what was considered "race music." The Wailers were playing exactly what those young white people wanted to hear and they did way better as far as local dances.

Losing their audience to these newcomers was frustrating for the Blue Notes—but then getting banned from playing in town was a much bigger problem. Various incidents, Buck Mann remembered, finally got the Blue Notes barred from performing in their own hometown: "It just got to where there was too much fighting and things going on at our dances at the Crescent and Oddfellows Hall. A few guys that followed us were fighters. Every night."

The Tacoma Police Department and the City Council both took notice of all this teen troublemaking. The immediate result was the passing of a new city ordinance that outlawed public dances for anyone younger than eighteen years of age. To Little Bill's great disappointment, "The city council finally kicked us out of Tacoma and wouldn't let us play anymore dances there."

One workaround for the band emerged when some local promoters booked them for a gig at Art Mineo's New Yorker Café. When the promoters went to City Hall to buy a dance permit, they dutifully pledged to not allow any minors entrance to the dance. "And so, of *course*," Little Bill recalled with a twinkle in his eyes, "they promised the officials that no one under eighteen would be allowed in. And, of course, they let in anyone who had a dollar. Well, then these plainclothes police came up to the stage and they said to me, 'OK, partner. That's it. You'll never play in Tacoma again.' And Robin said, 'Let us do one more song so that there's not gonna be a problem'—'cause the place was packed! And so he finally talked them into it—and we did 'Louie Louie' for about forty-five minutes! [*laughter*]."

Exiled, the Blue Notes made the best of the situation by playing Teen Age Hop gigs regularly out at Breeseman's Resort on Lake Spanaway and at the Little JEM burger shack plopped halfway between Tacoma and Fife, near the Eleventh Street Bridge on Highway 99—and right next to the Tacoma city limits sign. After a few months of holding their dances in the banquet room located in the back of the Little JEM, city officials in Fife put on the clamps and the band was no longer welcome there. It was time to look further afield for gigs, like up at Angle Lake near Des Moines and down in Olympia, Centralia, and Aberdeen.

With the Blue Notes banished from Tacoma, the rise of the Wailers accelerated when they started playing Saturday night dances at the Midland Community Hall. This room was a country joint where "Pop" Avera and the Wildwood Boys played weekly gigs. But after Avera saw the size of the crowds the Wailers could draw, he figured he could make even better money by letting them take over one night a week.

Meanwhile, as Morrill told the *Seattle Post-Intelligencer*, the band "started printing up our own posters, renting a little hall. We were lucky to make $5 each. It was really funky back then. We didn't have a P.A. system. I used to walk through the crowd and yell out the songs." Those gigs were billed as "Wailers House Parties"—dances held at various rentable venues like the Fellowship Hall (in the basement of the circa 1926 Temple Theatre), the Crescent Ballroom, and the Tacoma Armory.

But it was at the latter venue where problems arose in early 1959, when city leaders took note of all the teen action. As the *Tacoma Sunday News* reported, the "only sour note in The Wailers' picture at this moment, and not one of their own making, is Tacoma's ordinance prohibiting juveniles from attending public dances unless accompanied by parents or guardians. It was this ordinance that stopped a dance at the Armory a week ago, an affair sponsored by a service club. Nearly all the girls were underage. . . . Enforcement of the ordinance means that The Wailers can't play much in their home city."

All the band's scheduled gigs that season were booked at out-of-town venues like Olympia's Elks Lodge and American Legion Hall, Puyallup's Liberty Theatre at 116 West Main Street, and Parkland's Parkland Theater. From there they began branching out, playing gigs everywhere from Yakima to Walla Walla, Spokane, Caldwell, Boise, and Vancouver, Washington.

Some of the legal and logistical hurdles to throwing a dance in Tacoma were soon eased with an amendment that allowed public youth dances if they were sponsored by "churches, schools, or government agencies." It was at about that point when a businessman named Dick

Cope entered the picture, offered to help promote the Wailers, and somehow managed to get control over the Tacoma Armory. Finding ways to skirt the rules, Cope booked the Wailers there. But then a tragic evening caught the attention of the Tacoma City Council and brought more troubles for the band. "They finally," Rich Dangel recalled, "barred the Wailers from playin' in Tacoma a couple times because somebody got shoved over the balcony at the Armory and got his neck broken. And that's a drag, it's not somethin' to laugh about, but at the same time it was strange the things that went on at that time and were taken pretty lightheartedly."

But as the Wailers solidified their sound—which was largely based on rock songs by Chuck Berry, Link Wray, and Little Richard—their reputation grew. Before long they became the band preferred by a number of local hotrod clubs, including the Toppers, Demonos, Drag-Ons, Henchmen, Kounts, Steeds, and Stompers.

"There'd be a thousand-some-odd people in this dance hall that holds five hundred," exclaimed Dangel. "And there would always be a fight. But I remember a couple of them. It'd start at one end of the dance floor and the whole place would be fighting. So we'd get scared and pick up a mic stand just in case, you know. There was chicks running around with black eyes and bloody noses and torn clothing. I mean everybody fought. Cops were knocked out. Their cars were wrecked. They broke the windows. Cut their tires up. They went *nuts*! I mean, *fighting* was the trip. Get drunk. Fight. And fuck. *That* was it."

One particular night, the Wailers and Blue Notes engaged in a Battle of the Bands dance where the Wailers' fans—including hotrod club members and bikers—clearly outnumbered the Blue Notes' fans. Little Bill's frustration boiled over, and he quickly devised a revenge plan. At the end of his final turn onstage, he grabbed the microphone and made an announcement along these lines: "Hey everybody, after this show there is going to be a party over at Ken Morrill's house—come on over!" Well, by the time Morrill packed up his gear and drove home—where his parents both happened, luckily, to be away for the night—the party was well underway.

"My house was full of about 500 people, you know, Hell's Angels types," Morrill shared with *Blue Suede News*. "My parents were out and they had climbed in through the roof. There was nothing I could do, so I joined the party. The next morning I woke up on the living room floor and there were like 10,000 beer bottles around. Guys were in my parents' bed and lying out on the front lawn. It was quite a scene."

Score one for the Blue Notes. But as Morrill was able to clean up the mess before his parents returned, there were no hard feelings. But by now, everyone had the sense that this rock 'n' roll scene was beginning to expand; as John Greek informed the *Tacoma News Tribune*, "Rock 'n' roll is just catching on in the Northwest and is becoming more and more popular every day. Even older people are admitting they like some of it. A year ago Tacoma had no rock 'n' roll combos, now there are half a dozen and Seattle has eight or ten."

There were seemingly more teen bands popping up every week. In Tacoma alone, the Converters, Princetons, Roamers, Rockers, Searchers, Sensations, and Solitude were surfacing. But these Tacoma groups largely lived in their own ecosystems and didn't interact much with outside bands.

"There were definite lines drawn," Ron Holden admitted:

There were boundaries. The Frantics more or less played the North End, and we more or less played the Sound End. The Wailers played Tacoma, and Little Bill and the Blue Notes played the South [Puget] Sound area. And we kind of kept it like that for a while—but then pretty soon someone had the idea to start these Battles of the Bands. And then we would meet at like the Spanish Castle or the Encore Ballroom, the Tacoma Armory or the Evergreen Ballroom or Parker's and all these bands would get together and battle. Then the cultures meshed.

The stubborn social patterns that enforced these decades-old turf borders had surely been breaking down since the racially segregated musicians' unions had voted to merge in late 1956. And even though the actual melding of AFM Local 76 and AFM Local 493 would not occur until January 14, 1958, it was these younger players who were leading the way toward a better future. ★

CHAPTER *10*

STRAIGHT FLUSH

The Northwest's teen scene was gaining momentum by the late 1950s. But a number of components of a viable local music "industry" were still sorely lacking: a savvy, youth-oriented record label; any major radio support for local records; and print media that would do more than ignore or disparage any musical activities other than those that pleased the bland taste of mainstream society.

Still, the bands played on. Among the most ambitious were the Wailers, who on August 25, 1958—and accompanied by their new manager, Attlio "Art" Mineo—drove up to Seattle to record some tunes at Lyle Thompson's Commercial Recorders studio at 1426 Fifth Avenue. Mineo had moved here from New York, where he'd had some experience playing upright bass with big-time orchestras led by Paul Whiteman and Vincent Lopez, and now led a dance band at his Tacoma restaurant, the New Yorker Café. He'd signed the boys to a contract and assured them that his music-biz contacts back East would help the Wailers.

Mineo, alas, also thought his ear so good that during their two-and-a-half-hour recording session—when they were attempting to cut a Rich Dangel original called "Scotch on the Rocks"—he inserted himself into the creative process by insisting that the song needed an intro gimmick. Mineo went out to a nearby restaurant, brought back a pitcher of water and a cocktail tumbler brimming with ice, had Thompson roll the tape, and then in his thickest Italian American accent, said "Eh, *goomba*! How about a nice *tall cool one*?" He followed that by recording the sound of water being noisily poured into the glass. The band was aghast but, hey, Mineo was in charge, and his goofy bit was grafted on as the song's intro.

The band was so bummed with the result that when invoiced by Commercial for the $64.30 bill they neglected to pay it, and later received a billing reminder that included the threat that "if balance is not paid in full by September 10, 1958, all Master Tapes will be erased." For his part, Mineo moved ahead with his reference copy of the tape and began working his contacts to get the band signed with a big-time label. It was an uphill battle, though, because the Northwest had no reputation for either rock 'n' roll or hit records.

At precisely this same time period, a major breakthrough was unfolding in Seattle, where a brand-new label with adequate capital was being formed by a group of music-biz veterans and record-distribution professionals. The story started way back in 1946, when Lou Lavinthal (and his partners Stan Solman and Stan Jaffe) had founded C&C Distributing Company at 708 Sixth Avenue, which quickly became the region's biggest independent record wholesaler.

Aside from the major record companies of the day (like RCA, Capitol, Columbia/Epic, and Decca/Coral) who had their own exclusive networks of retail shops, smaller labels (like Imperial, King, Atlantic, Mercury, and Dot) typically needed regional distributors, and C&C was there to serve. Along the way, C&C became a force, and one factor in their success was the hiring of a sharp new sales account representative named Bob Reisdorff.

Reisdorff loved jazz and began hanging out at various Black nightclubs where he soaked up the music. His first music-biz job was back in '55 when he was hired by the local outpost of Decca Records—a major label that had long prided itself on its deep classical catalog, its unrivalled hillbilly roster, and its blue-chip moneymaker Bing Crosby. The timing was perfect. Decca had, for unfathomable reasons, signed Bill Haley and His Comets, and Reisdorff found himself helping to promote the recordings by that game-changing act.

It was against that backdrop that C&C saw Reisdorff's worth and kicked him up to the position of promotion manager. One of Reisdorff's innovations was to begin publishing a little mimeographed newspaper called the *Platter Pulse*. It was his way of getting the region's DJ's attention focused on the particular independent-label records C&C was pushing. Reisdorff was also demonstrating an uncanny ability to spot promising tunes before they became hits. And so, in 1958, Reisdorff decided he wanted to form a new label. He felt he could produce hit records as well as all those guys in New York and Hollywood. Lou Lavinthal agreed, bought in, and committed to throwing C&C's corporate weight behind a new venture: Dolphin Records.

With this business foundation set, all Reisdorff needed was some promising talent to groom, record, and promote. Making his weekly rounds for C&C, word spread that he was forming a label and he began hearing tips and receiving tapes from all sorts of "talents" wanting to make a splash. But his interest wasn't fully piqued until early in the summer of '58 when he listened to a tape submitted by three Olympia High School kids who called themselves Two Girls and a Guy.

The two pretty, blonde cheerleaders, Gretchen Christopher and Barbara Ellis, first sang together as a duo called the Saturns. They performed a few times with the Blue Comets, a combo that boasted ace guitarist Donny Ulrich—the same Tumwater High School kid who'd played with Little Bill and would soon go on (as "Don Rich") to widespread acclaim as a key member of Buck Owens's Tacoma-based country band.

When Olympia High's 1958 spring quarter talent show came along, the girls recruited three more girlfriends, rehearsed a bit, and added a trumpeter from the school's pep band—Gary Troxel. The sextet worked to arrange a version of "Stormy Weather," but in the end those three other girls chickened out and Christopher, Ellis, and Troxel scrambled to produce something quick for the fast-approaching assembly. With their backs against the wall, they began toying with a song idea that Christopher and Ellis had already been messing around with.

"Gretchen and I were walking downtown to the local record store, the Music Bar," Troxel reminisced, "and I was humming my part of the song—only I was doing it about twice as fast as the record turned out! And she said, 'Slow that down, 'cause Barb and I have been working on this'—their 'come softly' part—and that's how the two parts came together. I slowed it down to the speed of her and Barbara's part of the song and it just went together very easily. We sang in the halls together. I suppose that probably sounds silly or crazy to a lot of people, but we would do that."

Silly? Crazy? Far from it. Instead, what the teens had created was a classic example of blue-eyed doo-wop—a tune with the improbable, and eyebrow-raising, title of "Come Softly to Me." And it made its public debut at their school's talent show.

"I was singing lead initially," Gretchen Christopher recalled:

Barb was harmonizing and Gary was doing the "dum dum" background in counterpoint. And at the end I leaned into the microphone and said "Come" very breathily, very dramatically, and everything was absolutely silent and it brought down the house—which I didn't attribute to that word. Just to the song. I thought they loved the song. But afterwards, Barb took me aside and said, "You can't *say* that! You *mustn't* say that!" "Why not?" "Because it means . . . *you know!*" And I just didn't believe it when she told me. I'd never heard that expression, so I couldn't believe it when she told me what it meant.

Well, their more worldly fellow students must have had a clue. After the trio sang the song again at a postgame school dance with the backing of the Blue Saturns, numerous audience members rushed up and told the singers they should record it. The trio proceeded to make a demo recording and Christopher scored a summer job at the Colony Club, a popular Seattle nightspot owned by the jazz impresario Norm Bobrow.

"Gretchen had this tape and asked Norm to listen to it," Reisdorff recalled. "The title was 'Come Softly'—and he was chuckling about it. He said, 'Can you imagine calling a record "Come Softly"?!' [*laughter*] So, he said to her, 'You should have Bob Reisdorff listen to it 'cause he has connections.' So Gretchen brought this thing to me—and it was just beautiful. And I thought it was a *natural* hit."

Even though the tune seemed like a surefire winner, Reisdorff stumbled into an opportunity to get a second opinion from a seasoned music-biz professional: "Bonnie Guitar" Tutmarc. A veteran of the country scene, she and her music-instructor husband, Paul Tutmarc, had performed on Seattle's KVI and KOL radio throughout the 1940s and recorded a handful of 78s for some of the town's pioneering record labels. In 1955, she headed off to Hollywood, where she got a gig as a session player; in 1957, she scored her first of several international hits with the country-pop classic "Dark Moon."

That led to an appearance on CBS-TV's *Ed Sullivan Show*. Upon her arrival at the airport in New York, she got the full pop-star treatment: Bonnie's limo was rocked by crowds of teenagers chanting her name. As "Dark Moon" soared to number 6 on *Billboard*'s pop chart, she embarked on a string of concert dates with other stars including Gene Vincent, Jerry Lee Lewis, Sam Cooke, the Del Vikings, and the Everly Brothers. Bonnie was a talented singer and player, and later she served as one of the few female A&R heads (for RCA's country music division). Beyond all that, Bonnie's hands-on studio experience and considerable talents in the technical aspects of cutting hit records were about to contribute dramatically to advancing the recording arts in the Pacific Northwest.

In 1958, Reisdorff was taking ukulele lessons at the home studio of Paul Tutmarc. There he met the thirty-five-year-old Bonnie and they struck up a conversation, and he jumped at the chance to have her listen to the Two Girls and a Guy tape. All it took was one playback and she knew exactly how the song ought to be produced. Her enthusiasm was obvious; Reisdorff and Lavinthal cut a deal by offering Bonnie one-third ownership of Dolphin, and the trio were immediately signed. Reisdorff suggested that their bulky name be shortened or changed to something with a more modern ring to it. Glancing down at the old Olympia telephone exchange prefix, he blurted out, "How about . . . oh, the *Fleetwoods*?"

Time was booked at Joe Boles's studio and Bonnie led the session, adding simple, gut-string guitar backing. In January 1959, Reisdorff took the tape to Los Angeles, where he expected a positive response from record company bigwigs and various influential radio DJs. One by one they gave it a thumbs-down, saying it just didn't have the magic. Returning home, he went straight from the airport to Seattle's KING-AM. A friendly DJ aired the tape and the radio station's switchboard suddenly lit up with callers raving about the song.

A rush order was placed with a pressing plant, and within days the Dolphin label had boxes of their debut release in hand. They began distributing the 45s both to retail shops and regional radio stations. That's about when Dolphin received a cease-and-desist letter from a New York firm that already had an active corporate division called Dolphin Records. The Seattle crew reacted fast by creating a look-alike brand: *Dolton* Records.

Meanwhile, various industry sharks became aware of the song and started circling. Reisdorff began hearing from bullies who demanded that Dolton turn over the track to their better-established labels. Or bullies who threatened to issue sound-alike recordings of "Come Softly to Me." Or bullies who leaned on him to transfer the publishing rights over to their companies.

But if anyone thought Reisdorff was just another rube from the sticks, they were dead wrong. Reisdorff sprang into action. First, he stalled while he sent the group out on a quickly scheduled concert tour to shore up the song's position in various markets. Then, he solicited help from the management at KING Broadcasting—an NBC affiliate—to step in, and they happily encouraged all the other NBC stations to support the Fleetwoods.

With that momentum, the whole matter resolved itself. Dolton cut a distribution deal with Liberty Records in Los Angeles, soon after which the *Seattle Post-Intelligencer* reported that one hundred thousand copies had already shipped. Then Reisdorff and the trio jetted off to Philadelphia, where they appeared on Dick Clark's *American Bandstand* show where the host also presented them with gold record awards. Then it was off to New York, where they appeared on the *Dick Clark Show*. Two days later, "Come Softly to Me" jumped to the top slot on both the *Billboard* and *Cash Box* charts—and to number 5 on *Billboard*'s R&B chart—and became a huge international smash, hitting number 1 in the UK and selling a million copies. Success was coming at these kids from all angles. Next came their appearances on the *Ed Sullivan Show* and the *Alan Freed Show*, and then the *Cash Box* Awards designated them as the Most Promising Vocal Group of the Year.

"Come Softly to Me" itself represented a historic breakthrough: the gold record presented to the group by Dick Clark was the first such honor earned by a recording of Northwest origin. Although the dreamy disc was decidedly *not* an example of the emerging, bluesy Northwest Sound, it did launch Dolton onto an amazing trajectory.

The label's utterly surprising success with the Fleetwoods instantly made obsolete the old doubts about the possibility of striking gold with homegrown talent. And that dramatic shift in perception affected local pundits and critics—and even the entertainment industry establishment in Los Angeles and New York.

Indeed, after the runaway success of the Fleetwoods, Liberty Records was suddenly open to damn near anything the Dolton brain trust presented them. If Bob Reisdorff and Bonnie Guitar's prescient pop vision saw merit in a particular recording they'd produced, Liberty assured them that they'd be willing to finance the pressing and distribution of it. As it would turn out, this blind faith was not misplaced, as each of the first seven Dolton singles issued would score on the *Billboard* or *Cash Box* charts. It was a remarkable streak, and one that would energize the careers of some of the Northwest's finest young rock 'n' roll talent—including Seattle's crosstown rivals, the Frantics and the Playboys.

It was back in January 1958 that the Frantics had first attempted to record some tunes at Joe Boles's studio. That same year they also booked some time with Kearney Barton at Northwest Recorders, where they cut a version of an old chestnut, "St. James Infirmary Blues." In addition, they also laid down a few numbers at Chet Noland's Dimensional Sound studio, but nothing ever came of these efforts. Still, the band didn't lose hope and kept brainstorming ways to raise their profile.

One night after rehearsing, they had the wild idea of packing their gear into a couple of cars, driving over to the broadcast studios of KOL radio, and trying to meet the popular on-air DJ Art Simpson. Upon their arrival, they waved at him through the windows. Simpson opened the door and they explained they were a rock 'n' roll band, and that's all it took. He invited them to set up their instruments in KOL's ad-jingle production studio and let the tape recorder roll. Simpson captured a take on the Frantics' new original instrumental "Checkerboard." Then, as Jim Manolides would later recall, Simpson shocked the boys: "He put the son of a bitch on the air! *Right* then!" Simpson also advised them to meet with Bob Reisdorff at Dolton Records. Reisdorff dug "Checkerboard" and offered them a contract on the spot. Next thing the Frantics knew, they were over at Joe Boles's studio recording additional originals, "Straight Flush" and "Young Blues."

As it happened, the Frantics debuted "Straight Flush" in February '59 on KING-TV's new *Seattle Bandstand*. This program was a teen record-hop show modeled on Dick Clark's national program. The two-hour Seattle version—as hosted by local radio DJ Ray Briem—kicked off Saturday afternoons at one o'clock, featured touring stars like the Four Freshmen or Bobby Darin, and occasionally spotlighted local acts. And in the wake of that exposure, the band's new Dolton single was welcomed by Reisdorff's contacts at area radio stations like KING (which debuted the disc), KOL, KMO, KXRO, and KJR.

A contemporary newspaper article quoted Briem reveling in all the excitement:

> *Seattle Bandstand* . . . has become a real star-maker. The Fleetwoods made their first appearance on the show. Now their "Come Softly to Me" is pushing the million-seller mark. "Straight Flush" by

the Frantics is #2 on the local charts and skyrocketing. The song was first heard on *Seattle Bandstand*. . . . Seems like Seattle is loaded with talent and the rest of the country is beginning to find out about it. . . . Keep an eye on the Wailers. This is a group of Tacoma teenagers. . . . We hope to have them on *Seattle Bandstand* in the near future. ★

CHAPTER 11

TOUGH BOUNCE

There were more than a few people down in Tacoma in 1959 who'd been watching in awe—and let's face it, even some *envy*—as Seattle's Dolton Records had rocketed to success within just a few short months. Among them were the Blue Notes' leader, Little Bill Engelhart, and across town, the Wailers' manager, Art Mineo, who had been hustling to score the band a recording contract.

Mineo had tried and failed to convince numerous labels—ranging from Atlantic in New York to Dolton in Seattle—each of which had declined to sign the band. Finally, he announced to the boys that he'd negotiated a deal. The Wailers would be recording for the New York–based Golden Crest Records. While the band members were undoubtedly pleased, they could also be forgiven if none of them had ever heard of the tiny company. Golden Crest was a small-time label with a penchant for issuing marginally commercial spoken word and weak jazz recordings. "High Fidelity in Good Taste" was the wishful corporate motto of this label that had virtually no experience in rock 'n' roll.

Golden Crest's owner, Clark Galehouse, made the trip out to Tacoma and set his portable recording gear up at the Lakewood Knights of Columbus Hall where the Wailers were booked to play a Saturday night dance. When the gig ended at about 2:00 a.m., he and Mineo placed one microphone near Rich Dangel and John Greek's guitar amp and another near Kent Morrill's poorly tuned piano and the boys cranked it up one more time, laying down five songs: a new take of "Scotch on the Rocks" along with "Dirty Robber," "Roadrunner," "Mau Mau," and "Snakepit."

Meanwhile, Golden Crest evidently decided that issuing a song called "Scotch on the Rocks" by a teenage band was probably *not* "in good taste" and altered the song's title to the tamer "Tall Cool One," which could at least be interpreted as referring to an innocent mug of soda pop.

Written by Rich Dangel, who thought it would be "cool" to make a song based on ascending half-step "power chords"—and this at a time well before anyone had heard that phrase yet—"Tall Cool One" had other catchy elements as well. It showcased a tinkling, jazz-tinged piano that grooves along until the halfway point, when said riff is utterly decimated by the harsh squall of a saxophone solo. Golden Crest felt this song was the band's best shot at a hit and issued it in early April 1959 as the Wailers' debut single. However, rather than celebrating a hometown band's achievement, on May 3 the *Tacoma News Tribune* dissed them by instead complimenting Mineo's acumen, taking care to note that his "own inclinations lean to a more musical type of performance but he recognized a lively possibility when he heard The Wailers."

Regardless of such skepticism, within weeks "Tall Cool One" was climbing up the playlists at Tacoma's KMO and a few additional Northwest radio stations. By early May, it had sold twenty thousand units locally. This activity led to other stations across the country picking it up, and on May 18, 1959, the song entered the *Billboard* charts, where it appeared for thirteen long weeks; peaking at number 36, the single eventually racked up sales of around three hundred thousand units.

That same month, the Fleetwoods struck again, hitting number 39 on the *Billboard* chart with Dolton's third release, "Graduation's Here"— and from there, *everything* seemed to accelerate. Three Northwest teen acts already had nationwide hits, and additional action was now taking place at Joe Boles's studio.

The Blue Notes had watched all this and naturally wanted to get in on the action. For his part, Little Bill recalls that the band asked around and heard that Boles's studio was *the* place to work and so went there on their own volition. Bob Reisdorff, on the other hand, would later insist that the band had contacted him and he declined to sign them; instead, he suggested they first cut a demo with Boles. Two different stories, which later became a point of contention that would make things rather sticky.

As Little Bill described the situation, "The Blue Notes were basically an instrumental group—which most groups were back then. We had Rockin' Robin with us, and I sang a little—but it was mostly an instrumental group. And we just wanted to see what we sounded like, so we went up to Joe Boles's studio in West Seattle. We'd saved up our money and booked a couple hours of time. We went through all the instrumentals and then Joe came in and said, 'You've still got a little extra time. Do you have anything *else* you'd like to do?'"

The Blue Notes' repertoire went deep—they knew plenty of rockin' R&B favorites and had already written a few instrumentals, including "Spook" and "The Boogie," the latter of which they'd recorded back in 1957. But now, poor Rockin' Robin had been sitting there quietly with nothing to do, and hell, by this point he was just dying to get a crack at recording. But instead of letting him cut a song and getting to hear his own voice on tape for the first time, Little Bill wanted to record a vocal number he'd penned called "I Love an Angel."

"So, we did it and Joe comes *flying* out of the control room," remembered Little Bill. "He was *all* excited—he hadn't been impressed by any of the instrumentals we'd just done. You know it was like [*bored*] 'Take one. Take two.' But he said, 'Is that an original?' And we said, 'Well, yeah, it is.'" Lassie Aanes also remembered that moment: "He says, 'Man! I know we got a million-seller right *here*! I can probably get you ten thousand dollars for this thing right now if you want to hook up with a record company.'" Little Bill continued: "He said, 'Everybody sit down. I'm gonna make a call.' And so he called Bob Reisdorff and Bonnie Guitar from Dolton Records and they came down and just *flipped* over this song. He had contracts with him and everything!"

In fairness to Reisdorff and his newfound interest in the band, it should be stated that not only was Boles's engineering work a marvel to behold, but the song itself was a gem of teen angst. In addition to the endearing lyrics—"I love an angel, but does she love me?"—and the sweet appeal of Little Bill's youthful voice, the song featured a sax choir chart to die for. Pairing Buck Mann's grunting bari sax with twin tenor sax lines from Frank Dutra and Tom Geving, the arrangement by Geving was simply stunning. Casting back over the years, Geving recalled, "The song stayed pretty much the way Bill wrote it, but I did a lot of work on the arrangement. Especially the *horns*. I'd gotten the idea for the harmony solo part from seeing Little Willie John's group down at the Evergreen. And all of a sudden the song just came together."

It sure did. Joe Boles could hear it. Bonnie Guitar could hear it. And Bob Reisdorff could finally hear it as well. Little Bill remembered what happened next: "So, Bob Reisdorff asked us, 'Well, what's the name of the band?' And we said, 'The Blue Notes.' And he said, 'No, no, no, no. *That's* no good. We need somethin' *more* than that.' Then Buck [Ormsby] says, 'Well, Bill's grandmother calls him "Little Bill."' And Reisdorff goes, 'Little Bill and the Bluenotes': I *like* that!'"

Meanwhile—unbeknownst to the ecstatic band—Boles was having second thoughts about having steered the band to Dolton. Indeed, as an engineer, a de facto producer, and the co-owner of a song publishing company, Boles must have kicked himself for having ever telephoned Dolton. It was *he*, after all, who'd spotted this potential pop hit. And so, not too long after everyone had cleared out of his studio, Boles got right back on the phone to Reisdorff to reclaim *his* discovery. "Well, so Joe jumped in there and wanted to take the record himself," remembered Reisdorff. "And I went to him and I said, 'Joe! *What* are you *doing*? I'm using your studio exclusively. I'm *sending* you people, I don't expect you to intercept me.' And Joe was upset about it. Just *terribly* upset. He had stars in his eyes. . . . He liked that song. He liked that a lot, and he was going to put it out on his own label. I think that would have been a mistake."

Sidestepping the issue of whether Reisdorff had actually "sent" the band to Boles, Reisdorff reluctantly decided that to settle the matter he would offer to pay Boles "a penny a record" as a royalty on future sales. Having ironed out that wrinkle, Little Bill and the Bluenotes were brought back to Boles's studio on March 28 and work on the song proceeded from scratch—this time guided by Bonnie Guitar, who took great care in helping capture the band at their very best. She and Reisdorff were taskmasters that day, making the combo cut the song scores of times seeking pop perfection. At session's end, the anxious and excited boys drove home to Tacoma with assurances that they'd be receiving checks—at union rates—for contributing to the recordings.

From Tacoma's KMO to Seattle's KOL and KING, the song began picking up chart momentum. Then the record was featured for a couple of weeks on the *Dick Clark Show*. This was, of course, ideal promotion (even though Little Bill claimed that his subsequent royalty statements would show significant deductions to pay for some sort of fee for these airings), and "I Love an Angel" broke into the *Billboard* Hot 100 on June 22, 1959.

Right about then, Dolton booked a tour that would see the Fleetwoods, Frantics, and Little Bill and the Bluenotes performing big concerts in Spokane, Pasco, Portland, and Seattle's Orpheum Theatre. Now Little Bill really felt like a star and was ready to tell the whole world about it. One night he went down to the Evergreen Ballroom to see Little Willie John, the R&B singer who'd scored a major hit with "Fever" back in '56:

> When I told him I was a singer with a record out, he asked if I would like to sing a song or two with the band. With the Upsetters! In those days, you didn't get up on a bandstand without at least a sports jacket on, and since I wasn't wearing one at the time, he took me back into his dressing room to select one of his. It looked like a small men's clothing store back there. Since we both stood about five feet two, all of the jackets fit me perfectly. I picked one out and within a few minutes I was on stage singing with the Upsetters. What a trip.

Heady times, to be sure, for Little Bill and everyone else in the Bluenotes. Everyone, that is, *except* Rockin' Robin. As the Bluenotes' main singer, he was, understandably, feeling slighted. And he began to whine about how he wanted to record something. It seemed to him as though a coup d'état had occurred now that Reisdorff had interceded and renamed the band *Little Bill* and the Bluenotes. Even worse, now those Dolton know-it-alls wanted Little Bill to wear a *different* stage outfit from the rest of the band members during their live appearances.

Then Dolton did something that irked Rockin' Robin *and* some of the other Bluenotes. When the *Portland Bandstand* and *Yakima Bandstand* TV shows expressed interest in having the Dolton acts perform on the air, Reisdorff chose to take along the Fleetwoods, the Frantics, and Little Bill without the Bluenotes. It was becoming obvious that Reisdorff saw Little Bill as the key talent—and this flattering attention was not something to which Little Bill was immune: "There was a lot of 'Why's yer name in bigger print on the records?' and 'Why do *you* get to dress different?' And you know . . . well, I think if you asked the other Bluenotes they'd tell you [what] I was leaning towards: I wanted to be a star!"

Although the Bluenotes were obviously a talented bunch, they *were* a bit scruffy. But what Reisdorff objected to most was Rockin' Robin's unpredictability. Onstage he was wild, impulsive, and fun as heck. So, keeping this in mind—but against his better judgment—Reisdorff booked the band—along with the Frantics—to perform for a two-day KTVW-TV mental health telethon that was being broadcast live from Seattle's Civic Auditorium on May 9–10, 1959.

The Bluenotes were also booked to play a dance down in Centralia that night, so it was *after* that gig wrapped up at 1:00 a.m. that the boys loaded up all their gear and drove the ninety miles up to Seattle. By the time they'd arrived and were set to play for the telethon, it was 3:00 a.m. But viewers were still tuned in and the phone banks started ringing and ringing. Donations flowed in. The show's producers asked the band if they could hang out and perform again around 6:00 a.m. And then again at 9:00 a.m. And again at 10:00 a.m. But up until that point, Robin had been shunted aside and hadn't yet sung a single note.

The boys in the band began pressuring Little Bill to do something. He walked over to Bob Reisdorff and pleaded that Robin should sing the next song. But Reisdorff resisted, saying "No. Robin's too crazy. You never know what he'll say." Facing further pleas, he made Little Bill promise that Robin wouldn't blurt out anything questionable. And so, Robin made his live TV debut, singing Larry Williams's 1958 barn burner "Dizzy Miss Lizzy." The Bluenotes were on fire, Robin was a swirling dervish, and the show's emcee was floored. At song's end, he interviewed them on camera, focusing on the fact that the band had been up and willing to perform for so many hours.

Still laughing about it many years later, Little Bill recalled what happened next: "He says, 'How do you do this?' And Robin says—real straight-faced—'Oh, we take pep pills.' And we didn't! But Robin had a real weird sense of humor. Reisdorff almost fell down behind this camera and he said, 'I told you he'd say something like that!' This was live TV—can't cut *that* one!"

This was the final straw: Dolton resolved to separate Little Bill from his band. With "I Love an Angel" becoming a national hit, Liberty Records successfully licensed the tune for Dolton to various European record markets and it took off in England and Germany. Liberty was so excited by this that they invited Little Bill down to Hollywood for a meet and greet. To Little Bill this development was yet another sign pointing toward his inevitable stardom.

Little Bill and Buck Ormsby drove to California to attend and the bigwigs there were reasonably pleasant but soon after, the label's promotion machine seemed to stall out. His hit song lost its momentum after climbing steadily up to *Billboard*'s number 66 slot by August.

Speculation has long swirled that in that era of all-American pretty boy stars like Bobby Vee, Bobby Vinton, and Bobby Rydell, Little Bill, with his gaunt appearance and steel crutches, presented too much of a marketing challenge for the teen-dream biz. His sweet voice and songwriting skills were not enough to overcome Liberty's reticence. It was a rude awakening for Little Bill, but Liberty would never again show interest in his career. He went back and briefly rejoined the Bluenotes, who had in the meantime recruited Bill Johnson to replace him on guitar.

Bluenotes sax man Frank Dutra recalled that "Bill had a record out now, so we brought him up to do like twenty minutes out of every set—like we did with Robin, who was doing the same thing. It was better for Bill and everybody to make him a feature—not being on the bandstand the whole time. We were trying to push the group—and Bill. And you can't do this by having Bill standing there all the time. It looked better to have him as a feature only."

Meanwhile, Seattle's KJR had jumped on the Wailers' debut single, "Tall Cool One," in April 1959. By the first week of May, it was triumphantly poised at that station's top slot—and the single's rockin' flipside, "Road Runner," was revving at the number 5 slot! The momentum behind this record was stunning: in its first ten days in local record shops, "Tall Cool One" sold twenty thousand copies. And from there the record took off nationally. *Cash Box* magazine's charts had the tune at number 45 and gave it a big thumbs-up: "The Wailers serve up a lidful of solidly rocking instrumental music. All the necessities of infectious rock 'n' roll are here: honking sax, twangy guitars, pounding drums." The disc had a strong thirteen-week run in *Billboard*, peaking at number 36.

With all this success, the *Tacoma News Tribune* continued covering the Wailers' activity, which was great for them. But the attention and publicity conversely irked some of the Bluenotes' young fans who felt that their favorite hometown band—who also had a national hit—were being ignored. One of them penned a miffed letter to the editor, which read, in part, "I am speaking for the public. I believe that you have been unfair to the local band-groups. You always manage to have an article in the newspaper about the Wailers etc., never a word about the Bluenotes. This is unfair! These groups have made Tacoma known all over the nation. In return, nothing is done for them. You are showing favoritism to the Wailers. Nothing has ever been written about the Bluenotes. . . . I think Tacoma should be ashamed of its actions. . . . I think a special tribute should be paid to them."

Well, too late for any remediation on that front, as the Bluenotes were spiraling downward. Meanwhile, Golden Crest was ecstatic to finally have their first *Billboard* Top 40 hit and Clark Galehouse raced back to Tacoma with his tape deck for a second session, which yielded some good original instrumentals: "Tough Bounce," "Long Gone," "Swing Shift," "Driftwood," and "Gunnin' for Peter."

The label was fired up and determined to go all out in pushing the Wailers' career. That is, *if* the combo would agree to relocate to New York. But there were issues. The band members—aged sixteen to eighteen—were still obligated to attend high school through May. Another complication was that Art Mineo was claiming rights to a full 50 percent of the band's earnings, though he was eventually squeezed out by Golden Crest.

Meanwhile, when school let out—and with a cash advance of $1,200 (almost $12,000 in today's dollars)—the Wailers (with Kent Morrill's mother, Lucille, acting as chaperon) all crammed into a new trailer-haulin' '59 Plymouth Fury station wagon and headed east. Once they'd arrived in New York, Golden Crest took the boys directly over to the offices of one of the country's top talent agencies, General Artists Corp. (GAC)—the same firm that booked tours for stars like Buddy Holly and the Platters.

GAC had big plans for the Wailers. First, on June 11, the band made an appearance on the *Dick Clark Show*, where they did a pantomime of "Tall Cool One" that was greeted by the ecstatic shrieking of the girls who thought they were cute. After that, the Wailers were off to do the *Buddy Dean Show* in Baltimore, the *Milt Grant Show* in DC, the *Roy Lamont Show* in Richmond, Virginia, and record-hop shows in Ocean City, Maryland, Harrisburg, Virginia, Fort Wayne, Indiana, Jackson, Michigan—and later, a two-week engagement at the Cold Spring Resort in Hamilton, Indiana.

It was on June 26 that Golden Crest released the second Wailers' single, "Mau Mau" / "Dirty Robber," and the band went back to New York for appearances at the Apollo Theater and on Alan Freed's popular *Big Beat Show* on WNEW-TV. That's when two problems surfaced. First, Freed refused to air "Mau Mau," saying that the song title alone would offend his show's Black fans. The Wailers' well-read leader, John Greek, was aghast and tried to explain that he'd named the song after reading Isak Dinesen's popular 1937 book *Out of Africa*—and in *sympathy* with the eleven thousand Kenyan Mau Mau rebels whom British colonial forces had slaughtered in the early 1950s. Nonetheless, Freed wouldn't play it: case closed.

The second problem arose backstage at the Apollo, when the boys were informed that some other musicians wished to speak with them. Expecting to meet some new fans, the Wailers were caught off guard when those players happened to be the members of the Royal Teens, who had scored a Top 20 hit the previous year with "Short Shorts." It quickly became clear that the Royal Teens were *not* there to fawn over the boys from Tacoma. They were on a mission to confront the Wailers with a complaint that Mark Marush's sax solo on "Tall Cool One" was a note-for-note copy of the one on their hit. The Wailers had never noticed this before and were chagrined over the whole situation. Marush instantly lost credibility within the band and never lived it down.

Meanwhile, "Mau Mau" went Top 10 back in Seattle on KJR, causing it to break out on the *Billboard* charts, where it peaked at number 68 in a five-week national run. Golden Crest considered that a decent sophomore effort and geared up for a third try. This time, the Wailers were taken into Golden Crest's modest studio out in Huntington, Long Island, to record more songs. The tunes cut there had considerably better fidelity than the field recordings from the Knights of Columbus Hall. Plus, the new songs were demonstrating the band's growth as composers. "Devil's Island" was a spy movie–style instrumental rocker named after the brutal prison camp off of South America (which Golden Crest renamed "High Wall"). Then there was "Beat Guitar," "Wailin'," plus a tuff knockoff of "Tall Cool One" called "Shanghaied." Now Golden Crest had enough Wailers' tracks in the can to release an album.

Rich Dangel remembered how things transpired:

> They said, "OK guys, we want you to stay back here and we'll do the whole deal for you." GAC wanted to have us stay somewhere in Rhode Island and they'd fix us up in a nice pad, you know: give us the car, they were going to tutor us through school, and straighten us out. Probably give us clothes, you know that sort of thing. They were going to try and do a big whammy on us. They foresaw a

good thing. They were pushin' us hard. We were one of the *only* teenaged rock 'n' roll bands. That's a fact. It just happened to be the beginning of a new thing that happened.

But, by the end of all this road travel and other excitements, the boys were tired and homesick. In addition, Dangel and Burk hadn't completed their senior years of high school yet. "So," Dangel admitted, "everybody goes, well, you know, 'I miss my girlfriend' and: 'I wanna work on my hotrod.' *Whatever*, you know: 'I miss my *mom!*' OK? [*laughter*] And we knew the parents wouldn't go along with this program anyway, so back home we go. I think looking back on it now we should have gone with the flow of the thing."

Although the Wailers walked away from that big opportunity, they didn't stop pushing ahead on their own terms. Once back, they embarked on a road tour through Northern California along with the pop star Jimmy Clanton and Pat and Lolly Vegas. Then, in March 1960, Golden Crest issued *The Fabulous Wailers* album. No doubt disappointed that the band had headed back home, the label neglected to provide the release with much promotional fanfare; while it ultimately sold around eighty thousand units, it never did hit the charts.

The LP never really sold all that well—except to other young musicians. Even George Harrison of the Beatles once enthused that he'd had the LP in his collection "since day one." Closer to home, numerous Northwest bands would later record "original" songs whose debt to "Tall Cool One" was inescapable, including the Blue Jeans' "Cool Martini," the Mad Plaids' "Cool It," the Notations' "Ram Charger," and the Converters' "Lost City."

The Wailers, however, had created a unique sound that owed remarkably little debt to the school of Western guitar buzz and twang employed by Arizona's hitmaking rocker Duane Eddy or the braying saxophone–led hits by Ohio's Johnny and the Hurricanes. With two guitars, piano, sax, drums—and no bass guitar—the Wailers' slinky brand of rock 'n' roll was like nothing else around.

Indeed, *Hit Parader* magazine later dissected the Wailers' sound, describing one song, "Driftwood," as "primeval Jazz-rock. . . . The rest are a little more in the hard-rocking three-chord bag (usually 12-bar blues progressions). But, however elementary the tune structures and melodies were, the group went at them essentially like a jazz group. The tune is played through, and then there is some genuine improvisation on guitar, piano, and/or sax before it comes back in its original form. This was not quite the usual thing in 1959, though it became so shortly thereafter."

Over time, *The Fabulous Wailers*—which featured an iconic band photo that had been shot at the New Yorker Café back in the spring of '59—would come to be recognized as a landmark album in rock history. That cover shot alone has been noted as groundbreaking for visually depicting the five guys as coequals—a brotherly status that the subservient bands behind, say, Gene Vincent or Chuck Berry never evinced.

One song on *The Fabulous Wailers*, "Tough Bounce," was so cool it inspired John Greek's sister Marsha and a girlfriend to concoct a new dance of the same name, which they demonstrated live on the *Seattle Bandstand* TV show. Of the album's music, *Hit Parader* magazine later noted, "The Wailers' hit, 'Tall Cool One,' set a new standard of quality for the rock instrumental idiom, which had previously consisted almost entirely of such novelties as 'Tequila.'" Moreover, the magazine gushed that *The Fabulous Wailers* "LP was astounding when it was issued in 1959. And cut for cut, it remains the best LP by a white rock instrumental group made before the coming of the modern blues and San Francisco scenes." *The Fabulous Wailers* also marked their last hurrah with Golden Crest. The band was now on their own. ★

CHAPTER 12

MR. BLUE

In the summer of '59, the Pacific Northwest's rock 'n' roll eruption continued to play out. In September alone, Dolton Records scored again—twice. First, the Fleetwoods' "Mr. Blue" reached *Billboard*'s top slot, and then the Frantics hit the Hot 100 with "Fogcutter." This was an excellent instrumental tune that was dubbed after a famous cocktail first concocted at Trader Vic's, a historic nightspot that had been granted the very first post-Prohibition license to serve mixed drinks in Seattle.

By this time, the Frantics had solidified their reputation locally as superior musicians and were now often hired to support touring stars like Gene Vincent, Frankie Avalon, Ray Stevens, and Bobby Darin. In addition, Dolton began employing them—as a group or individually—to back other artists in studio sessions, including on the Fleetwoods' "I Love You So" and the Four Pearls' "It's Almost Tomorrow."

But a bit of music-biz trouble was brewing. Bob Reisdorff was still miffed with Joe Boles over that tussle regarding Little Bill's hit. That strained relationship led Reisdorff to scout around for a different studio to work with. He and Bonnie Guitar stepped into Northwest Recorders, an older downtown facility recently purchased by a staff audio engineer named Kearney Barton. Bonnie did a test recording there, they were pleased with the results, and a decision was made: all of Dolton's future Seattle sessions would be conducted here, not back at Joe Boles's place.

"At that time," Barton recalled, "there were only about three studios in town. When I started there, I had never run a studio, and I had to teach myself to do the actual recording and disc-cutting and so forth. I mean, I was teaching myself how to record these groups and I'd really never done that much. My first real exposure to rock 'n' roll was when I got in the recording business 'cause I'd been working in a radio station doing [*laughter*] *classical*."

The Dolton execs found Barton easy to work with; in fact, they hit it off *so* well that Dolton soon moved out from the C&C shop and into a small office space in the same building as Northwest Recorders. The situation was ideal: Dolton would be only a few steps away from a decent studio. And the front-burner project for Dolton at the time was to cut enough tracks to fill a debut LP for the Fleetwoods. The first tune they laid down was the international hit "Mr. Blue." Not bad for Barton's first try! Then, in October 1959, that single's flipside, "You Mean Everything to Me," also charted, and suddenly Dolton had a two-sided hit on their hands. On a serious roll, Dolton proceeded to release its first of many albums, *Mr. Blue*, which earned the Fleetwoods yet another gold record award.

By this point, running Dolton had become a full-time venture for Reisdorff, and C&C began looking for a new promotions rep to replace him. Reisdorff himself suggested that they consider hiring Jerry Dennon, an ace record promo man down in Portland. Dennon was young, had solid connections in that market, and understood the biz. A born hustler, Dennon had even—like Reisdorff—published his own industry tip sheet, *On the Record Beat*, in an effort to direct attention to records he wanted to push. By getting to know every radio station's program director, he began to have considerable impact on what records sold in his market.

Hired by C&C, Dennon moved to Seattle to be their Northwest promotions manager. Following in Reisdorff's footsteps, Dennon's job would amount to pushing all the independent label product C&C handled—but *especially* the Dolton stuff.

Meanwhile, success kept flooding Dolton—in March 1960, *Cash Box* magazine featured Reisdorff and Bonnie on the cover. But the music biz will drive you crazy, and the duo was already butting heads over the label's direction. By this time, Bonnie had proven her skills at picking tunes and assisting with arranging and recording songs, so she naturally wanted more input on A&R decisions. But Reisdorff—though no musician—was a great promoter who also possessed an ear for pop.

The driving issue became the fact that Bonnie was discovering more local talent than Dolton was able to market. After she mentioned her frustrations to Jerry Dennon one day, the two began scheming. Perhaps working together they could launch a new label of their own. With only a concept and a name derived from a contraction of Dennon's name—Jerden Records—they devised a way to launch their firm. But before they were ready to reveal their plans, Reisdorff caught them examining rough sketches for the Jerden label design and threw a fit; Lou Lavinthal axed Dennon and settled accounts with Bonnie.

Now free to compete with Dolton for local talent, Bonnie and Dennon were set to reach for the moon. So, instead of reinventing the wheel, they signed up Bonnie's discovery: a teen trio—two girls and a guy!— that was a dead ringer for the Fleetwoods. These high school kids from Vancouver, Washington, Darwin and the Cupids—Darwin Lamm, Bobbi Brown, and Janet Peters—were brought up to Northwest Recorders and Kearney Barton cut a few songs including "How Long," which both Bonnie and Dennon thought that was a sure shot. It took a few months for Jerden to raise the capital to get the record pressed, but upon its release in June, KJR and Vancouver, British Columbia's CFUN radio pushed the single up their charts. Seattle's newest label was off and running.

For the first couple weeks it appeared Jerden just might pull a Dolton all over again by scoring a hit with its debut release. "How Long" gained support daily on more and more stations across the region, and Dennon was able to quickly cut a distribution deal with Liberty Records—perhaps *too* quickly.

"Liberty was the label that *Dolton* was distributed by—and in hindsight," Dennon confessed, "I suspect that was a stupid move on my part. At the time we were thrilled to get a national distribution deal for our first record, but the reality is: we were competing with a substantial star [Dolton and Liberty's Fleetwoods]. Liberty distributed our record nationally and, well: nothin' ever happened. And looking back now, I'm not sure whether the record would have happened or not. But my sense is had we gone with somebody else we probably would have had a better shot."

Even though Liberty had failed Jerden by not taking their regional hit and promoting it nationwide, Dennon was not ready to throw in the towel. He carried on by issuing a pair of cool local instrumental 45s—"Little Genie" by the Adventurers and "Four Banger" by the Exotics—both of which sank without a trace. But Dennon pushed ahead by signing and recording a whole slew of other local acts—until, that is, Jerden's financial reserves ran out. About that sad period Dennon has ruefully admitted, "We had some wonderful grandiose thoughts that just didn't materialize."

And so, just before year's end, Jerden folded and Dennon and Bonnie each went their separate ways, though both ended up in Hollywood: Bonnie as a recording artist with RCA (and then as an A&R rep with Dot Records), while Dennon worked as a promo man for independent labels like Era and Fabor Records. And just as Bonnie would return to the charts with a string of country hits, so too would Dennon return to the Northwest, where he would eventually become as successful—and ruthless—a businessman as the local music industry would likely ever see. ★

Seattle bluesman Clarence Williams singing and playing
the electric guitar with the Leon Vaughn Band at the Basin
Street Club (411 Maynard Street), in 1948. (*left to right*)
Ralph Stephens (piano), Leon Vaughn (trumpet), Aaron
Davis (tenor sax), Clarence Williams (guitar/vocals), and
Milton Walton (alto sax). Photo courtesy of MOHAI, Al
Smith Collection.

Seattle's Jazz Age icon Oscar William Holden "tickling the ivories" at his Central District home, 1920s. Holden arrived in town gigging with the famed ragtime player Jelly Roll Morton and went on to raise a brood of talented children who would all contribute greatly to the local jazz or R&B and rock 'n' roll scenes. Photo courtesy of Linda Holden Givens.

Seattle's Gala Theater (2203 East Madison Street), 1937, just prior to being revamped as the Savoy Ballroom, circa 1943—and later, as the Eastside Hall, and finally as the Birdland in 1955. Located at the heart of the Black community business strip along East Madison, the facility played a key role in the rise of the region's jazz, R&B, and early rock 'n' roll scenes. Photo courtesy of the Puget Sound Regional Archives.

The Savoy Boys onstage around 1944 at the Savoy Ballroom (2203 East Madison Street). Their ace saxophonist
choir comprised (*left to right*) Billy Tolles, Gerald Brashear,
George Francis, and Floyd Franklin. Photo courtesy of
MOHAI, Al Smith Collection.

The Charlie Taylor Band—(*left to right*) Eddie Beard (trumpet), Quincy Jones (trumpet), Oscar Holden Jr. (sax), Charlie Taylor Jr. (sax), and Grace Holden (piano)—in performance at Seattle's East Madison YMCA (1700 Twenty-Third Avenue), 1947. Photo courtesy of the Charles W. Taylor Jr. family archives.

The Down Beat Record Company's display ad promoting Seattle's Maxin Trio—(*left to right*) Ray Charles Robinson (vocals/piano), Garcia D. "Gossie" McKee (electric guitar), and Milton S. Garred (bass)—*Billboard*, March 12, 1949. Courtesy *Billboard* magazine.

The Bumps Blackwell Junior Band—(*left to right*) Billy Johnson (bass), Harold Redmond (drums), Charlie Taylor Jr. (sax), Buddy Catlett (sax), Quincy Jones (trumpet), Robert "Bumps" Blackwell (vibes), and Major Pigford (trombone)—in Seattle's Trianon Ballroom (218 Wall Street), 1949. Photo courtesy of the Charles W. Taylor Jr. family archives.

The Maxin Trio's debut recording, "Confession Blues" / "I Love You, I Love You," Down Beat Records (no. 171), 78 rpm disc, 1949. Courtesy of the Northwest Music Archives.

Seattle teens helping mount exterior signage promoting an
All-City PTA Dance in Seattle's Civic Auditorium (225 Mercer
Street), in the summer of 1954. The first annual all-city high
school Christmas dance occurred in 1930; by the 1950s there
would be four dances per year, including two in the summer.
Photo courtesy of the Seattle Municipal Archives.

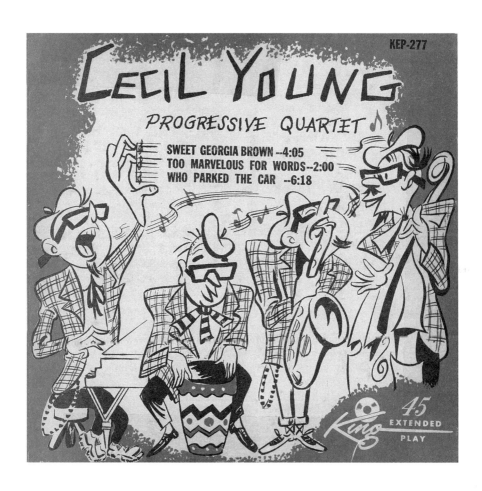

The Cecil Young Quartet, *Progressive Quartet,* 45 rpm record of their concert at Seattle's Metropolitan Theater, King Records (no. KEP-277), 1954. Courtesy of the Northwest Music Archives.

HALLOWEEN MASQUERADE BALL

Eagles Auditorium

Seventh at Union

FRI., OCT. 31st

Introducing

Billy Tolles

AND HIS NEW SWINGING
7-PIECE ORCHESTRA

featuring

Clarence Williams

AND HIS GUITAR &
BEA SMITH, Vocalist

Prize for Best Halloween Costume

Adm. $1.20 plus tax

ROCK & ROLL

WITH

BILLY TOLLES

AND HIS

VIBRATORS

PLUS

DAVE LEWIS COMBO

AND

**THE 5 CHECKS
THE 4 TEARDROPS**

PARKER'S BALL-ROOM

170th and Aurora

Tonight, July 20, 8-12

COME EARLY FOR THE
TV SHOW
9 P.M. TO 10 P.M. CHANNEL 13

Display ad promoting a Halloween Masquerade Ball in Seattle's Eagles Auditorium (700 Union Street), featuring Billy Tolles's latest dance band along with Seattle bluesman Clarence Williams and blues singer Bea Smith, *Seattle Times*, October 31, 1952.

Display ad promoting Billy Tolles and His Vibrators Rock & Roll dance at Parker's Ballroom (170th and Aurora Avenue North), with the Dave Lewis Combo—plus the 5 Checks and 4 Teardrops doo-wop groups, *Seattle Times*, June 6, 1956.

FOR TEEN AGERS UP TO 19

"BOP CITY"

FEATURING

BILLY TOLLES

AND HIS NEW 8-PIECE BAND

EVERY 1ST & 3RD FRIDAY

EAGLES AUDITORIUM

STARTING TONIGHT, MAR. 20

Dancing from 8:30 p. m. - 12

80c. plus tax

Display ad promoting one of Billy Tolles's trailblazing Bop City teenage public dances in Seattle's Eagles Auditorium, *Seattle Times*, March 20, 1953.

Promotional photo of Seattle's pioneering R&B honker
Billy Tolles onstage at Seattle's Downbeat nightclub (110
Third Street at Yesler Way). From the author's collection.

Promotional photo of the Frank Roberts Trio—(*left to right*)
Don Osias (organ), Jay (drums), and Frank Roberts (sax)—
in 1958. Courtesy of Frank Roberts.

The Dave Holden Combo—including legendary Northwest bassist Freddy Schreiber, Bernie Wolfin (drums), and Dave Holden (piano)—mid-performance in Seattle's Norselander Hall (300 Third Avenue West), 1956. Photo courtesy of Angela and Dave Holden.

This promotional disc—Joe Boot and the Fabulous Winds, "Rock And Roll Radio" / "That's Tough," as released by Seattle's Celestial Records (no. 111) in 1958—was the very first rock record produced in Seattle. Courtesy of the Northwest Music Archives.

Celestial Records, circa 1958, promotional photo of the Fabulous Winds. (*left to right*) Robert Ayers, Charles Thompson, James Foster (electric guitar), Deacon Brown, and Rogers Wright. Courtesy of the Northwest Music Archives.

Promotional photo of radio DJ Fitzgerald "Eager" Beaver (*center*) posing in 1957 with the Portland band that was recording for his Alzene "Bop" City Records, Chuck Moore and the All-Stars. Courtesy of the Northwest Music Archives.

Promotional photo of the Dave Lewis Combo—(*left to right*) Dave Lewis (piano/vocals), Chuck Whittaker (electric bass), J. B. Allen (sax), Bud Brown (electric guitar), George Griffin (drums/vocals), and Barney Hilliard (sax)—onstage in Seattle's Birdland (2203 East Madison Street), 1958. Courtesy of Barney Hilliard.

The Los Angeles–based R&B star Big Jay McNeely recorded the biggest record of his career at Joe Boles's West Seattle home basement studio in 1958. "There Is Something on Your Mind"—as issued by Swingin' Records (no. 614)—became a national hit and was covered later by legions of Northwest teen bands. Courtesy of the Northwest Music Archives.

The fabled Evergreen Ballroom located on the old Tacoma and Olympia Highway (at today's 9121 Pacific Avenue SE in Lacey, Washington), 1940. Dances held here by jazz, R&B, blues stars, and early rock 'n' roll stars, including Charlie "Bird" Parker, Ray Charles, B.B. King, Hank Ballard, and Little Richard, directly inspired the Northwest's first generation of teenage rock musicians. Photograph courtesy of the Thurston County Assessor, Washington State Archives.

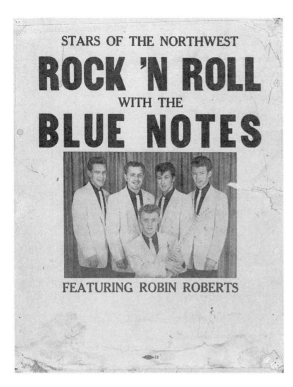

STARS OF THE NORTHWEST

ROCK 'N ROLL

WITH THE

BLUE NOTES

FEATURING ROBIN ROBERTS

Teen dance promotion poster by those teenage rockin' R&B "Stars of the Northwest," the Blue Notes. (*left to right*) Buck Mann (sax), Frank Dutra (sax), Little Bill Engelhart (electric guitar), Lassie Aanes (drums), and Buck Ormsby (steel guitar). Even though their new singer, Rockin' Robin Roberts, is mentioned, the undated 1950s poster's photo does not include him. Courtesy of the Museum of Pop Culture.

May 1958 Teen Age Hop promotional poster advertising weekly dances by the Blue Notes at the Coney Island Room within Attilio "Art" Mineo's Tacoma restaurant, the New Yorker Café (1501–7 Sixth Avenue). Courtesy of the Museum of Pop Culture.

TEEN AGE HOP

EVERY SATURDAY
MATINEE 2 - 5 P. M.

STARTING MAY 31

NEW YORKER CAFE
Coney Island Room

Music by the Blue Notes
AND GUESTS

Girls 50c   Boys 75c

SEASON TICKETS AVAILABLE

The Northwest's first white teenage R&B band, the Blue
Notes, live onstage on Halloween, 1957. (*left to right*) Buck
Ormsby (steel guitar), Buck Mann (sax), Lassie Aanes
(drums), Rockin' Robin Roberts (vocals), Frank Dutra (sax),
and Little Bill Engelhart (electric guitar). Courtesy of the
Oyster Bay Archives.

CHAPTER 13

RADIO DJS AND TEEN DANCES

Local broadcasting stations have proved to be a significant cornerstone of most every vibrant music scene since the dawn of the commercial radio industry during the roaring twenties. A great station not only airs good music but also weaves its way into a particular community by supporting or creating public events, especially dances and concerts.

For decades, the singular giant of the AM dial in Washington was KJR, which began broadcasting in Seattle in March 1922. Unlike many other stations that would follow, it managed to navigate the subsequent decades' musical changes and establish itself as the dominant broadcaster throughout the Pacific Northwest region.

Initially the airwaves in many regions were, logically enough, filled with the music preferred by most local listeners—meaning pop, classical standards, church hymns, country and western hits, and big band orchestra tunes. But as the post–World War II years unfolded, a string of youth-driven cultures emerged; as jazz, swing, R&B, and rock 'n' roll each picked up steam, the industry was, generally speaking, reluctant to embrace them.

In the Northwest in particular, Black-oriented musical forms were scarcely heard on the radio. And the discs of that nature that ever did get spun were typically aired only by a few pioneering Black DJs at the smaller stations.

The first such DJ of note was "Bass" Harris, a man whose on-air moniker was aptly descriptive of his sonorous, remarkably low-pitched voice. He had begun his career in Boston as a member of the Exposition Four vocal quartet, which found fame and even toured Europe. By early 1948, he was hosting his *Bass's House of Joy* radio show on Seattle's KING-AM. Although employed by a mainstream station, Harris managed to spin some interesting tunes by the likes of Louie Jordan and the Ink Spots during his late-evening shift.

Following in Harris's footsteps were two additional Black DJs, Bob "Bop" Summerrise and Fitzgerald "Eager" Beaver. Summerrise got his start in the late '40s at Bremerton's KBRO. Then, in 1952, he bought Seattle's only hip record store, the Groove Record Shop, renamed it the World of Music, and for years served the local jazz and R&B community's record-buying needs. As rock music came along, he began advertising the place as Seattle's "Rock 'n' Roll Headquarters." Summerrise was in the perfect position to keep tabs on what new music was hot. His cultural impact increased greatly in 1954 when Tacoma's KTAC hired him as a radio DJ and he began airing R&B and rude-jazz records that hadn't been heard before on local airwaves. He also bonded with area teens by broadcasting some of his shows live from Tacoma's Burger Bowl.

Meanwhile, Eager Beaver had begun working at Puyallup's KAYE station and by '52 was spinning R&B and jazz discs on his *Eager Beaver Show* at KFIR in North Bend, Oregon. In 1955, he raised the stakes by founding his own Broadway Broadcasting Company in Tacoma and doing crazy things to win over the local youth—like broadcasting remotely from another popular burger joint, the Last Round Café, and from his Broadway Record Shop. Back in Oregon by 1958, Beaver cofounded Portland's Bop City Records in the Black-oriented Albina neighborhood. His partner was Wilson Smith Jr., a porter with the Union Pacific Railroad whose job allowed him to bring back quantities of hip new records from the East Coast. Beaver also worked with a local doo-wop group called the Monterays and launched the "Bop" City label, which issued a rockin' R&B single, "The Flip Side," by the town's hottest Black band, Chuck Moore and the All-Stars.

Back in Seattle—and after KJR's Wally Nelskog had established a viable business model of regularly held teen dances over a five-year period in the early 1950s—things got more challenging. The Seattle City Council enacted a new ordinance that required any organization wishing to hold a dance for teenagers within city limits to guarantee that at least 50 percent of the proceeds would go to a local charity—which would then, in effect, become the dance's sponsor.

So, under this system, most of the area's rock 'n' roll sock hops were consequently presented under the aegis of local Catholic schools, various YMCAs, or public school PTAs. Thus came the monthly PTA-sponsored sock hops at Seattle Parks Department fieldhouses and the quarterly All-City Dances held down at the Civic Auditorium. Perhaps not quite as wild or fun as Nelskog's earlier Music Makers Dances at the Eagles Auditorium or Billy Tolles's Bop City dance events, these teen dances were nonetheless well chaperoned and well attended.

Indeed, after attendance records started being set at PTA dances thrown at venues like the Green Lake Field House, a few enterprising local AM radio DJs—led by KJR's "Big Daddy" Dave Clark and Lee Perkins, and KOL's Dex Allen—wanted to find ways to host their own profitable dances. And to get around the new half-to-charity rule, they just needed to rediscover a solution employed since the Prohibition era: find a venue outside the city limits.

"In 1958," Big Daddy remembered, "I was with KJR, doing the afternoon traffic slot. I was asked if I would be interested in coming to the YMCA in West Seattle once a month to do record hops. Being a natural-born ham, I said, 'Sure.' I not only played records, but the bongos, and did funny material. And if there was a new dance step, I got out and taught it. I put on a real show. Well, one night somebody came to me and said, 'Hey, we need something like this up in the North End.' I asked, 'Where?'"

He was pointed to the Lynnwood Rollaway skating rink, about sixteen miles north of town. Finding that the owners were amenable to renting the place out for a dance, Big Daddy booked it, promoted the event, and was thrilled when seven or eight hundred kids paid to dance to the records he spun. But at his second dance there only five hundred showed up. Even fewer came to the third one. He naturally became concerned they were losing interest, but he didn't know why exactly. Big Daddy asked around and learned the kids were bored dancing to recorded tunes.

That's when he booked Little Bill and the Bluenotes at his next dance and, as Big Daddy proudly recalled, at least one thousand kids showed up:

> I think that records just weren't able to keep up with the trend
> that was happening in popular music right then. Rock was really

coming on with what I would identify as very good music: a Ray Charles form of jazz. And dances—with live music—were the best place kids could get this. Plus, most of those kids had never been exposed to live entertainment, so they just ate it up. Finally, most dances that were being held right then were restricted to one school, while my functions were open to everyone. It was one place where kids could go and meet kids from other schools entirely.

After booking the Bluenotes for his next few monthly dances, Big Daddy branched out and booked the Frantics and then the Wailers. Following that, in mid-1959, he had a brainstorm: producing a Battle of the Bands event between the Bluenotes, Frantics, and Wailers all on one night. Well, two thousand kids showed up and packed the place so tight that a couple dancers fainted, which scared everybody and resulted in the owners installing an air-conditioning system before the next event.

Big Daddy wanted to start throwing dances more often than once a month, but the rink had limits due to their commitment to continue their roller-skating activities. So, he started scouting around and set an eye on the Spanish Castle: "I went to the people running it—about my coming in on Friday nights—and they were receptive. I started booking live bands and the first was a group from Yakima called the Checkers. They were great musicians. From then on, the Castle was the place to go every week. It did so well, in fact, that I felt that me being at the castle every Friday night was too much exposure. Subsequently, Dick Curtis—the all-night man at KJR—was there one Friday, and 'Jockey John' Stone, the afternoon disc jockey, was there another night."

It was in mid-1960 that Big Daddy opted to leave both the radio and dance businesses. Meanwhile, "Jockey John" Stone had become program manager at KJR, where he would quickly earn a reputation for denying airtime to local records. In one example, that same year Tom Ogilvy and Joe Boles took a fresh pressing of their new Seafair label production—Billy Saint's "Polly Ann"—over to KJR. But their reception by Stone was extremely unsettling. He reluctantly agreed to spin the record, but only after throwing a tantrum and tossing a few other records around his office for effect.

After listening briefly to Saint's record, Stone, Ogilvy would recall, calmed down a bit: "Then he looks at Joe and me and said, 'I want you fellas to know that I *despise* you.' Just like that. And Joe said, 'You do,

John? *Why* is that? What are you mad at us for?' 'I just don't *like* you. You're just a couple of small-timers.' But he said, 'I'll tell you this—I'm going to play your record. It's just an accident, but it has a good sound. And I respect a good sound.'"

From there, other KJR DJs followed Stone's lead, the record began selling well, and Dot Records quickly stepped up and licensed the recordings for wider distribution. With that commercial success, Billy Saint—a guitar-playing singer whose real name was Billy Osborne Jr.—was also in good shape and carried on recording additional singles for the Seafair, Dore, Jerden, and A&M labels. Meanwhile, in 1960, Stone also brought aboard a new DJ named Pat O'Day, a young on-air talent who would have the biggest impact of any of these men on the growth of the Northwest's teen scene. Indeed, by the mid-1960s, O'Day would come to dominate the Northwest region as only a very few other broadcasters would be able to do elsewhere in America.

It seems like destiny that O'Day's first break in the biz was provided by none other than Wally Nelskog—who, since leaving KJR, had cobbled together the largest chain of radio stations in the region. His fourteen outlets came to be called the "Cutie" network (including Seattle's KQDE, Everett's KQTY, Renton's KUDY, and others like KUTI, KUTE, KQDY, etc.). Nelskog's stations adopted the new Top 40 format—one essentially committed to airing whatever songs happened to be selling well based on sales statistics gathered from retail record shops as well as phoned-in requests. If a song was popular—be it pop, country, or rock 'n' roll—Top 40 stations gave it a try. And thus did the Cutie stations bring some of the first rock 'n' roll music to our local airwaves.

O'Day (born Paul Berg) was raised in Bremerton and had early exposure to radio thanks to his preacher father's weekly radio show. His two favorite local on-air personalities as a teenager had been KJR's Nelskog and Bob Salter. After graduating from a radio school in Tacoma, Berg was hired at Astoria, Oregon's KVAS. He debuted there in September '56, where in between reading lost-dog reports and funeral home ads he spun a few records. Eventually the management at KVAS agreed to his *Paul's Platter Party* concept for a live remote broadcast of a Tuesday night sock hop.

After a season in Astoria, he was hired away by KLOG in the lumber mill town of Kelso. To supplement the meager income Berg made spinning country discs, he hit on the idea of throwing a teen dance. He hired a local rockabilly combo, Vinnie Duman and the Rhythmaires, and their first shindig turned a good profit. Berg deduced that promoting dances was a far more lucrative vocation than spinning discs.

In August of '57 Berg was working solo one day at KLOG when Nelskog—who had been scanning various stations as he drove up the highway—tuned in and discovered a natural-born motormouth at work. He pulled up to the tiny station, walked in, and hired Berg on the spot to come and work at KUTI in Yakima. The offer was attractive in part because Nelskog's stations had already adopted this exciting new Top 40 format.

This chance to move up in the biz and spin Top 40 sounds was enticing enough for Berg to up and move to Yakima. However, just as he was settling in, with no warning whatsoever, Nelskog sold KUTI. Then, when the new owner suddenly announced a switch from Top 40 to an easy listening format, Berg rebelled and was fired on the spot. A few months later, midway through '58, he lucked out and was hired at Yakima's KLOQ. While at that station, Berg got his first real look at another facet of the music biz, dance and concert production. He soon met up with Pat Mason, who was bringing touring rock 'n' roll stars to the Yakima Armory. At first, Berg began to do radio-ad voice-overs to promote Mason's dances before also serving as emcee for shows by the likes of Bill Haley, Gene Vincent, Jerry Lee Lewis, Fats Domino, Eddie Cochran, Lloyd Price, and the Everly Brothers.

Meanwhile, like many other stations across America at the time, both Seattle's KJR and KOL also soon adopted the Top 40 format. Then, in the fall of '58, the underdog station, KAYO, recruited Berg over from Yakima. Alas, at this same point, a rising chorus of complaints about radio content began to take its toll and a remarkable number of stations across the country abandoned Top 40 for easy pop. In Seattle, KING conducted a quick "scientific" poll and claimed to have discovered that their audience preferred the music of Tommy Dorsey and Vaughn Monroe over rock 'n' roll. Accordingly, station management announced that "raucous rock 'n' roll will be completely excluded." That KING dropped rock 'n' roll was no great surprise, but it was shocking when even KJR, the greater Seattle area's Top 40 AM powerhouse, followed suit.

Berg, to his horror, arrived in Seattle only to discover that his new employer, KAYO, was experiencing cold feet. The station's general manager, speaking with the certitude of an oracle, announced that "the listening public is turning off rock and roll music" and therefore KAYO would now be switching to the "sweet side" of a new Top 50 format. Worse yet, the station was also hyping its call letters with a pointless promo campaign based on the concept that KAYO was KAYO. Management required all their DJs to select Celtic-type air-shift names—that is, monikers that began with the letter *O*. Berg showed his keen sense of humor by lifting the name of a Seattle school—O'Dea High—and he was soon performing his shift as "Pat O'Day," the host of the KAYO *Housewives Hit Parade* show.

All this change left KOL as the area's lone Top 40 holdout—and by early '59 it had skyrocketed straight to number 1 in the ratings. It somehow took several months for the once-mighty KJR to realize that KOL was plundering the teen audience and come crawling back to Top 40 and rock 'n' roll. Meanwhile, KJR's "Jockey John" Stone was getting testy about having to compete against KAYO's popular *Housewives* show and soon convinced KJR to lure O'Day onto their team.

For their part, KAYO management was livid over O'Day's defection and even threatened a lawsuit to prohibit him from using his air-name, which they'd legally registered. O'Day told 'em to shove it—he was keeping the name. Once he was comfortably ensconced at KJR, O'Day got down to business. And that business would include the promotion of teen dances featuring local bands like the Wailers, whom he first met when the boys had stopped by KAYO to show off their "Tall Cool One" single. Along the way, O'Day effectively built the foundation for a regional teen dance empire unequalled anywhere else in America.

But O'Day soon came to understand what Big Daddy and others had already learned: given Seattle's laws, making a decent profit producing dances for minors was an iffy proposition. But there was the Spanish Castle solution. And so, in the fall of '59, O'Day rented the joint, booked the Wailers, and every time he aired "Tall Cool One" or "Shanghaied" on KJR he managed to squeeze in a few plugs for the upcoming dance. This formula worked splendidly and the golden era of Northwest teen dances had truly begun. ★

CHAPTER 14

BLOWING THE BLUES

By the late 1950s, America's rock 'n' roll concert industry had matured to such a level that nearly every major national rock star had toured through Seattle: Bill Haley, Little Richard, Elvis Presley, Fats Domino, Buddy Holly, and on and on. But one name is conspicuously absent from that list: the Chicano rock pioneer from Los Angeles, Ritchie Valens.

Even though Valens did tour to promote his two late-1958 hits— "Donna" and "La Bamba"—the fellow who was booking his Northwest dates had grown wary of working in Seattle. Pat Mason had already experienced getting bogged down by City Hall's endless red tape and was exasperated to the point of giving up on Seattle for good: "That town will eat you *alive*." So, he concentrated on smaller markets. Thus it was that Valens's only gig in Washington took place in November '58 at the Holiday Ballroom roadhouse outside of rural Burlington.

The local band Mason hired to open for Valens was the Swags, a combo formed in 1957 by some Bellingham schoolmates. Seattle's Northwest Recorders is where the Swags' new manager Jim Bailey, a DJ at Anacortes's KAGT radio, took the band to record with Kearney Barton. Bailey then formed his own Westwind Records label and issued a two-sided instrumental single: an original, "Blowing the Blues," and "Rockin' Matilda," an instrumental rock version of the folk chestnut "Waltzing Matilda." From there, Bailey booked the Swags to appear on the newly launched *Seattle Bandstand, Yakima Bandstand,* and *Portland Bandstand* TV shows. "Rockin' Matilda" began charting in the Anacortes and Bellingham radio markets, and then Bailey pulled off a miracle: he persuaded grumpy "Jockey John" Stone at KJR to give the disc a little airtime in the Seattle market.

That's how a music-biz bigwig in Los Angeles took note of the record. Bob Keane—owner of Del-Fi Records, the label riding high with Richie Valens's hits, and the very same man whose Keen label had helped make Sam Cooke's "You Send Me" a hit back in 1957—swooped in, cut a deal with Bailey, and rereleased the Swags' single on Del-Fi, which resulted in "Rockin' Matilda" airing on Dick Clark's *American Bandstand* on consecutive weeks.

If anyone had thought that Seattle's Dolton Records had locked up all the best young talent in the Northwest, Keane was about to prove them wrong. In the wake of the February 3, 1959, airplane crash that silenced three of rock 'n' roll's brightest stars—Buddy Holly, J. P. "The Big Bopper" Richardson, and Ritchie Valens—Keane got to scouting even more new talents to sign. One can only imagine the shouts of glee that rang out at the Del-Fi offices after Keane received a letter from a KBMY radio DJ up in Billings, Montana, named Don "Weird Beard" Redfield, who mentioned that there was a seventeen-year-old in town named Robert "Chan" Romero. The singer later recalled that his teenage combo were the regulars at Billings's Teen Disc Club: "I had a small rock band called the Bell Tones. We played sock hops, school proms, just mostly all teenaged stuff. At that point I think most of the Montana bands were all country. . . . I think we had the *only* rock 'n' roll band in town. In that whole area!"

Redfield had already brought the Bell Tones into KBMY's jingle studio and recorded three of their tunes. So along with that letter he also sent a reel with those originals—"My Little Ruby," "I Don't Care Now," and "The Hippy Hippy Shake"—which he figured Keane ought to hear.

Mere days later, Keane was on the phone with Redfield raving that he thought Romero's rockabilly-informed songs were killer. A management deal was agreed on and they made plans to record. Romero hopped on a California-bound bus and was soon in Hollywood's fabled Gold Star Studios with the exact same musicians who had recorded Valens's hits. Released in July, "The Hippy Hippy Shake" was a full-on blast of red-hot Chicano rock that instantly found favor at a few Southern California radio stations. Meanwhile, back home in Billings, the town was thrilled with Romero's sudden success—one local burger stand even celebrated by opportunistically marketing their new ice cream desert feature as "The Hippy Hippy Shake."

Truth is, "The Hippy Hippy Shake" was just too wild to be accepted at most American radio stations. Other far-flung markets, however, embraced it. In England, the up-and-coming Beatles incorporated it into their live sets. In addition, another Liverpool group, the Swinging Blue Jeans, scored a British number 1 hit with their version in 1965. British music historian Rob Finnis would later write that various stars on the Merseybeat scene had acknowledged that Romero's single had "sparked off the entire movement." Furthermore, "it was not merely the song but the actual sound of the record—all hollow trash-can drum sounds and edgy layered guitars—which proved such an influence."

Following his success with Romero, Keane welcomed word from the Northwest about another promising talent. This time he was contacted by a couple go-getters from Seattle, Larry Nelson and Chuck Markulis, who had already garnered a bit of record-biz experience when they'd hustled a notable deal for their biracial doo-wop group the Shades.

After the Shades had cut a demo of their original tune "Dear Lori" at Seattle's Dimensional Sound studio, Nelson and Markulis made a sojourn to Hollywood and surprised everyone by successfully striking a deal with the seminal R&B firm Aladdin Records. The catch though was that the label's execs asked that the tune be rerecorded. This time the Shades booked a session at Seattle's Commercial Recorders and cut a new version, which Aladdin promptly issued as a single.

That's where Nelson and Markulis's education really began. They had to hustle to get the attention of any radio station, but the effort paid off when "Dear Lori" started receiving airplay in a few markets. Then Seattle's KAYO jumped on it and the song reached their Top 10. But their experience working in the Shades had taught them a couple of things: singing wasn't for them, and the Northwest teen scene had a not-so-secret racial fault line. Two distinct scenes were coexisting, with very little overlap. While the area's white kids were dancing at large venues, the Black kids had far more modest options open to them—venues like the CD's YMCA and YWCA, Garfield High School, and the Washington Hall.

This realization led Nelson and Markulis—who were now seeking a talent or two to manage—to think there were still some undiscovered Black groups around. And that's when Nelson—who'd also taken on a part-time job at the King County Jail—and Markulis began scouting around the CD and some South End sock hops for promising R&B talent. By '58 they were working with a couple of excellent acts: Ron Holden and the Playboys and the Gallahads.

By late 1957, the Playboys were getting frustrated because the Dave Lewis Combo was dominating the scene, and they were rarely able to get booked at the Birdland. In response, they began promoting gigs over at the Encore Ballroom. But that move brought its own complications. As Andy Duvall recalled, "We started throwing our own dances at the Encore Ballroom, but the law got on us because we weren't paying taxes." For whatever reason, the Seattle police began doggin' the joint, and more trouble followed.

"I was singing with my band at the Encore Ballroom," Holden would recall, "and during the intermission we went out to the parking lot to drink some whiskey, and maybe smoke one of those funny little cigarettes. So, the boys in the band and a couple girls were in the car. All the windows were steamed up and so one of the security policemen at the place came around the corner, pulled us all out. He checked everyone's ID."

Doing so revealed that Holden was over eighteen but that the other partiers were underage—including his girlfriend, and her father would step in and demand punishment. The result was that Holden was prosecuted on charges of contributing to the delinquency of minors and sentenced to ninety days in the King County Jail.

It was the summer of '59 when the slammer doors clanged shut on Holden. On the upside, he was inspired to pen love letters to his underage girlfriend. One of those seemed suitable as song lyrics; after he began whiling away the time singing along with a jailhouse doo-wop group, Holden honed it into the song "Love You So." Before long, a sheriff's deputy heard them, took an interest in Holden, and began treating him to daily cigarette breaks outside the cell. As it happened, that deputy was none other than Larry Nelson, who explained that he was about to retire and—inspired by Dolton Records' success—launch a new label.

Nelson and Markulis didn't waste a second after Nelson heard Holden and his fellow jailbirds singing "Love You So." First, they finagled Gene Autry's Challenge label into the unprecedented written commitment to issue a single sight unseen. Then, because the Playboys had replaced Holden with a Jackie Wilson–style soul man named Aaron Stewart, the duo found another good R&B band for Holden to work with: Little Willie and the Thunderbirds. After gigging together for a few months, Holden and the Thunderbirds were ready to record.

They booked a session with the cheapest sound engineer in town, Fred Rasmussen, whose Ravenna neighborhood home studio was called

Acme Sound and Recording. The goal was to cut Holden's "Love You So" and the Thunderbirds' scorching rendition of "Louie Louie."

With both "Love You So" and "Louie Louie" in the can, the band was asked to lay down one more tune; because they hadn't rehearsed anything else, Holden improvised a rockin' little ditty they would call "My Babe." With the session mercifully completed, the managers contacted Challenge, only to be informed that the label was switching from R&B to country and therefore had no interest in any R&B teen tunes. Reminded by Nelson and Markulis of their contractual obligations, the label reluctantly agreed to press and ship five thousand label-less singles, no strings attached.

While this offer was not at all the same as having an LA label promoting a new single through established radio connections, it was the best that could be achieved under the circumstances. It also pushed Nelson and Markulis to found their own company, Nite Owl Records, and arrange to have ten thousand labels printed. Upon the arrival in September 1959 of five thousand copies of "Love You So" backed with "My Babe," they and Holden proceeded to spend weeks gluing those labels on by hand. Meanwhile, the band's "Louie Louie"—the very first Northwest-produced version of the tune—remains unreleased to this day.

With all that effort invested, it came as a keen disappointment when "Jockey John" Stone refused to air "Love You So" on KJR—as did Seattle's other top stations, KAYO, KOL, and KING. The song wasn't a hit, they said: its intro was too long, and it had an odd beat that didn't really rock. Asked to flip it over and try "My Babe," word came back that it rocked too hard. That's about when Bob Summerrise finally broke the song on his late-night radio show. But even with that support, the bigger local shops didn't show much enthusiasm for stocking the single.

Nite Owl was not the only local label to experience resistance while promoting a record by a Black teenage rockin' R&B group. Even Dolton Records, still on a roll, had their first commercial flop when they signed Holden's former combo, the Playboys. It was after the band had played a few gigs at the Lynnwood Rollaway for "Big Daddy" Dave Clark—who loved their original instrumental "Icy Fingers"—that the Playboys first thought about cutting a record. Contact was made with Bob Reisdorff, who took the band into Northwest Recorders to work with Kearney Barton.

"Kearney was doing the recording," Playboys drummer Andy Duvall recalled:

Bonnie Guitar did the arranging. She screwed up "Icy Fingers." By the time it came out, it wasn't even like we had it. The song had had a real bluesy feel to it but she changed it around to a more commercial thing. But by now the Frantics' record was going pretty hot, so Dolton decided to release their second [single] before they released ours. In the meantime Bonnie Guitar found some guy [Gary Hodge], so his record came out next. We were always down there buggin' them: "Well, why can't *ours* get out?" We finally talked him into it, but he was reluctant.

That Dolton single—"Party Ice" / "Icy Fingers"—arrangement quibbles aside, was a two-sided instrumental gem, as good as anything the Frantics had ever done. But Dolton just couldn't make it click beyond a modest amount of radio play on Seattle's KAYO in October 1960. That failure likely caused the Playboys to switch allegiances and hook up with Nelson and Markulis over at Nite Owl, who surreptitiously took the band over to Joe Boles's studio to cut some tunes.

"The guy had outtasite equipment," Duvall enthused. "He really knew what he was doing. . . . But we couldn't release, or even tell anybody about the Nite Owl single, because we were still under contract with Dolton." True enough. And although Nite Owl would eventually issue the Playboys' second, excellent instrumental single, "Southbound Express" / "Cross My Heart," that release would have to wait until Dolton was thoroughly distracted with all their other hits—and after Nelson and Markulis had promoted the other local group they'd just discovered.

It was while checking out a sock hop sponsored by Wally Nelskog's Renton-based radio station KUDY that the duo stumbled across a Black doo-wop group called the Gallahads. This Seattle group had been around awhile, originally forming as the Echoes back in 1954 when they were attending Meany Jr. High School. The Echoes' original lineup—Clifton Jones, Joe Hardy, Bobby Dixon, Anthony "Tiny Tony" Smith, and Jimmy Pipkin—were all members of a neighborhood "club" called the Strokers.

In time, the Echoes' personnel shifted as Hardy got booted out and Jones drifted off, so the lineup stabilized as a quartet: Pipkin (tenor), Smith (baritone), Dixon (lead), and newcomer Ernie Rouse (bass). They started singing at assemblies, school funfests, the YMCA on East Madison, and a few after-school "mixers."

It had been KUDY DJ "Hey Hey" Steve Wray who first took an interest in the Gallahads and began booking them at station-sponsored sock hops. Wray even bought the members matching white chain-stitched, bulky sweaters. Now the Gallahads had a good act *and* looked sharp.

A session was booked with Kearney Barton at Northwest Recorders, where the Gallahads—with the backing of the Thunderbirds—recorded two songs: "Gone" (which featured Bobby Dixon's soaring lead) and "So Long." Nite Owl's second release, however, met the same fate as had the first. Undaunted, Nelson and Markulis recorded a demo version of a third Gallahads song, "Lonely Guy," right in Nelson's living room and shipped it down to Del-Fi Records in Los Angeles. It was in September 1959 that Bob Keane responded, according to Tiny Tony. "We got the call: 'Hey man, pack your bags and come on down!' You know, 'Let's record these tunes!' And us being kids and all—and anxious and everything— that's what we did. We jumped in an old '49 Ford and went down to LA."

The group was signed to an exclusive, five-year contract and promptly recorded two songs with Keane's orchestra, "Lonely Guy" and "Jo Jo the Big Wheel." The Gallahads stayed for only a week, but they had the time of their lives. One evening, they went across town to the famous 5/4 Club—the same R&B joint that the Barons had performed at a few years before—and did a spotlight set during a break by James Brown and the Famous Flames. However, just as the Barons had been ill-treated by the Modern label, Del-Fi offered the Gallahads no signing bonus. No cash advance. No per diem allowance. No performance fees. No royalties. Nothing.

"We were on our *own*," a downcast Tiny Tony later confessed. "It was the hard knocks days, man. We got lost in the big world down there, too. You know, it's embarrassing to admit this, but: we kinda got *flamboozled* down there. 'Cause it was all 'Bright Lights and Big City'—and we weren't concerned too much about our welfare and contractual agreements and whatnot. And so, we got screwed—there's *no* doubt about it—but on the other hand, we had fun. We lived a life while we were livin' it."

Released on Del-Fi, "Lonely Guy" began receiving airplay at scattered stations in late '59. In the Northwest, Wally Nelskog's KQDY came through with some airtime for the Gallahads, and then its sister station KQDE added Holden's "Love You So" to its playlist. That's about the point when Seattle's biggest record shop—the Ware House of Music—agreed to stock Nite Owl's records.

At that time, the Ware House of Music's storefront featured a "fishbowl" window where KAYO radio DJs could be seen by passersby broadcasting their shows live. And because the records they aired were those selling best at the store, it was a system easily manipulated. Holden and his bandmates simply recruited their pals to buy the single there and also to call in and vote for "Love You So" when it was pitted against other new songs in KAYO's hourly Battle of the Records contest.

"It was perfect for me," Holden recalled, "because now I sell twenty-five copies—gone in one week—and bang! I'm number 33 the first week. So the next week, sales go up, and I go up to number 22. Now bang! Both sides are in number 11. And bang! Next we're number 1! It was a *tremendous* hit here. It was *hot*."

"Love You So" was now sitting in KAYO's top slot, and its rockin' flipside, "My Babe," was at number 2. It was in January '60 that KJR belatedly began airing the tune and charting its rise in their Fab 50. This was exactly the kind of chart action to grab the attention of the record-industry big boys, and representatives from a slew of big-time labels—including Argo, Capitol, Chess/Checker, and Decca—raced to Seattle with licensing offers in hand. But they all seemed to want to sign up Holden and slowly develop his career—which was a sensible approach, but it wasn't as exciting as the offer made by Bob Keane.

Holden remembered how the deal went down: "He says, 'I've got $10,000, and I'll take it and run with it. Let's make a hit!' And we said, 'Hey, is this what we wanted or *what*?' We took the ten thousand, signed a lease deal, and he took it to Hollywood and made it a national hit."

Rereleased on Keane's new Donna label in late March 1960, "Love You So" broke the Top 5 on San Francisco's influential KYA. Then Los Angeles's top DJs, Hunter Hancock and Huggy Boy, jumped on it. By the first week of April, "Love You So" hit *Billboard*'s pop charts, chugging ahead toward the nation's Top 10. Meanwhile, over in England, the song became a decent hit, but it was "My Babe" that was the Brits' enduring favorite.

All this action led to Holden appearing on both the *Dick Clark Show* in New York and *American Bandstand* in Philadelphia. Holden then moved to Los Angeles and began cutting enough tracks for Del-Fi to release his *Love You So* LP, and he scored again when the "Gee but I'm Lonesome" single broke out briefly on the R&B Top 40 charts. From there, Holden set out on what became a long string of hard-core R&B

tours; at one point, feeling overwhelmed, he called back home and asked his older brother Dave to join him on the road.

Meanwhile, Del-Fi enjoyed continued success when the Gallahads' "Lonely Guy" finally entered the *Billboard* pop charts at number 111 on August 15, 1960. Now the label needed the group back in California to promote the tune by appearing at a few teen dances and TV sock hops. Problem was, over the prior months Tiny Tony had married and taken a job with the postal service and Dixon had just dropped out. Things stabilized, though, when Pipkin took over the lead spot and Ray Robinson was added on tenor.

When the Gallahads arrived, Hunter Hancock began giving the group airplay and took them around to a few lip-sync parties at high schools around town. Between the support of Hancock and Wolfman Jack, "Lonely Guy" became the top song in Los Angeles for about eight weeks, which led to an appearance on the *Wink Martindale Show*. The group also appeared on a local variant of the *Bandstand* model every Saturday for months.

As Pipkin would recall, "Then in 1961 our second single, 'I'm Without a Girlfriend,' came out. I was back home again then and Ernie got on the phone and called me one day and said, 'Jimmy, turn on the TV! Dick Clark's playing 'I'm Without a Girlfriend!'" That airing by Clark, however, marked the high point of the Gallahads' brush with fame. After regrouping in Seattle—reunited with Tiny Tony—the group continued making live appearances and even cut a couple more singles, including a 1964 take on Richard Berry's "Louie Louie" follow-up, "Have Love, Will Travel." But the doo-wop era had drawn to a close. The good news for the Gallahads was that many of the formerly instrumental-oriented combos around town were seeing the advantages of having singers out front, so the individual Gallahads found themselves in demand at dance gigs. As for Larry Nelson, he went on to a thirty-year career as popular host on Seattle's KOMO-AM radio. ★

CHAPTER *15*

COOKIES AND COKE

Dolton Records' streak of success kept picking up momentum, scoring ever more hits with the Fleetwoods as well as a slew of hit singles by newly discovered talents. But Bob Reisdorff didn't just sign up every kid who wandered into Dolton's offices. However, in being choosy, he almost let slip away the greatest discovery Dolton would ever make.

The act in question was none other than the Ventures, a Tacoma combo that would go on to be acknowledged as the best-selling instrumental rock group of all time. Remarkably they were led by two bricklayers who had only been playing their guitars together for about a year and a half prior to hitting the big time. It was back in 1958 that Don Wilson and Bob Bogle met and discovered a common interest: electric guitars. Their inspiration came from different sources. Bogle had been taking lessons with the Frantics' guitarist Ron Peterson and listening to a lot of Chet Atkins records. Wilson was more into Duane Eddy's trademark deep buzz–twang thing.

At one point, their day jobs took them to the tiny college town of Pullman. The duo—now equipped with student-quality, Sears, Roebuck guitars and amplifiers—found themselves drawing crowds of young people during informal practice sessions at the Washington Hotel banquet room. Before long, they were attracting job offers. Billed as the Impacts for their first couple of performances, the duo chose a new name that they felt better reflected their versatility—that is, the fact that they switched back and forth on rhythm and lead guitar duties. They became the Versatones and, with the help of a local drummer named Buddy Dumas, began gigging at the Pullman Elks Club.

Soon after, Wilson and Bogle moved to the construction company's next jobsite, in Tacoma, where they found a bassist, Earl Herbert, and a regular drummer, George Babbitt. Eventually the Versatones were hired to perform each week on Puyallup's KAYE. Then the station announced a talent contest, for which the Versatones were recruited to back the contestants. The winner was a fourteen-year-old gal from Kent named Nancy Claire, who specialized in Brenda Lee's country-pop repertoire. The prize was her very own fifteen-minute weekly show, which soon expanded to a full hour. Before long, Claire and the Versatones were performing live at the Belfair Barn and at other country dances and rodeos.

That's about when the Versatones changed their name to the Ventures and also decided they wanted to cut a record. The guys were aware of Dolton's ongoing success and made an appointment to meet up with Bob Reisdorff up at the label's Seattle headquarters. Once there, they played him a few tunes on their guitars, including a couple of originals and a driving rendition of a jazz instrumental called "Walk—Don't Run," which they'd found on a Chet Atkins album.

The Ventures saved their money for four months and booked time on September 20, 1959, at Joe Boles's studio, where they cut two songs, "Cookies and Coke" and "The Real McCoy." With master tapes in hand, they—with the complicity of Wilson's mother, Josie Wilson—launched a new business venture: the Blue Horizon record company. They arranged to have five hundred singles pressed and proceeded to learn how tough the record biz really was—the record was a flop.

Meanwhile, the band got hired to play regularly in Tacoma at Mike's Blue Moon Tavern—however, as Babbitt was only sixteen years old, he had to drop out, so the band used a succession of pickup drummers for a while. On Saturday night, November 28, the band performed on KTVW's *Dance Party* TV show, and on New Year's Eve they played their first big teen dance out at Fort Lewis.

From there, the Ventures were hired for a gig at a roughneck Tacoma country tavern called the Brittania, where Buck Owens and his Bar K Gang headlined six nights a week. But on Saturdays, Owens had a regular dance gig at the huge Bresemann's Pavilion out at Lake Spanaway. So, the Ventures began filling in, performing at the Brittania from noon 'til midnight every Saturday. And the boys had their eyes opened as never before. "It was *rough*," Don Wilson recalled. "I remember beer bottles flying around, and a paddy wagon parked right outside. You had a lot of soldiers and a lot of air force guys coming, getting totally wasted."

Before long, the Ventures struck up a friendship with two of Owens's bandmates, Nokie Edwards (lead guitar) and Skip Moore (drums); when they decided to try recording once again with Joe Boles, they invited these two pros to help out. Wilson remembered what happened next: "We went to Skip Moore—he was working in a gas station—and I remember going to him and saying 'We need a drummer to do this session. We want to record "Walk—Don't Run."' And he said, 'Well, I don't know. I'm kinda *busy*.' And I said, 'Well, I'll tell you what: we'll either give you twenty-five dollars or a fourth of what the record makes.' And do you know what he *took*? He said, 'Oh, just give me the twenty-five bucks.' So I said, 'OK.'"

That March 1960 session produced a tape of "Walk—Don't Run" and another instrumental, "Home"—both featuring stellar guitar work (Bogle on lead, Wilson on rhythm), Edwards's tight bass playing, and Moore's snappy drumming. Having learned from their unsuccessful attempt to independently distribute their first single, the Ventures knew that they wanted to work with a distributor who had some promotional experience. Maybe Jerden Records could help.

"Reisdorff had already turned us down," Wilson chortled, "so what we did was, we took 'Walk—Don't Run' to Jerry Dennon. He said, 'No. I don't think so. It doesn't sound like a hit to me.'" Kicking himself years later, Dennon willingly admitted his great error, confessing at that point he was simply distracted with Darwin and the Cupids, the Fleetwoods' dead-ringer teen trio he'd recorded: "My head was so into Darwin and the Cupids that I couldn't even hear this 'Walk—Don't Run' thing. They were saying 'Help!'—and I coulda said, 'OK, I will. I'll put it out. You don't worry about it.' *Instead* [laughter], I was putzing around with Darwin and the Cupids and 'Walk—Don't Run' went right by me!"

With no help in sight, the Ventures once again saved up their money and Blue Horizon issued its second single. This time, they were rather more conservative, pressing only three hundred copies. Prepared to again suffer rejection from all the local radio stations, the boys nevertheless went straight to Seattle's top dog, KJR. Determined to bypass "Jockey John" Stone, they met instead with Pat O'Day, who was by now holding down KJR's important afternoon shift. The ever-ebullient DJ took a chance: "We put it on the air instantly. We always played an instrumental going up to the newscast at the top of the hour, so we put it on every hour as that filler there, and of course, you know what happened after that. What was happening in Seattle was so startling—there was no question: it was a *stone* smash."

And as it happened, one of the first callers was Bob Rcisdorff from over at Dolton. He'd been listening to KJR and now—a mere week and a half after Blue Horizon had issued the single—he finally heard the magic. Don Wilson could relish a small moment of schadenfreude: "When Reisdorff called the station he said, 'Jeez, *what* is that?' And Pat O'Day told him, 'Well, it's a local group.' And he was amazed. Reisdorff called my mom—she was doing our legwork for us then because we were too busy—and he didn't even remember us having been in his office. He said, 'No, I *couldn't* have heard that. That's a natural hit.' And we said, 'Yeah. You *did*.' So he says, 'Jeez, I want to make a deal with ya.' So we got together with him and we signed to Dolton Records."

Before rereleasing the single on Dolton, Reisdorff wanted to run it by Liberty to see if they thought it was as great as he did. "And so," said Wilson, "Reisdorff sent it down to Al Bennett (who was the president of Liberty). He played it and said, 'No. It's not a hit. I don't want it.' And Reisdorff said, 'I'll *guarantee* it! You put it out and I'll guarantee it. If it loses money I'll pay.'"

Well, not one red cent was paid to Liberty by Reisdorff. Plenty of greenbacks, however, went in the opposite direction, though, because the song was an instant smash. "Walk—Don't Run" spent eighteen weeks on the national charts, peaking at number 2 with *Billboard* and breaking out across the globe, including England, Germany, and Japan. Dolton—and Joe Boles—had done it once again.

The Ventures needed to begin touring—but because Skip Moore passed on the offer to join them on a permanent basis, the boys set out to find a new drummer. They decided to track down Howie Johnson, who'd been performing with Buck Owens in Seattle at the Circle Tavern, and he accepted their offer.

Evidently still feuding with Boles, Reisdorff rushed the Ventures into Northwest Recorders to cut enough tracks with Kearney Barton to fill out their debut LP. With "Walk—Don't Run" an international hit now, the Ventures appeared on ABC-TV's *Dick Clark Show* in New York. "We went to New York and did the show, and came back immediately and packed up and moved to Hollywood," Bob Bogle recalled. "And by then Reisdorff had already lined up a tour for us. On that tour we were playing like skating rinks and armories and things like that. We started that tour way down in Arizona and we went on up through New Mexico and then on into Colorado—and I can't remember where from there, but we were gone about a month. I remember the fans were screaming so loud we could hardly hear our amplifiers most of the time. And they'd try and tear yer clothes off. We had to have constant security. We *loved* it!"

From skating rinks and armory shows, the Ventures next found themselves playing the famous Hollywood Bowl for Alan Freed's KDAY Spectacular event on June 25, 1960, a thrilling show that also featured the Fleetwoods, Brenda Lee, Bobby Vee, and the Shirelles. But a few months later, Howie Johnson, tiring of all the travel—and the residual neck pain caused by an earlier car wreck—chose to withdraw.

Another change came when Nokie Edwards and Bogle switched roles. Although Bogle's admirable lead playing had driven "Walk—Don't Run," it had become apparent that Edwards was an undeniable guitar master with a far-ranging grasp of jazz, classical, flamenco, country, and rock 'n' roll. Finally, the band met their permanent new drummer while hanging out at North Hollywood's Palomino Club, where they were invited to sit in for a couple numbers with the house band. As the drummer, Mel Taylor, knew "Walk—Don't Run" from the radio, he nailed the jam session and was easily recruited to join the Ventures. It was October 1960 when their latest Dolton single, "Perfidia," began its thirteen-week run up the *Billboard* charts, giving them a solid number 15 hit. Soon thereafter they embarked on the first of many successful international concert tours.

That same fall, Dolton concluded negotiations with Liberty Records, with the result being that Seattle's most successful label was sold in a deal that saw Reisdorff running Liberty's Dolton division from a brand-new office complex in Los Angeles. This was fantastic for Dolton; for Josie Wilson, who tagged along for the move, bringing her Blue Horizon label into new offices there as well; and for the careers of both the Fleetwoods and the Ventures.

The latter had begun to make their mark. As *The Rolling Stone Illustrated History of Rock and Roll* proclaimed in 1976, "The year 1959 yielded a bumper crop of instrumental hits. By now every American city claimed an instrumental band as hometown favorites. . . . By far the most important instrumental band of the era was the Ventures." Judged by quantity of output alone—the Ventures eventually produced more than two hundred albums—the band was riding a phenomenal wave of success. Not only would their record sales exceed thirty-one million units, but their music was having an even greater societal impact: the Ventures would in time be recognized as "the band that inspired a thousand rock bands," and in particular the one that kick-started the surf rock movement of the early 1960s.

But for Seattle's fledgling music industry—not to mention all the other Dolton acts that were unceremoniously dumped—the day Reisdorff closed up shop in Seattle was a sad one. An exciting era had come to a close, and no one knew if some other local label would ever arise and thrive as Dolton Records had done.

In the two years that Dolton had been pushing hits out of Seattle, the label's success had served as an inspiring example—one that got other people to thinking optimistically that maybe, just *maybe,* the town could support a real music industry. Oddly enough, even the label's sudden bug-out from the scene in late 1960 had a silver lining: everybody and their brother began labels and scoured the area for the next Ventures or Fleetwoods.

Though that was quite a formidable bar to meet, a few new labels—Penguin, Seafair-Bolo, and Camelot—did score notable successes. Penguin Records had been founded in 1959 by Jim Hammer, a young record librarian and assistant engineer at KOL radio. He had watched Dolton's success and was determined to give the record biz a go with releases by area bands like the Continentals, Royals, and Dynamics.

The Continentals were formed by a mix of Blanchet High and Lincoln High kids, including Eldon Butler (sax) and Don Stevenson (drums). They got their first gigs playing on the CYO circuit well before they were qualified for the job. Soon the Continentals came up with a couple of what might be called "original" teen-R&B tunes: "Cool Penguin"—which essentially was "Fogcutter" turned inside out—and "Soap Sudz," whose inspiration Butler said came from the Playboys.

After connecting with Jim Hammer, in May 1959 the Continentals were whisked into Joe Boles's studio, where their two songs were recorded and then issued by Penguin. Butler would recall that "Jim Hammer somehow decided that since a competitive station was pushing the Frantics that his station needed something to push. He said, 'We're gonna make this record.' And then it got on the station. Instant play. There was no problem. I think 'Cool Penguin' finally went up to number 7. Blanchet girls called the station over and over. I think we only made about fifteen dollars from it! [*laughter*] But we were rock 'n' roll stars and *that* was fine!"

Typical of radio-biz politics at that time, KJR, KING, KAYO, and most of the area's other stations offered no support to Hammer's product—so, by June, "Cool Penguin" was a Top 10 hit only at KOL. But that fact alone enabled Hammer to strike a national distribution deal with Era Records in Los Angeles, and the single was reissued and given another, bigger push—one that got "Cool Penguin" aired on the *Dick Clark Show*. The Continentals' career high point was playing a number of big out-of-town gigs with the Fleetwoods.

Hammer's next discovery was a West Seattle combo called the Dynamics, who traced their origins back to the Keynotes, a group originally formed by a few Chief Sealth High School chums including Terry Afdem (piano). By mid-'59 the band shifted personnel a bit, adding Afdem's thirteen-year-old brother Jeff on sax and a few others. Now named the Dynamics, they hooked up with Hammer in August '59 and recorded two original instrumentals, "Aces Up" and "Baby," in the Afdem family's living room. The disc, issued by Penguin, was again rejected by the local stations—KING-AM's Al Cummings hated the record so much he called it "Hammer's folly." But Hammer again got air support from KOL and successfully another distribution deal, this time with New York's Guaranteed Record Co.

Two months later, Penguin released its third rockin' single, "Thunder Wagon" / "Teen Beat" by a Tri-Cities combo, the Royals (which included the future jazz guitar star Larry Coryell). Then came one additional single, "Hopeless Love" / "Let the Good Times Roll" by teen songbird Lynn Vrooman (backed by the Royals). Everyone's hopes were naturally high, but all the excitement came to a sudden and tragic end when Hammer was found mysteriously murdered in his New York hotel room.

Meanwhile, Tom and Ellen Ogilvy's Seafair Records—which had lain dormant since their "Old Rooster Tail" hit back in 1956—got reenergized and began pumping out singles in June 1960. In addition, the sister labels they owned in partnership with Joe Boles (Bolo, Nolta, and Virgelle Records) issued what would end up being the most consistent stream of high-quality teen-R&B of any firm in the Northwest.

In a quest to sign up talent, Bolo Records proceeded to scoop up a couple of Dolton's castoffs—the Frantics and Little Bill—along with two of the now-defunct Penguin label's acts: the Continentals and the Dynamics. Meanwhile, Seafair took on one of Jerden's former acts, the Exotics. Bolo Records quickly recorded and issued what would be the Continentals' second and final single. "The Turnaround" was a dance-oriented instrumental that became a minor radio hit on Wally Nelskog's KQTY, but Seattle's bigger stations failed to embrace it. A similar fate met a pair of instrumentals, "Onion Salad" and "Lonesome Llama," that Seafair released for the Dynamics.

Meanwhile, by 1960 the Dave Lewis Combo had once again undergone more personnel changes, this time poaching two players from the Playboys: Johnny O'Francia (tenor sax) and Carlos Ward (alto sax). This, Tiny Tony recalled, was a move Lewis made any time he needed fresh troops: "You know, I've seen Dave Lewis go through so many musicians. But he didn't go through 'em to run 'em out and all that—he went through 'em *training* 'em! I mean, some of the baddest guys in the world. The whole thing was if they could get a *chance* to play at Birdland with Dave Lewis. You know, that was the whole thrill. From a musician's standpoint the greatest thing was being able to play there, and seeing how the people appreciated that good music there."

All that experience served Ward well—he went on to work with John Coltrane and the funk group B.T. Express (who scored their number 2 hit "Do It ('til You're Satisfied)" in 1974), and from there to a long jazz career. But back in the day, this new incarnation of the Combo sounded better than ever, and it was in January 1961 that Seafair released an instrumental single for them. "Candido" was the nickname of Lewis's drummer friend Don Mallory, and the flipside, "R.C. (Untwistin')," was a tribute to Lewis's musical hero, Ray Charles. Everybody who had ever heard these two tunes—at dances or on record—thought they were great. Everyone, that is, except KOL and KJR. According to the Ogilvys, Pat O'Day claimed the tunes were just "too R&B" for KJR's audience.

The good news, though, was that on November 20, 1961, Seattle got a new FM radio station, KZAM, the first ever oriented to the area's Black community. With a veteran R&B DJ, Fitzgerald "Eager" Beaver, managing the operation, both sides of the Combo's single got considerable airplay and "Candido" became a modest local hit.

The Dynamics, meanwhile, had experienced a few rounds of personnel changes that would dramatically raise the band's stature on the scene. New additions included Pete Borg (bass), Ron Woods (drums), and a series of singers including Tiny Tony and, before long, the Ogilvy's teenage son Jimmy—who would later adopt his mother's family name, Hanna, for his own stage moniker.

Because of his parents' activities in Seattle's fledgling record industry, young Hanna had been exposed to music and musicians that would profoundly affect his tastes. As a white kid growing up in the CD, he had developed a keen appreciation of Black music forms, but he *really* got fired up after attending a dance at the Seattle Armory that featured Rockin' Robin and the Wailers.

From there, Hanna made the effort to sneak in to see R&B musicians at rooms like the Birdland, the Mardi Gras Grill, the Encore Ballroom, and the Eagles Auditorium. It was back in 1959 that Hanna had helped form a bluesy band called the Versitones with some fellow Garfield High guys—including Dave Lewis's younger keyboardist brother Ulysses and Ron Woods, a Meany Junior High kid on drums.

According to Hanna, though, their path wasn't an easy one: "We couldn't get the group *going*. Dave Lewis, Ron Holden, the Gallahads—they pretty much controlled the few places there was to play. There was no market for the group. There was no place to play. It was impossible to break out of the Central area with a [racially] mixed group without a following. It was hard to get support in the city because it was conservative. Blues music had always been so contained to places like the Encore Ballroom. We really didn't get a lot of opportunity to play."

Around June of '61—after Tiny Tony began drifting away—Hanna was invited to audition as a singer with the Dynamics. He was surprised to discover that unlike the band's earliest garage-rock-quality recordings, the Dynamics were now developing a new R&B edge.

This soulful kid was hired, and the revamped band debuted at a parking lot gig just outside the Rhodes Department Store at Seattle's University Village Shopping Center. From there, the Dynamics would blossom into one of the region's most popular dance draws. ★

CHAPTER 16

I'LL GO CRAZY

The Tacoma teen-band rivalry between the Bluenotes and the Wailers was, by the summer of '60, finally sorting itself out. When the dust had settled, the former was vanquished and the latter was gearing up for their long reign as top dogs of the Pacific Northwest teen scene. The action kicked as the summer of 1960 approached. The Wailers had now all graduated from high school and were ready to take their success to the next level, so their leader, John Greek, reached out to Golden Crest.

"At the end of the school year, Greek calls them up and sez, 'OK, everybody's out of school, we're ready to go,'" Rich Dangel remembered. "And they said, 'Forget it, man. It's too late.' It's like they gave us the one chance." So, that was that. Golden Crest didn't want to work with the Wailers any longer. In the band's view, Golden Crest had now broken its end of the deal by reneging on issuing more records. But those sentiments didn't necessarily mean that the band was free and clear to record for some other company. Their contract, after all, covered a period of five years. Beyond that, only John Greek had been of age to sign it—the other guys' parents had all signed for them. Uncertainty over their legal relationship with the label would cloud their immediate path forward.

That same summer, the Wailers realized they needed more vocal numbers than Kent Morrill could provide to fill out a whole dance set. So now, just at the point when the Bluenotes were most vulnerable (having been abandoned by Little Bill and Dolton Records), the Wailers dealt them a heavy blow by wooing Rockin' Robin into their fold. He made his debut with the Wailers at a big dance at the University of Puget Sound's fieldhouse. Still, his former bandmates understood Robin's reasons for leaving. "I think he felt he had more of a chance to get a record with them," said Little Bill. "And he was right." Buck Ormsby added, "All I can say is there was no unfriendliness or anything like that. He was just a real high-strung person and he needed more excitement—which the Wailers offered."

The Bluenotes' slow fade-out was inglorious, but they had certainly made their mark. The band's single-minded love for gritty R&B eventually influenced their old rivals—and now, with Rockin' Robin on board, the Wailers stage show was revved up considerably. Robin's new bandmate Kent Morrill was quite impressed: "He was a very high-strung person who appeared like he was on speed all the time, but I don't think he was. I don't think he did any kind of drugs. But he was so hyper that he couldn't sit still for five minutes. He had to walk and shake his hands like he used to do. And he was just a bundle of nerves and energy, and so when he would come onstage it was like a bull out of a chute."

Meanwhile, by late '59, the Frantics had added Little Bill on vocals, and their recording of his bluesy original "Sweet Cucumber" was issued by Seattle's Topaz Records. This new firm—founded by John Hill, the boyfriend of Fleetwoods' singer Gretchen Christopher—was in Dolton's old downtown digs. But in 1960, when the Frantics began booking more and more dance gigs in California, Little Bill started looking around for a new band to work with locally: "I talked to Pat O'Day and he asked me to come out to the Spanish Castle. He wanted me to meet someone and I said, 'OK.' So, I walked in and he says, 'This is John Stone, and he has a band.' And he says to John Stone, 'Bill's gonna be the singer with yer band.' [*laughter*] It was like, And that's that!"

Because O'Day controlled the weekly dances at the Castle, he suddenly had leverage over his boss at KJR. Stone had somehow imagined he was so talented as a singer that he should form a band, the Adventurers, and make records. God knows how he managed to finagle a recording deal for himself with the venerated New Orleans label Ace Records, but he did. Stone also had such little faith in Seattle's recording studios that he traveled to Los Angeles's Gold Star Studios, where he cut a couple of weak tunes with some heavyweight session pros. Then he had the gall to push his single, "Together," on KJR.

O'Day was appalled: "'Jockey' John Stone was one of the worst singers in creation. But I used to have to hire him and pay him to come to a dance and sing his *horrid* songs. [*laughter*] So, I figured, 'As long as I've got to hire these turkeys, we could have something here that makes sense.' So, we got Little Bill in there."

The Adventurers were scoring some great gigs, which Stone arranged outside of O'Day's orbit. They played with Roy Orbison, Gene Vincent, and other stars. And all the while, Stone was abusing his powerful position at KJR—a pattern that would soon bring his downfall. Others witnessed how he'd get on the phone and bully the managers of various rock 'n' roll stars, essentially informing them that if their act didn't come to Seattle and perform at some show he was producing and promoting, their current single would be dropped from KJR's playlist.

Relieved of his duties at KJR after similar incidents where—as Pat O'Day diplomatically recalled—"he *forgot* to pay some of the acts," Stone fled town. Meanwhile, the Adventurers carried on without him, even participating in the Stars of the Century extravaganza at the Civic Auditorium on November 20, 1960. That concert also featured the Fleetwoods, Frantics, Wailers, Checkers, Exotics, Casuals, Darwin and the Cupids, Billy Saint, and Ronnie Height. The show traveled to the Yakima Armory and the Spokane Coliseum, making it the closest thing there would ever be to a Northwest teen-R&B road show revue.

Originally formed back in 1959, the Adventurers were admired for the great sax work of Jim Michaelson and the exceptional guitar work of Joe Johansen, whose hard-core adoration of the blues was about to make him a pivotal influence on the early Sea-Tac scene. And like so many of his peers, it was the Evergreen Ballroom that had forever changed Johansen's life:

> Let me tell you how much the Evergreen Ballroom meant to me.
> . . . For a young white kid to see that stuff for the first time—I'm
> just agog. I saw Ike and Tina Turner there. And Hank Ballard and
> the Midnighters. Fats Domino. Etta James. You know, anybody who
> was worth a damn. And then I saw B.B. King there. I thought I was a
> pretty hot stuff blues player. I'd been listening to B.B. King. I'd been
> listening to the blues. I thought I knew what I was doin'. Uh, it wasn't
> *quite* true. Now, he had a big band—a thirteen-piece band—and
> they started this song and he played one note and it went out over
> the crowd and then just dripped down on everybody and I could
> feel it in my spine goin' down. And I can remember thinking, "Back
> to the drawing board, Joe."

After the show Johansen and Little Bill went backstage and met up with their idol—just as they would on other nights with touring R&B

stars at the Evergreen. "I just always thought it was great how nice these guys were," said Johansen. "Bobby Bland: I spent hours talking with him. And his guitarist, Wayne Bennett, was real cool. And the guitar player with the Upsetters spent forty-five minutes after the show showing me how to play the song 'Hold It.' Freddie King showed me how to play 'Hideaway' at the Evergreen. Those kinds of lessons that you learn— man, *that's* important stuff."

One night at an Adventurers' gig, the band crossed paths with Nancy Claire—that singer they'd been seeing on local TV singing all those Brenda Lee tunes with the Versatones. "I met them at a dance in Auburn and they had me sing," she remembered. "And they liked me. Little Bill asked me to join up with the Adventurers, but then Joe Johansen said, 'Quit singin' those cowboy songs.' [*laughter*] [Those were] his exact words—and he and Little Bill handed me Aretha Franklin's record called 'Won't Be Long.' That was the beginning of *my* rhythm and blues."

Having discovered R&B music, Claire would go on to become one of the region's most in-demand singers. Meanwhile, Rockin' Robin had been in the Wailers for months now and was harping about wanting to make a record. He desired nothing more than to have a disc out with his name on it, and the song he had brought over from the Bluenotes was one he was still nuts over: "Louie Louie."

"It was Robin," Kent Morrill admitted, "who really discovered that song. He was workin' in a record store. And you know when we wanted to rehearse and learn songs, we would bring records that we liked individually and the band would decide if they thought that was cool. We usually went along with whoever wanted to sing something. And I remember that Robin brought that record to us."

The Wailers had become the top drawing group in the whole Northwest and were ready to take it to the next level. However, with Golden Crest shunning them, they were a bit stuck. The band wanted to continue making records and knew that they couldn't just wait until the contract ran out way off in mid-1964. Yet, until they were free and clear of that, what other label would sign them? Something had to be done. Added to that, they were unable to resolve the dilemma of Robin's insistence on recording "Louie Louie."

"Now, the main controversy I had with him was he wanted to bill himself on a record!," John Greek, the Wailers' founder and leader, explained:

We were going to record "Louie Louie." He wanted to bill himself as "Rockin' Robin and the Wailers." And, well, then *Kent* wanted the same thing. He wanted to be featured as "Kent Morrill and the Wailers." So, naturally, I said, "Hey, wait a minute here!" [*laughter*] I said, "*No way. We can't do it!*" We were going into it *heavy*! So the thing as far as recording "Louie Louie"—that was a big block between me and Robin. Him wanting top billing. Label credit. There was no way to do it. I was *protecting* the band name, and to me it felt like they were overstepping. I mean, why weren't we calling it "John Greek and the Wailers" you know? We could have called it "Richard Dangel and the Wailers." That's bullshit to me. I told the guys in the band, "Not unless we're gonna go on and become professional backup for other singers and do that whole thing." But to me it was downgrading the band—in fact, turning us into a backup band. That was almost like shooting someone else's name out on top, and that wasn't the way the band operated.

It was this precise issue of "the way the band operated" that came into question in early 1960. And unfortunately for Greek, it was *he* who was now besieged with troubles. The problem began after Greek had gotten the band associated with a dance promoter named Dick Cope, who began booking them into the Tacoma Armory and taking what the band suspected was more than his share of the profits.

So, it all began with legit questions about that coupled with Greek's bookkeeping practices—like the matter of him, as the combo's leader, taking a solo "promotional" trip to radio stations down in San Francisco or trying to write off a few cases of beer as "business expenses." Little details like that caught the eyes of the boys' parents. So, things got real nasty when Mike Burk's father dragged Greek and Cope before the board of Tacoma's AFM Local 117 musicians' union. As Greek bitterly recalled decades later, "There was a hardcore thing against us there, *too*! There was a faction that was, you know, positive union, but there were some other guys, boy, they'd just as soon see us—and anybody else playin' rock 'n' roll—*gone*."

In the end, Cope was banned from hiring local musicians, and Greek suffered an even greater blow. Voted out of the union *and* exiled from his band, he had by June relocated to Hollywood and started working with Gary Paxton, recording lots of rock singles under various names—including Johnnie and Jeff, the Puddin' Heads, and the Beautiful Daze. He played (in costume) one of the Sacred Cows rockin' out on "Kill, Kill, Kill" during a wacky episode of the *Get Smart* TV show called "The Groovy Guru"; he also worked as a composer, arranger, and session player at Hollywood's Artist's Recording Studio and as an audio engineer at Quad Teck Studios.

But back in 1960, and within days of Greek's departure, the Wailers contacted Buck Ormsby, who had been struggling to keep the Bluenotes going, and invited him to sit in at their next dance. That night, the Wailers first heard how Ormsby's booming electric Fender bass guitar could dramatically fortify their tunes. His presence would influence the band's direction in major ways. There had already been ongoing discussions about whether they could escape their Golden Crest contract or attract a new contract from some other company.

But with Ormsby aboard, his general stubbornness helped convince the band to finally renounce their relationship with Golden Crest and launch their own label. Ormsby knew deep in his bones that he could do better than the professional record-biz executives: "They never got it. Nobody with a major company wanted to commit themselves to something new. In Hollywood, the national record guys didn't know anything more than we did—so we figured, 'Do you always have to depend on someone else? Hell, we'll do it ourselves.'"

And so, Ormsby, Rockin' Robin, and Morrill committed themselves to a partnership called Etiquette Records, and in August the first of two recording sessions with Joe Boles produced a version of "Louie Louie" along with a raving rendition of Ray Charles's "Maryann"—both featuring Rockin' Robin's maniacal lead vocals that dependably drove crowds crazy. "Everybody in the Northwest was goin' nuts over ['Louie Louie']," Rich Dangel exclaimed. "Whenever we played it at gigs they had fights and everything. They went *nuts*!"

So, the plan was for Etiquette to make its debut by issuing a single, but their master tape sat on a shelf for half a year while the Wailers wasted time bickering about label credits. The debate was whether to release the recording as "Rockin' Robin," "The Wailers," or "Rockin' Robin and the Wailers."

This delay invited disaster when, in March 1961, the Wailers' old rival Little Bill booked a session with Kearney Barton at his new studio,

Audio Recording on Denny Way. The plan was to record a version of "Louie Louie" using the Adventurers and a local, Black girl group, the Shalimars, to contribute backing vocals. Little Bill had agreed to a deal with Topaz Records, a label started by Gretchen Christopher's boyfriend, John Hill. Topaz hired a local jazz musician to produce the session, which was not without its problems.

Decades later, Little Bill's voice still betrayed a sense of frustration while explaining what happened next:

> Topaz had a producer named Bill Franklin and he kept coming into the studio saying "You're singing it wrong." I said, "What do you mean?" He said, "It's not 'Me gotta go.' It's 'I gotta go.'" [*laughter*] Well, we got it done. Boy, we worked on that. But we still had the girls' background voices being put on when my old friend Buck Ormsby comes by the studio and he says, "What are you doin' down here?" And I said, "We're puttin' the girls' voices on my record." He said, "Care if I go up and listen?" And I sez, "No, I don't care."

Oblivious to the fact that the Wailers had cut a version of "Louie Louie" the previous summer, the musicians were busily doing those vocal overdubs when Ormsby walked into the session and was stunned to see them working on a competing version. Freaked out because the Wailers had wasted months gridlocked over label credits and were about to be upstaged, Ormsby made a preemptory strike by racing a copy of the Wailers tape over to Pat O'Day at KJR.

Topaz did still issue Little Bill's "Louie Louie" single, but it never had a chance. Etiquette placed a rush order for several hundred singles—credited to "Rockin' Robin Roberts"—and it became an instant hit in Seattle. The records sold out, and Etiquette ordered more. And more. And more . . .

There are plenty of reasons why this "Louie Louie" sold even better than Richard Berry's original. The Wailers had transformed Berry's low-key R&B groover into a haunting garage-rock masterpiece. It kicks off with Mark Marush's sax blatting those famous three intro notes; then, instead of the original version's offbeat island guitar figures, Dangel applied blunt power chords to a stripped-down adaptation of the tune's main riff, all anchored by Mike Burk's perfect exemplification of the Sea-Port Beat.

One of Burk's greatest admirers was his guitarist, Rich Dangel: "He was doing certain syncopated bass drum rhythms and whatnot that most drummers weren't doin' yet. He was very influential. A lot of drummers came around to see him. To me a drummer is everything when it comes to the foundation of a sound. And he had a lot to do with the foundation of the Wailers' sound. And, he had a lot of influence on other bands playing in what you might term a 'Northwest Sound.'"

Topping all this, of course, was the electrifyingly frenetic lead vocal. In addition to the ad-libbed "yeahs" that Rockin' Robin interjected periodically, his shouted call to arms—"Let's give it to 'em, RIGHT NOW!" which teed up Dangel's iconic guitar solo—was an invitational hook that few teens could ignore. Whether on record or onstage, Robin's talents were impressive.

"When I saw the Wailers for the first time," said Jimmy Hanna, "I remember Robin singing a James Brown tune, 'I'll Go Crazy.' Robin did that *unbelievable*. [*laughter*] Un! Believe! Able! Rockin' Robin was just untouchable as far as singing. His energy on stage wasn't to be equaled. I thought his energy in person was as good as anybody I'd heard. And I'd heard some good ones! But Rockin' Robin—I mean, man: his pitch of intensity on stage was unparalleled. I mean, he was right in there with the top echelon. He could have been bigger than any other person that I can think of at that point."

And with his new single sitting at number 1 on KJR—and in the Top 5 over at KOL—Robin might have reasonably thought he could be the rock world's next big star. The record's retail figures around the Puget Sound area were phenomenal: in just a matter of weeks, Etiquette had sold nearly fifteen thousand copies of the single. Then it started hitting down on Portland radio. Next it began getting a bit of national attention when *Cash Box* gave it an overall grade of B+ saying "Fine Blues vocal by the songster on a catchy ditty that was an awhile back success by Richard Berry. Roberts receives striking combo support." But the darn disc still wasn't breaking out beyond the Northwest, where it had sold twenty thousand copies by this point.

"'Louie Louie' was a song Robin believed in," Pat O'Day testified. "He used to call me on the phone and say, 'How can we make that thing break through?' He said, 'Isn't the evidence there, Pat, that it's a hit?' And I'd say, 'Robin, the evidence is there in spades. And what we need is a record company that will believe in it.'"

The time had come to seek a distribution deal and try to catapult the record into national hit status. That's when O'Day—who by this time had been earning a reputation in the radio industry for successfully breaking new records at KJR—offered to help by talking it up with his peers at other big radio stations around the country and pitching it to a few record execs in Los Angeles.

"I flew down there *twice* and just *begged* them," a pained O'Day later emoted. "I said, you know, 'Release it not just for the guys in the band, but also for *yourselves*. *Believe* it. You know: Seattle's not that goofy. Look at the *sales* numbers!' . . . But I would talk to the other program directors and they'd say, 'Oh, Pat, that's just yer local group up there.' You know, 'We listened to it, but God . . . that *ain't* much of a record!'"

For all its success with Northwest teens, not everybody could hear the record's charms. This wasn't anyone's fault—given how different "Louie Louie" was, industry doubts about it were reasonable. As O'Day recalls, "It didn't sound like any rock 'n' roll of that time. It didn't sound like anything we'd heard. You know, 'Is it *Black*, or is it *white?*' Or 'Is it . . . *good?*' And I'd say, 'Gang, it's *magic*.'" O'Day's persuasiveness eventually prevailed: "There was one guy at Liberty that believed me and he had it released."

Etiquette got their distribution deal, which was a situation Jerry Dennon was keeping an eye on:

> In 1961 I was with Era Records in Los Angeles and the record was number 1 in Seattle and selling thousands and thousands of copies and I recall sitting at a meeting with the music director of the number 1 station in LA and the national sales manager and national promotions manager of a label that was distributing it nationally. And basically the dialogue was, they were "doing a favor for Pat O'Day by taking it," that "we really don't understand it." I'm sure they were just stroking O'Day by taking it. They probably didn't think that the record had any potential outside the Northwest. They probably thought, "Hey, you know, the band is obviously big up there, so let's not worry about it. Pat's gonna be happy." Little did they realize what they were overlooking.

"So the Wailers' record came out," O'Day explained, "but Liberty was, at that time, going through a whole bunch of ownership changes and they totally dropped the ball. They never, never put any emphasis behind it. And it's too bad. As a result they missed a record that was as big as anything they would ever have. And . . . I guess if there's one thing that's a shame, it's the series of circumstances that never allowed Robin's 'Louie Louie' to ever achieve its rightful number 1 position in the country."

While it is true that Rockin' Robin's "Louie Louie" never did break out nationally, in a very real sense it had already achieved enough. By striking a responsive chord (or rather three) with local teens, the Wailers had managed to supersede both "Tall Cool One" and "Walk—Don't Run" by establishing "Louie Louie" as *the* signature riff of Northwest rock 'n' roll—a heartbeat pulse whose legacy would reverberate through the decades. ★

CHAPTER *17*

LIKE, LONG HAIR

One measure of the expansion of the Pacific Northwest's rock 'n' roll scene was the remarkable growth of the teen dance circuit, which now wound through Washington and Oregon, over to the college towns of Idaho and Montana, and up into the Vancouver, BC, area. And it would be bands like the Dave Lewis Combo, Clayton Watson and the Silhouettes, the Wailers, Ventures, Statics, and Checkers whose touring was having an influence on other musicians.

For its part, Montana would see the emergence of pioneering bands, including the Renegades, Avengers, and Checkmates, just as Idaho had the Trebletones, Stompers, Fabulous Chancellors, Dick Cates and the Chessmen, and the Red Hughes Band. But it would be this latter band, from Caldwell, who would (under a new name and with updated personnel) achieve the greatest success of any Northwest combo thus far. Indeed, they would score a couple dozen international hit singles, release twenty-odd albums, produce a teen idol of the first order, and host a couple of their very own weekly ABC-TV shows.

The Red Hughes Band formed in 1957 when a few jocks began jamming after school in the music room at Caldwell High. A local tough named Red Hughes wanted to sing in a band and managed to corral the White brothers—Richard and Robert—on guitars, bassist William Hibbert, and a drummer, Dick McGarvin, to join in. Before long, they invited another local kid over to jam. It was Paul Revere, a bright fellow who'd been expelled from school for tossing a typewriter out the window and had instead graduated from a barber college. Having a real knack for business, he already owned three barber shops (and a drive-in burger stand, the Reed 'n' Bell) by age eighteen—and, as the boys would discover, Revere also played a mean boogie-woogie piano.

"I had been playing by ear since I was seven," recalled Revere.

"Boogie, blues and—when the craze started—rock 'n' roll. I idolized Jerry Lee Lewis, and I was determined to be as good as he was. I think I made it." It was, in fact, after seeing Lewis live at a local dance that Revere committed to being a performer. At that show, Revere had also loved the opening act, Clayton Watson and the Silhouettes, who impressed Revere because they were young Northwest guys sharing the stage with a legend.

But the Silhouettes weren't the only working band from whom he was learning. The Wailers had already developed a dynamic stage show, including their own synchronized move: the "Wailers High-Step," which numerous up-and-comers would copy.

"I remember . . . traveling to Caldwell, Idaho," Buck Ormsby reflected, "and I remember Mark Lindsay and Paul Revere coming to the edge of the stage and watching us play. After the show, it was 'How do you do this?' and 'We're starting to form this band.' And that's how we first became aware of them. They came to our gig and at that time we were doing all these steps and moving because we picked that stuff up from [James Brown's] Famous Flames and all those people."

After Hughes's band had held just a few rehearsals with Revere aboard, the Caldwell Elks Club decided to sponsor a series of fundraising sock hops and invited them to perform their first gig. As beginners, the boys played the absolute simplest of songs. "We'd rock in the key of F for ten minutes on a song," drummer McGarvin recalled, "then rock in A for ten minutes on a different song—except that it was the *same* song in a different key."

It didn't take long for Revere to decide to bypass the local dance promoters by renting a hall so the band could clear the profit themselves. Things went so well that he decided to devote even more time to the band, so he sold the barber shops and bought the Reed 'n' Bell hamburger stand in nearby Nampa.

Mark Lindsay was a shy Eugene, Oregon, trouble-boy with thick glasses who'd left home at age fifteen to stay with his grandmother in Nampa. Once there, he got a day job at McClure's Bakery and began singing with Freddy Chapman's Idaho Playboys, a country band that featured the White brothers, who also played in the Red Hughes Band. One night, Lindsay decided to attend a Red Hughes dance at the Oddfellows Hall over in Caldwell. Riled up by their loud rockin', Lindsay impulsively whipped off his glasses, charged the stage, and blurted out that he'd like to sing a tune. Hughes said sure, Lindsay cut loose, the crowd cheered, stage fright overtook the boy, and he fled.

The next day, Revere came by the bakery to pick up his regular supply of hamburger buns for the Reed 'n' Bell and a fateful friendship began. One telling described the encounter as follows:

> Covered in flour and with his coke-bottle glasses back on, [Lindsay] was soon visited by Revere, who had come in to pick up buns for his hamburger stand. While Mark wrapped the order, Revere started talking about an incident that had happened at the dance that he played the night before. "It was the weirdest thing!" said Revere. "In the middle of the show, this skinny kid with a crazy look in his eye came up to the stage and asked to sing a song. So we let him." Mark, knowing full well who the stranger was, casually asked, "How was he?" "Not bad," Revere admitted. "It was *me*!" replied Mark.

Charming story, but one suspects Revere was just toying with the kid. After further discussion, Revere told Lindsay that if he learned to play the saxophone he could join the band. Lindsay began taking sax lessons, and when Revere invited him to tag along to a rehearsal he gave it a shot. But his beginner-level "skills" didn't exactly bowl over the guys. McGarvin was tickled to share, "I remember Paul bringing Mark in. He wasn't singing, he was going to play tenor sax. He played the worst—it was just *awful*! . . . He'd squeak and honk and play out of tune, but he was sincere and really dedicated."

So, Lindsay began gigging with the band, and Red Hughes began resenting that his crowds were digging the cute new sax player. The rising tensions came to a head one night when Hughes was late to a dance and Revere asked Lindsay to help out and sing a few tunes until their leader arrived. When Hughes rolled in he saw Lindsay in action and erupted: "If you ever let Lindsay on the stage again, I'll fire the whole band!"

No need. The entire band quit on the spot and soon regrouped with Lindsay as front man. Having noticed a copy of the jazz-oriented *Down Beat* magazine at his sax teacher's place, Lindsay suggested their new name: the Downbeats. The group carried on, playing dances and adding more songs to their set lists. It was the early summer of '59 when the Wailers' "Tall Cool One" popped up on Boise radio and that *really* made an impression, especially on Mark Lindsay: "The Wailers' 'Tall Cool One' came out, and I remember going to Paul and saying 'Look, man, here's a band from the Northwest, they actually made a record that's on the charts. If they can do it, we can do it.'"

By 1960, the Downbeats had developed a repertoire that included the Wailers' "Tall Cool One" and "Roadrunner," along with some new originals—mostly piano-based instrumentals. Revere decided to book a couple of hours of recording time at the Boise's radio station KGEM. Although as he recalled, "It wasn't actually a recording studio—there was no recording studio in Idaho then. This was a radio station that had a little studio that they used to cut radio spots in. And so we all crammed into this studio and set up the drums and the guitar amps and the whole thing and we recorded this stuff in [*laughter*] a couple of hours."

Well, turned out that somebody at one big-time label listened to Revere's tape and told him to get his band, come back, and do some recording in a professional studio. The Downbeats—Revere, Lindsay, Robert White, Dick White, and their new drummer, Jerry Labrum—piled their gear into Revere's T-Bird and Mark Lindsay's Plymouth Valiant and raced down to Hollywood. Once there, they met up with that label executive, who arranged to get them into a studio. And that's when they got their first taste of reality in the big, bad music biz.

"He gave us checks for union scale on the session," Lindsay remembered, "but said, 'You know, it's standard practice to give the checks back after the session.' Paul went to the union and checked, and it turns out that we're not gonna be with this big label, but on this guy's own small label. He'd just quit his job as president of this big label. Paul told the guy to make a paper airplane out of the contract."

Revere was a never-say-die optimist who always had a backup plan. "Someone had suggested this guy in Gardena, California, who had a pressing plant. A lot of the smaller labels got this guy to press their records up. But every once in a while, this guy would put out a record on his own label, Gardena Records. And so I went down there and he instantly loved the stuff and he wanted to put it out."

Gardena's owner, John Guss, probably also liked the fact that instrumental rock had a proven market. And although Guss was interested in releasing the Downbeats' "Beatnik Sticks," he insisted on changing the band's name to something less jazzy. Revere balked at his first suggestion—the Nightriders seemed too country and western. He much preferred Guss's second idea: "How about Paul Revere and the Raiders?"

Back in Caldwell, the newly named Raiders were thrilled when in September 1960 they received a box of singles from Guss. The first thing Revere did was race one over to KGEM, where his former drummer Dick McGarvin was now working as a DJ. Right after he'd dropped it off and jumped in his car to hit another station, "Beatnik Sticks" came blaring out of his dashboard radio. Stunned, he could only pull his car over to the roadside, get out, and jump for joy, waving at passersby and yelling, "That's *me* on the *radio!*"

From there, "Beatnik Sticks" began charting on stations from Los Angeles to Vancouver, BC, to Boise. The tune got enough airplay in Southern California that Guss asked Revere to return with the Raiders so they could do a few promotional gigs, cut some new recordings in a better studio, and prepare a follow-up single. The Raiders arrived in California again and Guss paired them with the noted Sunset Strip scenester and wild man producer Kim Fowley.

Together they cut a few tracks, including a rerecording of one of Revere's earliest compositions, "Like, Long Hair." "I actually was inspired by something I heard on the radio," Revere remembered. "It was a Rachmaninoff thing and it went '*Bummn . . . Bommn . . . Bahdumn.*' And I thought, 'Man, *that's* a hook!' So I went home and I sat down at the piano and I just started messin' around with it and gave it a little rock 'n' roll flavor and a little boogie-woogie left hand and within about ten minutes I basically had the song 'Like, Long Hair.'"

Guss took Fowley's new production of the tune back to his plant, pressed it up, and once again radio programmers supported their efforts. A local teen dance TV program, Wink Martindale's *Top Ten Dance Party* show, invited the Raiders to appear, and soon thereafter Dick Clark aired the record on *American Bandstand*. Guss was so excited he promptly released an entire *Like, Long Hair* album, which included Mark Lindsay's first vocal recording, "Sharon" (as arranged by Gary "Alley Oop" Paxton), a tune penned in tribute to the waitress at Revere's Reed 'n' Bell hamburger stand—Sharon Darnell—who went on to marry him and bear his two children.

In late March 1961, *Billboard* listed "Like, Long Hair" as a new chart entry and ABC sent word that Dick Clark wanted the band to perform on his show. All signs were pointing toward an immanent breakthrough for the band, and Guss and the Raiders were all ecstatic. This excitement swelled for a few hours, until the mail was delivered and Revere received a draft notice from Uncle Sam instructing him to report for immediate duty.

This disruption caused serious problems: the *American Bandstand* offer was a major lost opportunity, and the Raiders were stuck fulfilling two weeks of live bookings by having a top studio pianist named Leon Russell fill in for Revere. Meanwhile, Revere secured Conscientious Objector status and exemption from military service due to his family's Mennonite religious beliefs. To fulfill his obligations to the Alternative Service Program, he worked as a cook in the psychiatric facility at Dammasch Hospital, located in a rural area just outside of Portland.

"When he got drafted," Lindsay recalled, "Paul said, 'It's all over now, because in two years no one will know who we are.' But I was a very determined person at that time and said to him, 'Listen, it's not over. I'll tell you what, do your thing in Oregon and I'll go down to California.'" While the rest of the Raiders headed back to logging jobs in Idaho, Lindsay settled into Hollywood, sleeping on the floor of Kim Fowley's apartment. He scrounged around, sought opportunities, picked up five-dollar studio session gigs, snapped portraits of tourists outside Grauman's Chinese Theater, and whiled away the days behind the landmark Hollywood sign, where he practiced his saxophone in seclusion.

That the Raiders—who were named by a national poll of radio DJs as one of the top up-and-coming instrumental bands in the nation—would be defunct for the foreseeable future surely concerned Guss. "Like, Long Hair" peaked at number 38 during its six-week *Billboard* chart run, selling about five hundred thousand units in the United States and another seventy thousand over in Germany, but it would be difficult to promote the record any further without Revere's help. Rather than give up, Guss gamely moved forward by issuing more Raiders singles—including "Paul Revere's Ride," which self-mythologized his original trip to California—and issued the *Like, Long Hair* LP, which joined *The Fabulous Wailers*, *The Ventures*, and the Fleetwoods' *Mr. Blue* among the first albums issued by a Northwest rock 'n' roll group.

Once Revere had completed his public service obligations in 1963, he was raring to get rockin' once again: "When I got out . . . I went down to Hollywood, grabbed Mark, who was literally starving down there, brought him back to Oregon, and got him a job. There were virtually no rock groups there, and I knew it was time to get started again." ★

CHAPTER *18*

SWINGIN' SUMMER

Eastern Washington had been a bastion of rockabilly music in the early days of rock 'n' roll, and the Yakima Valley area—with its big military base and legions of migrant Mexican farmworkers—proved particularly fertile for a dynamic teen dance scene that revolved around high school sock hops, armory dances, and even a couple of teenage dance venues: the Walk In Club and the 'el Bon Club.

Following the lead of Jerry Merritt and the Pacers, additional combos emerged in Yakima including the Checkers. This group would see a series of reincarnations and along the way become one of the Northwest's very best. In 1957, the Checkers comprised the Torres brothers Nick (vocals) and Bobby (bass), Glenn Dahl (vocals and guitar), Bob Campbell (piano), Norman Drake (sax), Ralph Gibson (drums), and a killer guitarist named Johnny Hensley. And just like their heroes Gene Vincent and His Blue Caps, the Checkers performed live with two "clapper boys" (who contributed rhythmic handclaps).

In 1958, the Checkers lost Gibson, so a new kid named Mike Mandel joined on drums. He was a blind musician's musician who knew theory inside and out and had come of age attending Pat Mason's shows featuring Little Richard, Little Willie John, and Jerry Lee Lewis at the Yakima Armory. When Campbell left, Mandel switched to piano and Doug Robertson became their drummer. Then, when Drake left, Mike Metko—a tenor saxophonist whose experience amounted to having been a member of the Jumps, a swing ensemble based at Sunnyside High School—joined. But it was Metko's job at Toppenish's 250-watt station, KENE, that provided the Checkers with their next opportunity. Through KENE he met Mason, who proceeded to hire the band to open shows by rockabilly stars like Jimmy Bowen, Johnny Burnette, and Jimmy Clanton.

The Checkers were now ready to make a record. Metko borrowed KENE's Ampex tape recorder and laid down two rockin' instrumentals, "The Big Cat" and "Buzz," at the Toppenish grange hall. Custom pressed for the band by the fly-by-night, LA-based Dottie Records, "Buzz" failed to garner any airplay from stations other than KENE. But the Checkers carried on by building up their onstage experience at gigs across the region, acquiring better musical gear, and adding new players.

Mandel was sorry when Johnny Hensley quit to join Clayton Watson and the Silhouettes, but he understood the temptation as he highly respected the musicianship of Watson's band: "He sounded just like the records—and for me that was everything! In those days I was shooting for record quality. Exactitude of sound. So when I saw Watson I was blown away. He had two or three saxes with him, and he did all the stuff that we didn't do: the multi-sax stuff, the Fats Domino stuff, the Little Richard stuff, the Little Willie John stuff. Great R&B. It was excellent to me at that time. He did the charts correctly. He was able to imitate the record stars really well."

For his part, Hensley was such a rockin' guitarist that he was soon poached by the Texas rockabilly stars Buddy Knox and the Rhythm Orchids. After a couple months of performing without a guitarist, the Checkers were desperate to find another player of Hensley's caliber. Eventually, the band was over in Richland shopping for a new Fender amp at Korten's Music Store and mentioned to the salesman that they were also in need of a new guitarist.

"And," Mandel chuckled as he related the story, "these guys said, 'Well hell, we know a little guy here named Larry Coryell. A *nice* little guy. He's fifteen years old and he plays the dickens outta that guitar'":

So, they asked us if we wanted them to call him and have him come down and audition. Our attitude was "Well look, we're seventeen and eighteen years old and we travel a lot and we're pretty free spirits here. I don't think a fifteen-year-old is appropriate for this band." They called him anyway, and the kid came down while we were making the transaction for the amplifier, and he sat down and played Duane Eddy just like we ordered. He played Chuck Berry fairly well. And *that* was it for me. If you can do Chuck Berry like that, well, yer hired!

Coryell's stepfather was a nuclear scientist who'd moved the family to Richland from Texas in 1950 when he was seven. Having lived in these two locales, he considered himself to be "a country boy, a real hick, man." Richland was literally in the backwater sticks: "I was never more than a hundred yards from the Columbia River. It was really out there. I didn't know what jazz was." However, "I always wanted to be a guitarist. I remember walking those dusty streets in Richland, with the tumbleweeds rollin' down the fields, and the desert air and all that. Just *nothin'* out there [*laughter*] and just dreaming about being a guitar player."

He took private jazz lessons at Korten's, but as there was no jazz scene in the Tri-Cities area of Richland-Kennewick-Pasco Coryell was soon performing country and then rock 'n' roll with a band led by Keith Colley (who would go on to his own solo recording career). After his stint with the Royals, Coryell took a big step up by joining the Checkers.

They were fast becoming the top band in all of Eastern Washington and loved nothing more than playing out-of-town gigs. It was just plain exciting to pack up a car or two with all their gear and head out on the road. And so, week after week they played every minuscule burg ranging from White Salmon to Ephrata, from Washtucna to White Swan.

In time, the Checkers worked their way up to gigging in the region's larger towns: Walla Walla, Spokane, and then eventually crossing the "Cascade Curtain" to Portland and Seattle. Coryell later recalled that "it was the thrill of our life to play the Spanish Castle," where they shared bills with Gene Vincent, Ray Stevens, and Dorsey Burnette. The latter star was so impressed by the Checkers' musicianship that he recruited them to back him in a recording session at Joe Boles's studio.

But playing over here brought a different level of challenge because this was indisputably the Wailers' and Frantics' turf. The Checkers' sax man Mike Metko reflected on those times: "The two main bands as far as we were concerned, when we used to come to the coast, was the Frantics and the Wailers. In fact, I'll always recall that we played the Tacoma Armory and the kids were all requesting 'Louie Louie'—and we'd never *heard* of it! Needless to say, we had to learn that after playing there. I think the next weekend we got on that song because it became almost the national anthem up there."

Once "Louie Louie" was committed to memory—which must have taken all of a minute or two—the Checkers were on a level playing field with the other bands and did their damnedest to pull out all the stops when they were here. The stage show they'd developed is now the stuff of legend: Coryell was known for doing backflips while playing his guitar, and Mandel thrilled crowds when he stood on his head and played his piano.

By this point, the Checkers longed to be a touring band—playing music late into the nights and cruising America's highways for weeks on end. But it was difficult to indulge that fantasy for long, always knowing they were but a day's drive from their parents' homes. They were aching to head out on a *real* road trip when Metko announced in the late spring of 1960 that he could get the band a booking in Phoenix, where his parents now lived. Most of the band was instantly sold, but young Coryell still had a few weeks until school let out for the summer. The Checkers were torn: they could hardly go without their guitarist, but it didn't appear there was any way to get him excused from the last days of classes at Richland High. Well, no way unless they absconded with him.

"We *kidnapped* Larry!" Mike Mandel hooted later. "We called his principal and requested that Larry come with us to Phoenix—where we were going to make our fame and fortune. (I don't know why we thought that was an entertainment capital but we did!) [*laughter*] So what we did was, we had an enclosed trailer that we had rented for the trip to carry our instruments and we put Larry in the trailer and wouldn't let him out to call his family until we got to Klamath Falls, Oregon. We had him call and say, 'Here I am and I *ain't* comin' back.'"

Upon their triumphant arrival in Phoenix, the Checkers discovered that their solitary booking was a performance after a basketball game in some high school gym. This was decidedly *not* the major tour they had all fantasized about. But while there, the band contributed to some recording sessions with a couple of local singers before scurrying back home. That same year, the band recorded a couple of original tunes— "Black Cat" and "Soft Blue"—which Jerden Records failed to release before closing shop in 1960.

Undaunted, the Checkers returned to Boles's studio and cut a few more songs, including a session backing the rockabilly star Johnny Burnette. But it was their original instrumentals—"Skooby Doo, Part 1," "Skooby Doo, Part 2," and "Swingin' Summer"—that they figured were winners, so they went down to Los Angeles to seek a record contract. Arriving at the door of Arvee Records, the Checkers were invited in by the label's young promotions man named Sonny Bono. He listened to their tape and agreed to license the tunes for commercial release.

Well, Arvee followed through by immediately issuing the single, "Skooby Doo, Part 1" / "Swingin' Summer"; when it bombed, Arvee reloaded and tried "Skooby Doo, Part 1" / "Skooby Doo, Part 2." This time the record got a little airplay, but a couple of months later the Checkers asked for, and were given, a release from their contract.

Just when the Checkers felt that they were foundering, an offer came through for a midwestern dance hall road tour starting in March of '61. The opportunity required that they sacrifice their young guitar whiz, as Coryell was stuck completing the spring quarter of his senior year of high school.

Before heading out on the road, Mandel remembered, "An agent named Bob Dawes called me and said, 'Listen: would you guys like to do a tour with Bobby Vee and the Ventures? There's only two Ventures—Bogle and Wilson—and they need a bass and a drummer?' Well, that was what I was looking for. So, we had to get another guitar player 'cause Larry couldn't make it. So we got Joe Johansen from a band called the Adventurers. Now, we had met him, but . . . Joe was not our first choice. We weren't knocked out. 'Cause, after *Coryell*, what *else* is there?"

The band voted to take the new offer instead, bought a '58 Plymouth station wagon, and set out from Yakima. Arriving in Iowa, they began rehearsals with both Bobby Vee as well as the Ventures. As it turned out, Vee hated the group—he wanted a Buddy Holly–type sound and didn't relate to the Checkers' Northwest-style teen-R&B. In fact, Vee's petulance made the tour difficult. For example, when they played his hometown of Fargo, North Dakota, Vee sidelined the Checkers and instead had his father accompany him on guitar.

Later, the Checkers (who had replaced Metko with Jim Michaelson from the Adventurers) were called to Los Angeles by two rockabilly stars, Johnny Burnette and Jimmy Bowen, who was establishing a new career as a producer. Bowen had the boys cut a couple of piano-based instrumentals that his publishing house controlled: Burnette's "Cascade" and Bowen's "Blue Saturday." Though the Checkers' hearts weren't in the tunes, that single—when released on Bowen's Skyla Records—did surprisingly well with radio stations in Seattle, Phoenix, and various midwestern towns where the Checkers had toured. The band looked to *finally* have a hit on their hands.

Mandel reveled in the thrill: "I remember riding around the Midwest. We were like in Iowa, and the radio station was in St. Louis, and I was blown away. Oh, it *messed* me up! I couldn't believe it. Hearing us on the radio like that on a distant station like that: it *blew* me away."

But while "Blue Saturday" went Top 10 on a smattering of stations, it just never built up the momentum to propel it to the national charts. By mid-'62 the Checkers had made their final road tour. And then, after wrecking their station wagon while returning from a late-night dance gig, the combo dissolved. It wouldn't be long, however, before both Mike Mandel and Joe Johansen relocated to Seattle and began to make their marks on Northwest music. ★

CHAPTER *19*

THE GIRL CAN'T HELP IT

By 1960, the touring R&B revues performing at the Evergreen Ballroom were attracting larger audiences and inspiring the young musicians in attendance. Those pro players were profoundly affecting their fans' tastes in music, their sense of appropriately natty stage attire, and their sense of how an effective show ought to be paced throughout an evening.

Back then, R&B performances typically featured a dapper emcee who served as the ringmaster, joking, working the crowd, and introducing each of the revue talents. Among those might be a whole string of seasoned singers, a few comely dancers, a comedian, and any number of individual players who would be called up front to cut loose with spotlight solos—and then, finally, the grand entrance by the headlining star. And throughout all this activity, the backing band's front line would all be doin' synchronized steps. It also didn't hurt matters that many of these entertainers were exceedingly kind and friendly to young local musicians.

"I remember one time Little Richard and the Upsetters were playing there," Buck Ormsby recalled:

> I was with the Wailers and this was like 1960–61—and they saw us white boys out there, and the sax player leaned over and said, "You guys play, don't you?" And I said, "Yeah." And he said, "You want to come up and play?" So, he asked us to come up and play. Me, Rich Dangel, and Mike Burk. And I think he was, like, trying to see if we could really play. . . . But we got up there and he kind of left

the stage, and we cooked and he came back up and grabbed his sax and started playing! I mean, we could *do* that sort of stuff. But the Black musicians of the time: they taught us stuff. . . . I think it helped us, the Wailers, a lot.

One of the knockout acts of the day was the one led by Ike Turner. Back in 1958, his Kings of Rhythm band had brought aboard Turner's young wife, Tina, as lead vocalist; and then a girl group of omni-shimmering backing singers, the Ikettes, in 1960, reemerging as the Ike and Tina Turner Revue. It was their onstage energy and admirable stagecraft that made a deep impression on anyone who was ever lucky enough to have seen the show. And for the local musicians, they learned what it meant to pull out all the stops to entertain an audience.

"We were inspired," Rich Dangel reflected, "by goin' down to the Evergreen Ballroom and seeing these acts, like Ike and Tina Turner, come through. Or you went to see Bobby Bland and he'd have the band do a couple tunes, and then Al 'TNT' Braggs would do a sax tune—and it was real exciting. So we got inspired especially by the groups that would have, like, the girl singers in the background, you know? And so we found out about Gail Harris."

Harris was a precocious Puyallup schoolgirl who already had years of experience singing country music with a bunch of old-timers on local radio and TV. At the age of nine, she became a regular on KING-TV's *Roy Gordon Show*, then she appeared on the *Jack Rivers Show*, and from there she moved on to Buck Owens's *Bar K Jamboree* on Tacoma's KTNT-TV. But, by 1960, Harris was looking around for a teen band to join. She auditioned for a combo called the Aztecs before eventually crossing paths with the Wailers, who were aware of the kid's country TV background but gave her an audition anyway.

Getting the chance to sing with Tacoma's top rock band, she jumped right in. "I started singing with the Wailers," Gail Harris fondly recalled, "when I had just turned thirteen. It was right at the time of 'Tall Cool One,' and John Greek was still there. . . . I used to listen to Etta James all the time, and I just tried to sing those kinds of songs. I sang pretty powerfully anyway and so kinda came up with my own style from that."

After Harris cut loose with a couple of Ike and Tina songs, the Wailers knew that they'd found their very own Tina. Rich Dangel remembered, "She was this thirteen-year-old singer that we thought sang great and we got her to join the group. Robin was already with us, and then we had the girl singers—the Marshans—who came along. So we had a sort of revue happening where we'd go up and do our instrumentals set. Then Robin would come up and do some tunes, then Gail would come up and do some tunes and then we'd have the girls come up and back up Gail. You know: *tryin'* to make it into a *show*."

Now the Wailers' ten-piece crew began developing what would be the most exciting teen-R&B stage act yet formed in the Northwest, and Harris would quickly become the most influential female singer on the local teen scene. Her spirited performances inspired untold numbers of girl singers across the region—including another, named Little Becky, who also gigged a bit with the Wailers. Musicians all across the Northwest—including Mike Mitchell, the guitarist from a new Portland-based combo called the Kingsmen—were quite impressed.

"The Wailers were the band," Mitchell freely admitted. "The Frantics were great, but the Wailers were the band to copy. The Wailers had everything: they had a band, and then they had a lead singer, Rockin' Robin, who would come out and do a few songs, and then Gail Harris would come out and do a few songs. And then she had backup singers that would come up and do a few songs, so they were a whole revue in themselves. So those were the guys we kinda emulated and followed. And so did Paul Revere and the Raiders."

Another band Harris auditioned with, the Statics, had also been influenced by the R&B revues appearing at the Evergreen. Learning their lessons well there, the band would go on to earn a region-wide reputation as an absolutely smokin' teen-R&B combo—one appreciated as much for their sound as for their synchronized dance moves, perhaps the best of any of their peers.

The Statics had originated in Burien in 1958, and their eventual leader, Neil Rush (sax), had gotten into rock 'n' roll after being inspired by the Frantics: "I saw the Frantics at a sock hop at Highline High School and I was about a sophomore so this would have been 1957. I was aware of Bill Haley and His Comets and all those people that really got the rockabilly thing started—but the Frantics were the first local band that I had actually seen that did it right."

Just prior to the Statics, Rush had formed his Renton-based combo the Amazing Aztecs, who went into Joe Boles's studio in January 1960. Their sole instrumental rock single, "Death Coach," got a bit of airplay over at Wally Nelskog's KQDE but then disappeared. The Amazing Aztecs eventually placed a "Looking for Female Vocalist for Recording Potential" classified ad, which attracted three respondents: Gail Harris, Nancy Claire, and Lynn Vrooman. The fifteen-year-old Vrooman didn't have the country television background the other two did, but she had already recorded that single for Penguin Records, and she had been hired to appear—with the Playboys backing her—on Fabian's November '59 tour stops in Seattle, Spokane, and Portland. Vrooman should have been the leading contender.

"Lynn Vrooman brought along an accompanist with her," Neil Rush snickered years later. "A girl named Merrilee Gunst. And Merrilee's parents sat outside in front of my dad's house waiting for the girls to audition. Anyway, to make a long story short: I fell in love at first sight. That's what happened. She was a sixteen-year-old girl and I was an eighteen-year-old guy, and I said, 'Can you do anything except play piano?' And she said, 'Well, yeah.' And of course Lynn—being her friend—said, 'Oh yeah, she sings real good!'"

Wrong answer. Merrilee was an effervescent North End kid with gorgeous dark eyes and long dark tresses who'd discovered rockin' R&B music dancing to the Frantics, Little Bill and the Bluenotes, and the Wailers at various Seattle dances.

As a student at Shoreline High School, Merrilee's performing experience was thus far limited to a few local USO shows with Vrooman. She'd been perfectly happy as the group's pianist, never harboring any thoughts of being a lead singer. As it happened, though, Rush had made his decision: Merrilee was his choice for the Aztecs' new singer. He had to admit, however, that "the Aztecs ground down to a halt in the summer of 1960. It broke up because of Merrilee. It actually split the band apart. The guys in the band didn't really want to push a girl singer. They thought that I was putting far too much emphasis on Merrilee. And by the way, by that time I was madly in love with her, okay? So, I was."

Merrilee agreed, remembering, "We basically had to form a new band because I was not well accepted by the guys in the band. Because it was a guy thing, you know? But, because Gail Harris was so strong with the Wailers, I really think that any female that they could bring in that they could feature was a real plus. But I wasn't real good, so it was hard for them to accept that."

As things turned out, it was Merrilee's parents who found it hard to contemplate Rush's true interest in their daughter. To create some space there, they hired Merrilee her own personal managers, which forced Rush to negotiate Merrilee's involvement in his band through them. The result was the formation of an all-new combo that spotlighted her: Merrilee and Her Men. Over the next year and a half they gigged around on the circuit the Aztecs had already forged.

It was at about this point that the Statics—who had brought in a new guitarist, Dick Gerber—decided that they needed a singer and asked Tiny Tony (whose main group, the Gallahads, were only working sporadically) if he might want to pick up a few extra bucks with them. As it turned out, he had already been working casually with a few other combos, including the Dynamics and West Seattle's El Caminos. But, in 1962, Tiny Tony opted to join the Statics because they had good connections and a big sound.

The only thing they seemed to lack was stage presence, and Tiny Tony was there to help. Having been the Gallahads' choreographer, so to speak, he began tutoring the Statics on how to do synchronized dance steps while performing. Soon the Statics would be known for their wild stage show, which was soon to be copied by countless other local combos.

Indeed, Paul Revere and the Raiders got schooled by the Statics one summer night when each band was booked to play different dances in Clarkston, Washington. As Neil Rush tells it, "At 10:30 that night, Revere was standing in front of us because we had a full house and they had nobody. I remember that later we—Tiny Tony and I—sat out there in front of a Chinese restaurant that night and basically taught them the basics of doing dance steps."

Such synchronized dance steps would later become a visual trademark for the Raiders. The Statics' moves were impressive—and funky enough to get Tiny Tony in hot water with the law on another night. "Tony got thrown in jail once down in Olympia out at the Evergreen Ballroom," Rush recalled:

> You know, we used to do some pretty graphic steps—we'd do the "bump and grind" kind of a thing. Well, one of the things Tony used to do: see, one of his girlfriends was a six-foot-tall Amazon-looking woman, very beautiful, and she was dancing out in the

crowd right in front of Tony. And Tony was with her—only he was on the stage. And Tony would take his belt and he'd pull his belt out and stick it out like a dick. He used to wear three-piece suits and he would have his belt sticking out about seven or eight inches, and the cops came and hauled him away. They hauled his ass away for that one. We had to go down and get him out.

For her part, Merrilee was becoming a major attraction for the Statics, and they decided it was time to cut some singles. Among them were "Harlem Shuffle," "Buster Brown," and Little Richard's "The Girl Can't Help It"—records that sold reasonably well to their fans despite the fact that Pat O'Day rejected every one of them for airplay on KJR. And while the DJ forthrightly told Neil that they just weren't *hit* quality, the band always believed the music was just too R&B-oriented for O'Day's tastes.

It was a criticism leveled by other artists as well. Yet O'Day always defended KJR's programming policies by stating that, at the time, airing any R&B that was rootsier than the slick "Motown sound" was a tough row to hoe on Seattle radio. If that were true, it spotlights an interesting dichotomy in the area's culture. Here you had Seattle—the home base of a thriving, indigenous teen-R&B sound that fueled countless numbers of O'Day's own weekly dances—yet the broadcasting of such local music (or the hard R&B that had initially inspired it) was risky business.

Meanwhile, the Wailers continued to evolve more toward an R&B sound. They announced auditions for their own version of the Ikettes, and a number of teenage girl singers showed up to try out at the Crescent Ballroom. In the end (and after working out parts backing Gail Harris on Ike and Tina's hit "Tra-La-La"), three—Marilyn Lodge, Kay Rogers, and Penny Anderson—were hired and given a group name of the Marshans. Soon after, Etiquette Records issued Harris's first single, "Be My Baby," an attempt at a girl-group pop sound.

It was the golden era for girl groups, and in addition to the Marshans, the Northwest was also home to the Chandels, Cordenes, Marvelles, Shalimars, Shampaynes, and, most successful of all, a Black teen trio called the Chanteurs, whose single, "No Doubt about It"—featuring Mike Mandel on keyboards—got frequent airplay on KZAM and became a good seller for Bolo Records.

Meanwhile, Etiquette issued a few records by the Marshans: "I Remember," "It's Already Tomorrow," "Don't Worry about Me Baby

(I Feel Just Fine)," and "You're So Fine," as sung by Marilyn Lodge under the name Mayalta Page. Lodge also had a thrilling experience one night down at the Evergreen Ballroom. The Ike and Tina Turner Revue was performing, and a girlfriend mentioned to one of the Ikettes that Marilyn was a talented singer: "The next thing I knew, I was in a back room auditioning for Ike and Tina. I guess I met with their approval because the next thing I knew I was being introduced on stage. I believe I sang the Mary Wells song 'Bye Bye Baby.' My knees were knocking for weeks."

But there was another local female singer whose experience would top even that big night. Kathi McDonald, who noted her two greatest musical influences as Tina Turner and Gail Harris, sang with a few Bellingham bands including the Accents and the Unusuals, whose first single was issued by Jerry Dennon. In 1965, the band headed off to San Francisco and scored a deal with Mainstream Records—the same label that would soon release Janis Joplin and Big Brother and the Holding Company's debut discs—resulting in the single "Summer Is Over." Then, while attending an Ike and Tina Turner Revue concert at the Carousel Ballroom, he noticed her singing along in the front row and signaled her to come and talk backstage. She auditioned and was hired as an Ikette, toured with their Revue, and appeared on their *Come Together* album. In short, Kathi McDonald's early dreams came true. ★

Promotional photo of the Wailers—(*left to right*) Rich Dangel (electric guitar), Mike Burk (drums), Mark Marush (sax), Kent Morrill (piano/vocals), and John Greek (electric guitar)—posing for Tacoma's Richards Studio on April 16, 1959. The same shot was used as the cover image for their debut album for Golden Crest Records, and it went on to influence the production of numerous later promo photos by other local bands. Courtesy of the Tacoma Public Library.

Tacoma's first rock 'n' roll band, the Wailers, onstage. (*left to right*) Mark Marush (sax), Rich Dangel (electric guitar), Mike Burk (drums), John Greek (electric guitar), and Kent Morrill (piano/vocals). Undated 1950s photo courtesy of the Oyster Bay Archives.

The instantaneous international success of Olympia's doo-wop stars the Fleetwoods—and the subsequent hits by their Dolton Records labelmates the Frantics, Little Bill and the Bluenotes, and Bonnie Guitar—led to the release of this compilation album in 1960 by the UK label Top Rank Records (no. BUY/028). Courtesy of the Northwest Music Archives.

Teen dance promotional poster for the Playboys and their star singer, Ron Holden at the Tacoma Armory (1001 South Yakima Avenue), on March 11, 1960. Courtesy of the Northwest Music Archives.

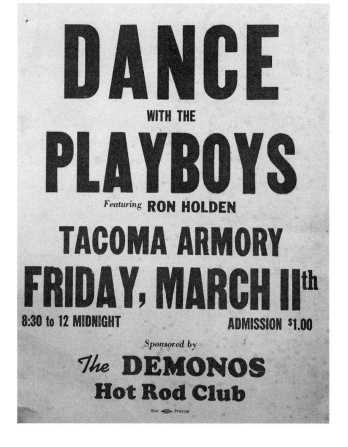

Ron Holden and the Thunderbirds' "Love You So" / "My Babe," Nite Owl Records (no. 10), October 1959. After "Love You So" became a surprise number 1 radio hit in Seattle, both songs were quickly licensed and pushed by the Los Angeles–based Donna Records label. "Love You So" became a Top 10 national and international smash, while "My Babe" was the more popular disc in the UK. Courtesy of the Northwest Music Archives.

Autographed promotional photo of Ron Holden, Donna Records recording star, circa 1960. Courtesy of the Northwest Music Archives.

Dolton Records 1959 promotional photo of the Frantics.
(*left to right*) Jim Manolides (electric bass), Chuck Schoning
(keyboard), Bob Hosko (sax), Don Fulton (drums), and Ron
Peterson (electric guitar). Courtesy of the Northwest Music
Archives.

The Ventures—(*left to right*) Howie Johnson (drums), Don Wilson (electric bass), Bob Bogle (electric guitar), and Nokie Edwards (electric guitar)—posing at Tacoma's Richards Studio, April 26, 1960. Photo courtesy of the Tacoma Public Library.

Promotional photo of Yakima, Washington's pioneering 1950s–60s rockers the Checkers. (*left to right*) Dick Ruthardt (bass), Mike Metko (sax), Doug Robertson (drums), Larry Coryell (electric guitar), and Mike Mandel (keyboard), circa 1960. Photo courtesy of Mike Metko.

Promotional photo of Burien, Washington's top teen-R&B combo, the Statics. (*left to right*) Former Gallahads doo-wop singer "Tiny Tony" Smith (vocals), Dick Gerber (electric guitar), Neil Rush (sax), Dave Erickson (drums), Merrilee Gunst (vocals/keyboard), and Randy Bennett (electric bass), circa 1961. Photo courtesy of Merrilee Rush.

The Counts—(*left to right*) "Tiny Tony" Smith (vocals), Peter Riches (electric bass), Al Scanzon (sax), Mike Leary (drums), Dan Olason (electric guitar), and Steve Lervold (keyboard)—onstage in Seattle's Parker's Ballroom (170th and Aurora Avenue North), 1962. Courtesy of Peter Riches.

Promotional photo of the Viceroys—(*left to right*) Nancy Claire (vocals), Mike Rogers (keyboard), Fred Zeufeldt (drums), Kim Eggars (sax), and Jim Valley (electric guitar), circa 1960s. Photo courtesy of the Northwest Music Archives.

Promotional photo of the Dynamics—(*left to right*) Jimmy Hanna (vocals), Mark Doubleday (trumpet), Terry Afdem (keyboard), Ron Wood (drums), Harry Wilson (electric guitar), Pete Borg (electric bass), and Jeff Afdem (sax), circa 1960s. Photo courtesy of the Northwest Music Archives.

Seattle's Dynamics paid tribute to their local musical hero, Dave Lewis, by recording the definitive hit version of his original instrumental song, "J.A.J." The 45 rpm disc was issued in 1962 by Seafair-Bolo Records (no. 730). Courtesy of the Northwest Music Archives.

A reconstituted Paul Revere and the Raiders—(*left to right*) Drake Levin (electric guitar), Phil Volk (electric bass), Mark Lindsay (vocals/sax), Paul Revere (keyboard), and Mike Smith (drums)—back on their home turf in 1965 at Pat Patory's dance hall, Casey's Ballroom (848 Main Street), in Lewiston, Idaho. Photo courtesy of April Patoray.

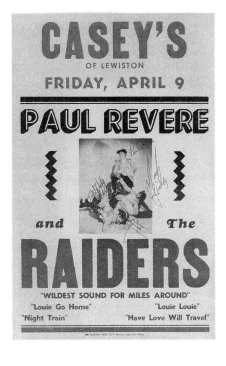

Autograph promotional poster for an April 9, 1965, teen dance at Lewiston, Idaho's Casey's Ballroom featuring Paul Revere and the Raiders. Courtesy of April Patoray.

PERSONAL MANAGEMENT
ROGER HART
HOLLYWOOD, CALIFORNIA
HO 4-5161
PUBLICITY
DEREK TAYLOR
CR 8-1911

Paul Revere and The Raiders

COLUMBIA RECORDS

Booked by
Pat Mason
Box 286
Seaside, Oreg. RE 8-7512

Columbia Records 1965 promotional photo of Paul Revere
and the Raiders live onstage—(*left to right*) Drake Levin
(electric guitar), Phil Volk (electric bass), Mike Smith
(drums), Mark Lindsay (vocals/sax), and Paul Revere (keyboard). Courtesy of the Northwest Music Archives.

The Kingsmen—(*left to right*) Don Gallucci (keyboard), Jack Ely (electric guitar), Lynn Easton (drums), Mike Mitchell (electric guitar), and Bob Nordby (electric bass)—posing in 1963 for the ace photographer Gino Rossi in the Chase teen dance club (12632 SE McLaughlin Boulevard, Milwaukie, Oregon). Photo courtesy of Gino Rossi.

Seattle's Dave Lewis Trio and two go-go dancers—(*left to right*) Dean Hodges (drums), Judy Shelman, Dave Lewis (vocals/keyboard), Patti Allen, and Joe Johansen (electric guitar)—posing in 1963 at Dave Levy's DJ's nightclub (2212 Fourth Avenue). Photo courtesy of Judy Shelman.

E.J.D. Enterprises Inc. Proudly Presents **DANCE**

HEAR ALL OF THEIR LATEST HITS

DON & The GOODTIMES

AFTER GAME DANCE

OSWEGO ARMORY - **Oswego, Oregon**

FRIDAY NITE **NOVEMBER 4** FRIDAY NITE

DOORS OPEN 9:00   Tickets $2.00

Teen dance promotional poster for Don and the Goodtimes—(*left to right*) Ron "Buzzy" Overman (electric bass), Bob Holden (drums), Charlie Coe (electric guitar), Don McKinney (vocals/sax), and Don Gallucci (keyboard)—Oswego Armory, Oswego, Oregon, November 4, 1966. Courtesy of the Northwest Music Archives.

Teen dance promotional poster for the Sonics—(*left to right*) Bob "Boom Boom" Bennett (drums), Gerry Roslie (vocals/keyboard), Rob Lind (sax), Andy Parypa (electric bass), and Larry Parypa (electric guitar)—American Legion Hall, Salem, Oregon, July 8, 1966. Courtesy of the Northwest Music Archives.

Carland & E.J.D. Enterprises, Inc. proudly present

"The Witch" **The SONICS** "Psycho"

Etiquette Recording Stars

Hear the Genuine Sonics play their top hits
"The Witch" & "Psycho"

FRIDAY NITE   **JULY 8**   FRIDAY NITE

American Legion Hall

7th & Jackson - Corvallis, Oregon

DOORS OPEN 8:30 TO 11:30

$1.50 before 9 $2.00 after 9

See the REAL SONICS in Corvallis for the first time

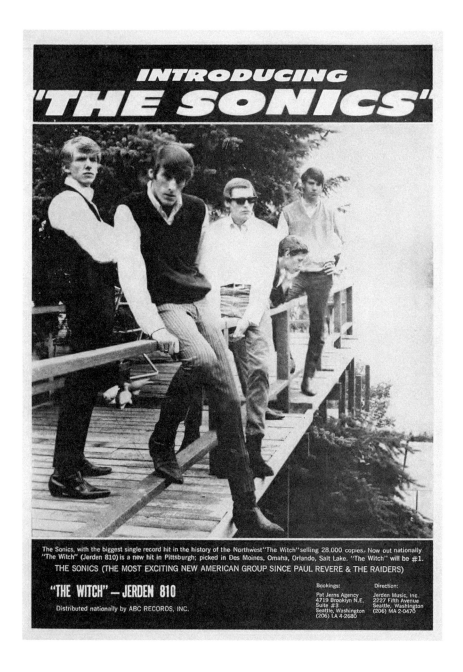

Jerden Records display ad with a photo by the noted photographer Jini Dellaccio to promote the Sonics—(*left to right*) Gerry Roslie (vocals/keyboard), Larry Parypa (electric guitar), Andy Parypa (electric bass), Bob "Boom Boom" Bennett (drums), and Rob Lind (sax)—and the Seattle label's November 1966 release of the single "Like No Other Man" / "The Witch" (no. 810), *Cash Box* magazine, December 10, 1966. From the author's collection.

Merrilee Rush (vocals/keyboard) and the Turnabouts—one of the Northwest's premier teen-R&B combos—live onstage, circa 1969. Photo by Hobart's Photography. Courtesy of Merrilee Rush.

Seattle's rockin' R&B band Thomas and His Tomcats saw their "Drive, Drive, Drive" / "One Day" single issued by Tom and Ellen Ogilvy's Nolta Records (no. RB-22) in August 1961. That was only a couple of months after their original electric guitarist, Jimmy "Jimi" Hendrix, had split in order to report for duty with the US Army at Fort Ord, California. Courtesy of the Northwest Music Archives.

Promotional poster for the Northwest Rock 'n' Roll Revival concert at Seattle's grand Paramount Theater (911 Pine Street) on May 14, 1972. Though there would be many more such reunion shows for those early generation teen-R&B and rock bands in the decades hence, none could boast as many of the original acts as participants. Of note: mid-performance, the Kingsmen symbolically tore off their vintage early 1960s matching jackets and tossed them aside to face their future together in a new era; *and* the performance by the Sonics would be their final one until, by popular demand, they reunited in 2007 and proceeded to tour the world and record for the next fifteen years. Courtesy of the Museum of Pop Culture.

CHAPTER 20

JIMMY'S BLUES

The Northwest rock 'n' roll scene was so robust by the late 1950s that scores of teenage bands were forming in the hopes of becoming the next Dave Lewis Combo or the next Wailers. Thus did hundreds of young players experience forming those bands and rocking a few dances. Most of those kids grew up and moved on to "real" careers. Among those who persisted, only a small percentage were blessed with the talent required to make a lifelong go of music, and a tiny fraction of that subset would ever attain mastery of their chosen instruments.

But only one individual among them all was fated to become the most globally famed guitarist of his generation: James Marshall Hendrix.

From the humblest beginnings—a childhood of hardship and neglect—Hendrix early on chose a path of self-soothing creative outlets: art and music. Young Hendrix came from a troubled home that long struggled to make ends meet. His parents, Al and Lucille Hendrix, had met on a warm summer evening in 1941 while walking to the Moore Theatre at 936 Second Avenue to see the boogie-woogie piano star Fats Waller making his first-ever appearance in Seattle. They started dating and then, months later, in March 1942, Al received his draft notice and Lucille informed him she was pregnant. They married on March 31, three days later he shipped out, and, right on schedule, Lucille gave birth to their son on November 27.

The wartime circumstances were tough. Feeling overwhelmed, the still-teenaged mother handed her baby off to others for safekeeping while she took on work as a server at various Jackson Street joints, including the infamous Bucket of Blood (inside the Hong Kong Chinese Society Club), where Lucille occasionally sang for tips. Upon Al's return from service in 1945, he finally met his son and the couple tried to make things work.

The years went by with Al working six nights a week as a janitor at the Pike Place Market; the couple liked to party and have friends over, though they often fought after drinking heavily. Meanwhile, young Hendrix found respite from this domestic tension in music—specifically the tunes in his parents' modest record collection.

"I was upstairs while the grownups had parties listening to Muddy Waters, Elmore James, Howlin' Wolf, and Ray Charles," Hendrix once recalled. "I'd sneak down after and eat potato chips and smoke butts. That sound was really—not evil—just a thick sound. The first guitarist I was aware of was Muddy Waters. I heard one of his records when I was little boy and it scared me to death, because I heard all these sounds. Wow, what is that all about? It was great."

But life in the Hendrix home was *not* all that great. Al and Lucille battled and she eventually moved out. Al began working as a gardener and often his young son worked alongside him. He and Lucille filed for divorce in 1951, and although he won child custody rights, he did not seem be a strong parent. Hendrix's boyhood pal Terry Johnson recalled how the neglected kid didn't have his own key and was often locked out of his own home well into the evenings. The two young friends would traipse over to the Mount Baker Tavern on Jackson Street, where, by peering in a window, they would find Al hunkered down at the bar and then go back to Johnson's home and play. Luckily, Hendrix's friends' mothers and grandmothers could tell from his shabby shoes and clothing—let alone the neighborhood tales about physical abuse at home— that the shy boy's needs were not being properly met, so they tried to watch over him as best they could.

Hendrix would later confess to his youthful frustrations: "I ran away from home a couple of times because I was so miserable. When my dad found out I'd gone he went pretty mad with worry." Asked when did he return home, Hendrix replied, "When I realized my dad was upset. Not that I cared, but well, he is my dad." It was on February 1, 1958, that Lucille was found unconscious in an alley behind a Skid Road bar just off Yesler Way and died hours later of a ruptured spleen. Al refused to allow Jimmy to attend her funeral. A year and a half later, Hendrix dropped out of Garfield High School.

"School wasn't for me," he explained. "According to my father, I had to go working. I had done it for a few weeks with my father. He had a not-so-good running contract firm, and in me he saw a cheap laborer.

I didn't see it that way. I had to carry stones and cement all day, and he pocketed the money." Beyond that, by most accounts Al never did fully support his son's musical aspirations. But he did recall the first indication of his son's interest in guitars back when the two were living in a shabby rooming house: "We had one room there, and I asked Jimmy to 'clean up the bedroom there; sweep up a bit.' And I went out, and anyway I come back and I seen a little pile of broom straw. And I said, 'I told you to sweep up. What all these straws doing here?' And, he said, 'I swept up and I was sitting here just playing the broom.' He was just making believe that the broom was a guitar."

One of Hendrix's earliest neighborhood buddies, Pernell Alexander, also remembered the early days: "We were friends even before music. We were friends even before we were playin' brooms! [*laughter*] It was grade school at Leschi. It wasn't even thinkin' about music—it was, I guess, tryin' to have girlfriends and learn how to dance!"

"My dad danced and played the spoons," said Hendrix. "My first instrument was a harmonica, which I got when I was about four. Next it was a violin. I always dug string instruments and pianos. Then I started digging guitars—it was the instrument that always seemed to be around. Everybody's house that you went to seemed to have one lying around. I was 14 or 15 when I started playing guitar."

Hendrix managed to acquire his own used acoustic guitar and plucked along while learning little licks from any possible source, including radio and television. A few of his favorites were "Summertime Blues" by Eddie Cochran, "La Bamba" by Ritchie Valens, and "Sleep Walk" by Santo and Johnny—all songs with exceptional electric guitar riffs. "I learned all the riffs I could. I never had any lessons. I learned guitar from records and the radio. I loved my music, man. I'd go out to the back porch there in Seattle . . . and I'd play guitar to a Muddy Waters record. You see, I wasn't ever interested in any other things, just the music. I was trying to play like Chuck Berry and Muddy Waters. Trying to learn everything and anything." Friends later recalled that among the first songs he mastered was the Wailers' "Tall Cool One."

His father remembered that one of the very first tunes his son gleaned from TV was the *Peter Gunn* theme, and Hendrix himself once told an interviewer of a more surprising source of TV inspiration: "The *Grand Ole Opry* used to come on, and I would watch that. They used to have some pretty heavy guitar players. But I didn't try to copy anybody.

Those were just the people who gave me the feeling to get my own thing together." But Hendrix's other source of guitar tips and techniques was a few neighborhood men, as he shared with *Beat Instrumental* magazine:

> I learned to play on a guitar that belonged to one of my father's friends who came to play cards. While the two men played, I would creep out onto the porch with the friend's guitar and see what I could get out of it. I didn't know that I would have to put the strings around the other way because I was left handed, but it just didn't feel right. I remember thinking to myself, "There's something wrong here." One night my dad's friend was stoned and he sold me the guitar for five dollars. I changed the strings around but it was way out of tune when I'd finished. I didn't know a thing about tuning so I went to the store and I run my fingers across the strings on a guitar they had there.

Hendrix also began picking up blues tricks from a hobbyist bluesman, John Williams, who lived at Twenty-Sixth Avenue and Marion Street, near the Hendrix home just off South Jackson, at 2603 South Washington Street. "He played the blues," Alexander remembered. "And Jimmy used to hang around Mr. Williams's porch a lot. And he learned to play, 'cause that's what Jimmy loved: the blues."

It was back around 1957 that Alexander—and Hendrix, thanks to the generosity of some of his friends' parents—were able to begin attending Sunday afternoon shows downtown at the Eagles Auditorium. In particular, they were excited to watch the great bands led by Hank Ballard, Bill Doggett, and Little Richard, whose Upsetters included a killer guitarist, Nathaniel "Buster" Douglas, who totally wowed the guys with his Fender Stratocaster.

Hendrix and Alexander sat in the front row for that show and afterward met up with Little Richard and talked with Douglas about his guitar. Another night, and after a Bill Doggett show, they met up with his guitarist, Bill Butler, who'd done the killer guitar work on their 1956 hit "Honky Tonk."

Another memorable rock 'n' roll concert Hendrix attended was Elvis Presley's show at Sick's Stadium on September 1, 1957. Then, a month or two later, Big Jay McNeely's combo was booked to headline a two-week engagement at the Birdland when he also agreed to perform an underage matinee show just up the street at the CD's YMCA. It was at this show that Hendrix and Alexander were wowed by brother Dillard McNeely's booming Fender electric bass guitar. After the show, they swarmed McNeely asking questions about the novel instrument.

Alexander also recalled that he and Hendrix were witnesses to a show by Hank Ballard and the Midnighters, whose guitarist Arthur Porter and bassist Alonzo Tucker made big impressions on the lads. But then the night took an unforgettable turn. This occurred on July 3, 1959, when Ballard's band were engaged in a playful little skit based around their 1954 hit "Annie Had a Baby." In an act that the band had been doing without incident for years, a costumed Ballard sang the tune while goofing around as Annie—and right on cue he reached under his skirt and pulled out a baby doll. The audience roared with laughter, but an outraged Seattle Police Department security squad stormed the stage, halted the show, arrested Ballard, and sent home the disappointed audience.

Another of Hendrix's sources of blues knowledge was Elven "L.V." Parr, a true bluesman from Arkansas who had learned to play guitar while in prison. In 1950, he began gigging around the South, playing gigs with the likes of Ray Charles, Albert King, Percy Mayfield, and Junior Parker and contributing to recording sessions at Memphis's fabled Sun Studios with Bobby "Blue" Bland and Johnny Ace.

"I came out to Seattle in 1959," Parr once explained. "I got into trouble with the law again, and was basically paroled to my dad, who was living out here by then. I played all over the Northwest when I got here. Things were jumping. We played at the Black and Tan, Birdland, the Drift Inn, the Cotton Club, the Mardi Gras—those clubs on Jackson Street."

Parr also gigged with the Playboys for a spell and began hangin' with James "Tomcat" Thomas—one of the Mello-Aires, a doo-wop group that had recorded at Joe Boles's studio in 1958—who held regular jam sessions at his house. That's also where "Jimmy Hendrix used to come around," Parr recalled. "He was just a kid then. I used to practice over at 20th and Madison with James Thomas and a couple of old guys. Every time we were over there, Hendrix would come over and be asking me things, asking me to show him this or that. I don't know if you'd call it teachin' him or not, but I used to show him a lot."

Like any budding musician, Hendrix took any opportunity to play anything, anywhere, with just about anybody. Terry Johnson played piano and sax, and as Mary Willix quoted him in her touching 1995 book *Jimi Hendrix: Voices from Home*, the two pals started learning together: "One of the songs we'd play back in those days was 'What'd I Say,' by Ray Charles. That was a big one. I had an electric piano then, a pink and white Wurlitzer, so we really were hot on that one. Ray Charles was one of our idols. In fact, of all the songs Jimmy and I played, that was one of our favorites."

At about this point in time, Hendrix and Alexander met up with a couple of other musical kids: Luther Rabb (bari sax), the son of a preacher man; and Anthony Atherton (alto sax), who once recalled how "we'd sneak in to see Ray Charles play at the Birdland. . . . At the Mardi Gras across the street from Birdland, I was about fourteen and the lady would let me go in and sit down by the stage. A couple of times me and Jimmy went in together."

Before long Hendrix, Alexander, Rabb, Atherton, and a couple other Meany Junior High School pals, Robert Green (piano) and Walter Jones (drums), formed their own teen-R&B band, the Velvetones. The group practiced in the basement of Green's home, the site of much music making as his parents' were friends with lots of southern musicians and their house had become a rest stop for numerous touring R&B stars including Junior Parker and Bobby "Blue" Bland.

"I formed this group with some other guys," remembered Hendrix, "but they drowned me out. I didn't know why at first, but after about three months I realized I'd have to get an *electric* guitar." Both Hendrix and Alexander were begging for electric instruments, but Al stubbornly resisted his son's pleas. There are a thousand and one stories floating around Seattle of folks taking credit for hooking Hendrix up with his first electric guitar, but it was Al who finally bought his son a white 1957 Supro Ozark in 1958: "I got a few dollars ahead and got him an electric guitar. I couldn't afford an amplifier, so he'd practice at home and then go off to a friend's house where they had an amp. . . . I never did get him an amplifier, although I'd planned on it. But he got music out of his guitar as it was."

Pernell Alexander had happy memories of that time: "Jimmy and I both started playin' guitar. The summer of '58. School was out, and we *had* to get 'em. And we got them about the same week. We had to learn and we really didn't know anyone to teach us so we spent that summer learning. We taught *ourselves*."

But this process was made difficult by Hendrix's ongoing lack of an amplifier. "My father was a preacher," Luther Rabb explained. "He also played the guitar and had some equipment. Sometimes I would sneak in and borrow his equipment. Matter of fact, one of the last times Jimmy and I talked we were joking about how we left my father's amplifier on overnight and totally melted it. My father always joked about that."

Alexander would laugh as he recalled how the Velvetones' approach was perfectly unschooled, and how they all still had so much to learn: "Oh, *primitive* wasn't the word for it. I mean, we didn't have a bass, and we just tuned our guitars to a piano chord in middle C, and that was it."

After the Velvetones had built up their set list—including foundational classics like Bill Doggett's "Honky Tonk" and Bobby Bland's "Further on up the Road"—they figured they were ready for the big time. Recollections about the band's earliest gigs vary, but a few of them were a junior high talent show, a luncheon for a local women's club, the Rosettes club, the Yesler Terrace Neighborhood House, local National Guard armories, and an outdoor show at Vasa Park.

"I remember my first gig was at an armory, a National Guard place," Hendrix told *Melody Maker*. "And we earned thirty-five cents apiece and three hamburgers. . . . In those days I just liked rock-and-roll I guess. We used to play stuff by people like the Coasters. Anyway, you all had to do the same things before you could join a band. You even had to do the same steps."

That Washington National Guard Armory (in nearby Kent) was more likely the Velvetones' third gig, and the band also started picking up others at the Rotary Boys Club, the YWCA on Cherry Street, and the YMCA on Olive Street. But regardless of where the band played, the shy Hendrix was experiencing raw stage fright: "Well, it was so very hard for me, 'cause at first man I was so scared, I wouldn't go onstage. You know, like, I joined this band—I knew about three songs—and when it's time for us to play onstage man, I was like this [*shaking gesture*], you know. And then; I had to play behind the curtains, you know, I couldn't get up front. . . . Plus you get very discouraged; you hear different bands playing around you and the guitar player seems like he's always much better than you."

There certainly were more experienced guitarists in Seattle but Hendrix was gaining skills, and another neighborhood kid who was lucky enough to own a new Fender Stratocaster guitar was actually intimidated by his self-doubting buddy. "We started messing 'round on the guitars," said Joe Gray, "but it kind of made me disgusted because he was musically inclined and I wasn't, you know. I mean, I had to study and read the music before I could play. I mean, he could pick up songs and just play them. Listening to them one time! So we would practice and he would help me."

Another tale from the early days involves the Holden family, where still *another* of Oscar Holden Sr.'s musical kids, Jimmy Holden, was a schoolmate and jam buddy of Hendrix's. As Holden's big brother, Dave, would recall, "My brother Jimmy—he also played the piano—he went to Garfield at the same time as Jimmy Hendrix, and they used to rehearse in our basement. And my dad used to sit in the middle room of our house—that's where his TV was—and he'd say, 'What's all that twangin'? That's not music. Would you guys stop that?' He'd bang on the floor. 'Cause it wasn't music to him. But that happened to be Jimmy Hendrix that was playin' this guitar that was soundin' so crazy."

Meanwhile, Hendrix, Alexander, and Johnson had also started hanging around the back door of the Birdland. They eventually slipped their way in to watch the Dave Lewis Combo, which at that point featured Bud Brown, a seasoned guitarist who had come to town from the jazz/nightclub world and whose playing impressed *everybody*. Another local band the boys watched was the Sharps, which also boasted a brilliant Black electric guitarist, Ranleigh "Butch" Snipes, who was also known for putting on a wild stage show. "Butch Snipes: he's the one that actually taught Jimmy and I," admitted Alexander. "He's the one that Jimmy got all the behind-the-back and playin'-with-the-teeth and all that from. Besides Buddy Brown, Butch was the only one we knew who could really play."

In 1959, the Velvetones accepted a challenge to enter a Battle of the Bands against a Washington Junior High–based rival combo, the Rocking Kings, which included Charles Woodbury (piano and vocals), Ulysses "Junior" Heath (guitar), Walter Harris (sax), Webb Lofton (sax), and the New Orleans–born Lester Exkano (drums). Along the way, Robert Green (piano), Terry Johnson (sax and piano), and Fred Rollins (sax) also played with them. Though the battle was on the Rocking Kings' turf—the Yesler Terrace housing project's gym—the Velvetones pulled an upset victory and were rewarded with a monthlong gig, playing dances there every Friday and Saturday night.

By this point, Hendrix's natural talent was becoming obvious, and he was recruited by the vanquished Rocking Kings to play bass on his guitar. The band rehearsed Tuesdays in the clubroom of the Yesler Terrace Neighborhood House. However, some members still had doubts about Hendrix. As Harris, their sax man, freely admitted:

> At first we were hesitant, because he didn't have an amp. But he always managed to find someone to plug in with. Junior [Heath] was one lead guitar and Jimmy was the other. Jimmy was better than Junior, and Junior knew it. They were good friends offstage, but onstage they were total enemies because Jimmy could play better. Plus, Hendrix was plugged into Junior's amplifier, and it wasn't too kosher to plug into someone's amplifier and then show them up. Junior was good, but Jimmy put more into his playing. You could see it in his face.

The Kings also performed at the Garfield Funfest's talent show in 1959, and then they got their first chance to play the Birdland. More gigs there would follow, including one where Hendrix' Supro guitar was stolen from the stage while he wasn't looking. With the help of his bandmates he was able to buy a new one—a bronze Danelectro (which he later painted red); however, Hendrix never did acquire his own amplifier during his Seattle years.

One night while walking home after a Birdland gig, the guys happened by the home of James "Tomcat" Thomas, just off East Madison at 918 Twenty-Fourth Avenue, and heard raucous R&B music wafting out. They walked up and Thomas invited them in, where he and his nephew Perry Thomas (piano) were jamming with some other players. Then all the guys played a few songs together, Tomcat liked what he heard, and he offered to begin acting as the Kings' manager.

Over the next few months, he actively booked them into different venues, including their first out-of-town gig down at the Congo Room in Tacoma. It was on February 20, 1960, that they played on the hallowed stage of Seattle's Washington Hall. This was where some of the town's first jazz shows had taken place in the early twentieth century and where other legendary shows by the likes of the Duke Ellington Orchestra, Billie Holiday, Mahalia Jackson, Lightnin' Hopkins, and Fats Domino had occurred.

By now, Hendrix was finding his groove and the band even began performing his first original tune, "Jimmy's Blues." As Terry Johnson would later recall, they started out just jamming on tunes like Little Richard's "Long Tall Sally," "Slippin' and Slidin'," and "Good Golly Miss Molly," Chuck Berry's "Johnny B. Goode," and a few Elvis Presley songs. But Hendrix's growth as a player was accelerating in a preternatural way: "I *know* how good he was, compared to other guitar players: They were trying to play the basic—you know, the Ventures—trying to get the licks down and concentrate on their rhythm, and trying to get the chords right and everything. And Jimmy was making his own chords up! And making his own sounds. Even back then he'd try to make it talk."

"We all knew Jimmy was good," Webb Lofton added. "He played behind his back and between his legs. Jimmy had a used guitar when he joined our group, but no amp. Eventually the group bought an amp, but we didn't have one then. When Junior Heath joined the group, he had an amp, so Jimmy could plug his guitar into Junior's amp."

Stories abound in Seattle regarding young Hendrix's drive to jam with anyone who would have him. Among the first to let Hendrix sit in down at the Carpenters Union at 2512 Second Avenue in the Belltown neighborhood were the Playboys. As their original singer, Ron Holden, told it:

> He used to come into the Carpenters Hall when the Playboys would be playing there. He'd come in there with just his guitar and cord and say, "Hey man, let me play." And I'd say, "OK man, but we're playing like 'Blueberry Hill' so, you know, just be cool!" And so I'd count it off—a slow "Blueberry Hill" tempo—and we'd get about three bars into it and he'd go right for the throat. He'd play a solo all the way through "Blueberry Hill." He'd play a solo all the way through "Louie Louie," et cetera, et cetera. So finally, I just had to tell him, "Hey man! I'm sorry but you play too loud! And you're soloing all the way through!"

Meanwhile, the Dave Lewis Combo's yearslong Friday and Saturday after-hours gig at the Birdland had continued to attract good crowds—*so* good that Wilmer Morgan had begun booking the Combo to also play an earlier slot on Sundays from 7:30 to 10:30 p.m., which soon involved hosting a popular open jam session. There were always players, instruments in hand, who made pilgrimages to the gig in the hope that they might climb the bandstand and sit in. It was a good way to learn if one's skill level would pass muster, both with Lewis the ringmaster as well as the room's musically sophisticated audience. Among the striving players who continued to show up was Hendrix.

"Jimmy used to come to Birdland regularly when we were there," recalled Dave Lewis:

> The thing about Jimmy was . . . well, see, the music back in the '50s wasn't as technically involved as it is today. But it was formatted—in that there were certain patterns you played for, like, the blues—and when we'd have jam sessions on Sundays, Jimmy Hendrix would come up with his guitar and he was playing it as a kind of style that he played even [later] when he got popular. And we couldn't relate to it. So a lot of times he was asked to leave the stage. And, you know, the people when they come into Birdland they wanted to dance and they couldn't relate to the loudness and the feed-back responses. And that's what he was playing at the time. And we weren't really receptive to him, and I don't know, he may have resented us or thought that we weren't giving him a fair chance, but if you were in the time you would know how it was.

As painful as that rejection must have been for Hendrix, the Bird-land was becoming ever more important to him—it was the main place he could study the town's young R&B bands. Among those was the Nite-sounds, a combo formed in 1960 by his former bandmate Luther Rabb, who allowed Hendrix to join in on occasion. But other bands, including the Wailers and the Dynamics, just didn't get the kid and are known to have rejected Hendrix's entreaties to jam.

The latter band's drummer Ron Woods explained that it was noth-ing personal, since their band seldom let *anyone* join them onstage: "The Dynamics turned him down. They wouldn't let him sit in. He was just *another* Black guy who wanted to sit in at the dance. We didn't let too many people jam, because it was too disorganized. We had our set [list] and nobody ever jammed with the band. The guys didn't know Jimmy, and he wasn't my best buddy, he was just a guy at Garfield that I knew by sight rather than name."

A lot has been made over the years about Hendrix's mixed feelings about his hometown, and such recollections from some of the town's top musicians indicate there may well be something to it. Such eyewit-ness statements seem to suggest that Hendrix was already a remark-able—if undisciplined—player. So Hendrix was likely frustrated that he was already exploring a unique style that clashed with the established aesthetic parameters of that era's R&B traditions.

It was 1960 when the Rocking Kings' manager, James Thomas, decided to form his own band, Thomas and His Tomcats. He would be the singer, and he recruited two of the Rocking Kings—Hendrix and Charles Woodbury (piano)—along with Richard Gayswood (sax), Leroy Toots (bass), and Bill Rinnick (drums). Perry Thomas also played piano at times. Thomas had an in with the military officers' club circuit so his band got steady work at venues like the US Naval Reserve Base at Pier 91, Larson Air Force Base in Moses Lake, Paine Field in Everett, Fort Worden in Port Townsend, and the American Legion Hall on Union Street. In addition, the Tomcats also gigged at the Masonic Temple, Cottage Lake Resort in Bothell, Vasa Park in Issaquah, as well as various dates in Ballard, Bellingham, and up in Vancouver, BC. The Tomcats also landed the gig for Seattle's annual summer Seafair Festival's picnic and dance. Soon the band was good enough to score a booking at the Birdland.

Though the Tomcats were working their way up, Hendrix's days as a Northwest player were numbered. From here on his story is well known. After transferring from Franklin High School to Garfield—and then dropping out altogether—he began to have minor run-ins with the law. More than once, according to friends, Hendrix participated in break-ins at area clothing shops and finally, in May 1961 and at the age of eighteen, he was arrested on two occasions while joyriding in stolen cars with his runnin' buddies. After spending a week in youth detention, Hendrix—in a typical scenario for a lad in his circumstances—faced a judge who offered him the choice of jail time or "joining" the army.

So, boarding a southbound train at the King Street Station on May 31, 1961, off he went to basic training at Fort Ord, California. In September, he returned to Seattle on furlough and caught up with his homies. What Hendrix would presumably learn is that Thomas and his Tomcats had caught a few breaks in his absence. Only a couple months after he'd split town, the band had signed a record contract with Tom Ogilvy, and a session at Joe Boles's studio led to the August release of their excellent Nolta R&B single "Drive, Drive, Drive"—a record that, according to Anthony Atherton, would soon catch the attention and earn the support of Bob Summerrise: "There was this disc jockey from KZAM by the name of Bob Summerrise who used to come by and listen and sometimes tape us to later play on the air."

In the wake of that exposure, the Rocking Kings soon hit what they thought was the big time: a regular Thursday night gig at the Birdland. But Hendrix's timing was off. So, while his former bandmates were now reveling in their successes, PFC James Marshall Hendrix dutifully returned to Fort Ord and then continued training for the infantry with the 101st Airborne Division down in Fort Campbell, Kentucky. ★

CHAPTER 21

DOIN' THE BIRDLAND

The Birdland had, since its founding back in 1955, served music fans well as *the* hub of R&B activity in Seattle. Toward the end of the decade, however, the joint's crowds were including ever-greater numbers of white people. In particular, young white musicians came to soak up the Dave Lewis Combo's sounds. Among them were Little Bill; Clayton Watson; the Wailers' singer Rockin' Robin, bassist Buck Ormsby and drummer Mike Burk; the Frantics' bassist Jim Manolides; singer Nancy Claire; the Dynamics' singer Jimmy Hanna, keyboardist Terry Afdem, and guitarist Larry Coryell; the Sharps' guitarist/singer Lee Parker; Buck England, an organist who would go on to work with Little Bill for many years; and Joe Johansen, guitarist with the Adventurers, the Frantics, and even the Dave Lewis Trio.

When asked decades later what the Northwest Sound was, Joe Johansen responded without pause, "It was the *Dave Lewis* sound. You know, there was the Wailers who were different. The Bluenotes were different. But I think the guy that brought everybody together—and who everybody respected the most—was Dave Lewis. The guy had a knack for takin' some real simple stuff and just makin' it real good."

Luther Rabb agreed: "Dave Lewis was our model. Dave's the God-father of the Seattle sound. The Dave Lewis Combo was more advanced musically than any other Seattle group. They knew all about overtones and music theory. They were my first impression of what a band should be. They had the fewest guys and made the biggest music."

The Continentals' Eldon Butler humbly admitted that "back in those days, Dave Lewis was just playing *so* far over everybody's heads, you know? His chord structure. His rhythm. The musicians he had with him were just . . . I mean, here we were studying 'Louie Louie,' and these guys were playing *music.*"

Lewis's grateful bandmate George Griffin confessed that "I know I have a gift, but Dave Lewis brought it out. When we were coming up Dave was a very shy person. But Dave is a genius. He has the ability to be where Quincy Jones is, or higher. For me Dave is the essence of the Seattle sound. The Dave Lewis Combo was the transition from rhythm and blues and rock to funk."

"The Dave Lewis Combo was the first rock group that I can think of that had solos coming from anybody in the band," Jimmy Hanna pointed out. "Not just the piano or guitar player. We all know that improvisation was going on much longer [before]. I'm talking about a rock group playing rock changes, playing with a rock beat, and then having solos coming in for choruses."

The Birdland's bandstand had been dominated by local Black musicians since day one. Some of those Black—or *mostly* Black—groups include the Barons, Four Pearls, Joe Boot and the Fabulous Winds, Doug Robinson Combo, Dave Holden Trio, Don Mallory Combo, Ron Holden and the Playboys, Skyliners, Les Gents, Gallahads, Velvetones, Rocking Kings, Thomas and His Tomcats, Ron Buford Band, Mr. Clean and His Cleansers, and the Boss Four. But the day came when Wilmer Morgan took a chance and opened the stage to a few white—or *mostly* white—rock 'n' roll groups who were demonstrating that they understood R&B, like the Thunderbirds, Continentals, Dynamics, Sharps, Counts, Nitesounds, and Pulsations.

Of course, just about anything can occur at an after-hours joint like the Birdland. Indeed, the neighborhood was rough: the Frantics' guitarist Ron Peterson recalled that a whole set of gear was stolen out of his car one night there. Yet, some of the wildest incidents—as the Continentals' sax man Eldon Butler recalled—were legit accidents:

I remember playing Birdland one night—and we might have been playing "Louie Louie"—and you'd look out there and all you'd see are their heads going up and down, all in unison: fwonk! fwonk! fwonk! *fwonk!* And the whole building is going: fwonk! fwonk! *fwonk!* And this big piece of plaster about eight feet in diameter let loose from the ceiling and it came down right in the middle of the dance floor and it cooled about three of 'em. Laid 'em out on the floor, and we kept playing and everybody just kept dancing and there was this circle with all these guys, [*laughter*] and all this plaster [was] laying in

the middle of the floor and the dance just kept going! Finally somebody came out with a broom and swept the whole thing up and the
music didn't even stop. [*laughter*] That's what I remember about Birdland. I don't know how many times I played there but I think Birdland
was the highlight of anything I played.

The Dynamics had been going to watch the Dave Lewis Combo at
the Birdland long before they ever got the chance to play there. In 1961,
the band lost their guitarist and was pondering whom to recruit as a
replacement. That's when they thought of Larry Coryell, whom they'd
first met back when he was with the Royals and again with the Checkers. Since then, Coryell had graduated from high school and, in prepa-
ration for journalism studies at the University of Washington, moved to
town in August of '61. The Dynamics—whose guitarist Dave Williams had
exited to go study physics—began wooing Coryell. Their bassist, Pete
Borg, sunk the hook—by squiring Coryell over to see the action at the
Birdland—and began reeling him in.

"The first week I arrived in Seattle I was knocked out by Dave
Lewis," Coryell fondly recalled. "All the Dynamics really dug Dave Lewis
and so we went down and we walked into the club and his band was
playing 'J.A.J.' And, you know, I'd never heard anything like it! I remember commenting to myself that it was a combination of Ray Charles and
Chuck Berry! That's the only way I could relate to it. And I sat in and
played something called 'D Natural Blues,' which is a blues of Wes Montgomery's. . . . It didn't fit. 'Cause I was trying to do a jazz thing and they
were trying to do a blues thing."

But it was the spirited action and atmosphere at the Birdland that
blew Coryell's mind. The kid from Richland had never seen anything
like it:

It was all African Americans. Their dancing style was unbelievable.
I had never seen so much uninhibited body movement. I was just
a white, middle-class Protestant from . . . the middle of the desert. In the Tri-Cities, man, like the only Black person in the whole
town was on the basketball team. . . . And I walked in there and I
was scared—there was so much prejudice and fear ingrained in
me—and of course I went back every weekend. . . . And you might
have been scared to death the first time you went, but after a while,
there's no problem.

The Birdland was a blast—and a great place to get educated about the blues and about stagecraft. But he also checked out other venues and grew especially fond of the Wailers' drummer Mike Burk and singer Rockin' Robin, as well as Little Bill and the Bluenotes, the Viceroys, Ron Holden, and the Frantics.

"The first time I saw Dave Lewis he was playing electric piano," said Larry Coryell. "And he had an original style, not a virtuoso in the sense of Oscar Peterson or Ray Charles, but he had an original style, he was a very effective composer, and he sang and had a great stage show. His stage presence was unbelievable."

Three months later, the Birdland was the site of a big Battle of the Bands event set for New Year's Eve. The combatants lined up: mainly Black bands plus a couple of white ones: namely, the Continentals and the Frantics with Nancy Claire. "And that was so strange," she marveled, "because I had never been into an all-black nightclub before!" It was that very same night that she met Larry Coryell, who was sitting in with the Continentals. Claire mentioned that the Frantics were moving up to nightclub work but she was too young to join them, and Coryell invited her to audition with the Dynamics. Thus began her relationship with yet another of Seattle's top bands.

Meanwhile, another pivotal moment had come in 1961 when the Washington State Liquor Board made a move that would permanently affect the local music scene. In anticipation of the millions of visitors expected to attend the upcoming Seattle World's Fair in 1962, the agency loosened the rules guiding the nightclub industry. Now venues could get licenses to pour individual cocktails; as a result, the old BYOB "bottle clubs" were suddenly obsolete. The Northwest's nightclub industry was entering a new boom time, and the associated increase in demand for musical entertainment had a positive effect on the scene.

Back in March of 1961—and just after the last of its members had turned of age and could at long last work legally in a nightclub—the Frantics became Seattle's first white rock 'n' roll band to score a gig in a downtown bar. They were hired by Dave Levy to play at his night-club, Dave's Fifth Avenue, which had been presenting jazz since 1955. Bringing the popular young band in was a surprise success and, due to popular demand, their nightly engagement lasted for months. At the summer's end, the Frantics received offers from a few California night-clubs; however, that opportunity to travel set the boys to bickering about whether they'd risk losing their cozy position on the Seattle scene if they hit the road. This debate became rather heated and Jim Manolides was ultimately ousted.

Coincidently, however, the very weeknight all this came to a head, Dave Lewis happened by Dave's Fifth Avenue to check out the action. He settled into a chair and watched a set or two by the Frantics. Between sets, he began shootin' the breeze with the guys when Manolides mentioned that since the Frantics were vacating the club to head south perhaps he and Lewis could team up and take over the gig. Lewis agreed and a new Dave Lewis Combo—Lewis (electric piano), Manolides (bass), Jerry Allen (guitar), and Don "Candido" Mallory (drums)—made their debut.

The Combo played the room six nights a week up through February 1962, before moving on to a residency downtown at the new Town House Tavern. However, because they had not given proper two-week notice to Dave Levy, he insisted that Lewis finish out two weeks of contracted work, which required that a few other musicians be brought in to help. Meanwhile, the Combo played their first dozen nights at the Town House with Seattle jazz pianist Overton Berry filling in for Lewis. Then, with Lewis rejoining them, the Combo played there throughout that World's Fair summer of '62. From there, the Combo moved over to a "bottle club," the Ali Baba in the Morrison Hotel, and then back over to the Birdland. That's about when Manolides bowed out to complete his studies at UW and Lewis acquired an Organo device, which was placed up on top of the piano keyboard and allowed him to take up playing bass lines, which meant the band no longer needed a bassist.

Meanwhile, across the street at the Mardi Gras Grill, the current house band, the Charlie Ross Trio, faced an emergency of sorts. Ross had to split briefly to attend to family matters back home in the Midwest. His drummer and sax man were desperate to find someone to fill in on Ross's Hammond B-3 organ for a few days. That's when they thought of Lewis, walked over to the Birdland, and offered him the gig to fill in for Ross.

Lewis—a pianist who'd never played an organ before—took on the challenge:

Because I only worked on Saturdays and Sundays at Birdland, I could work Monday and Tuesday and Wednesday nights there. And it went over so well and his group liked me, which I respected because they were older, more professional musicians. They knew *songs*. And I said to myself, "If I can at least *just get by* with these guys, maybe I'll be OK." They didn't expect me to do much other than back up those two guys, but during the third or fourth day I started getting my bit in there too—you know, after getting familiar with the tunes. At any rate, working that week, I fell in love with that organ. During the day I'd go in and rehearse, play around on it, and I got to find out what it could do. And then, as soon as I got paid for that job, I went down and put a down payment on one.

This switch from piano to a Hammond B-3 marked a major turning point for Lewis—he was now able to discover his very own sound. This became apparent with his first brilliant instrumental, the aforementioned "J.A.J." (whose name was a jab at the Combo's notoriously flaky guitarist, "Jive Ass" Jerry Allen). But the switch to organ also affected the evolution of the Northwest Sound because so many other top local bands (including the Wailers, Viceroys, Merrilee and Statics) followed his lead and also adopted Hammond electric organs. In truth, the idea of using an organ was nothing new in the wider world of jazz, where various jazzniks and R&B cats had been exploring the Hammond's rich overtones in nightclub and lounge settings since its debut back in 1954.

Indeed, a decade earlier "Wild Bill" Davis had begun recording and touring with an organ, and at some point the pianist Jimmy Smith heard him performing in Philadelphia and was inspired to acquire his own organ. But it was Smith who advanced the popularity of the organ-based jazz trio sound. From there seemingly every Black neighborhood bar in America sprouted organ-led trios some of whom became hitmakers including Bill Doggett, Milt Buckner, and Jack McDuff—each of whom had showed Seattle audiences their skills throughout the 1950s.

Meanwhile, tired of working so hard for the past five years to keep a band together and happy, Lewis had begun thinking about forming a more manageable ensemble. So, he began playing as a trio with Mallory and Guitar Shorty—a guitarist who had married one of Jimi Hendrix's cousins. For a while, they took a Central District gig at the Checkmate Tavern at 1431 Twenty-Third Avenue before moving back over to the Birdland.

Among the young white players who loved watching Lewis at the Birdland was Gordy Lockhard, a bassist whose band the Pulsations would soon get their shot playing the room:

I used to go there to see Dave Lewis. And at that time his trio had Guitar Shorty and they had the funkiest damn sound. They were the funkiest thing—to this date—that I ever heard. It was so bad I just can't even get started! What I loved about them was they were just fuckin' soulful. And groovy. I mean, they had the funk goin' on. Heavy, heavy funk. It just showed you how powerful music can be. But, man, it was a wild-ass club, I gotta tell ya. A typical night there was, you had the Five Steps and they were kinda a dance troupe and they'd get out and do their routine. Then you had a gal named Cree—she was kind of the queen of the ball and she'd be there. And there'd be smokin' goin' on in the back room—but I was just a teenager then and didn't get involved in all that. But I always grooved on the club—and then, we ended up playing there for almost a year. It was a *thrill*. It *really* was.

Meanwhile, in early 1962 Bolo Records issued the Dynamics' next single—this one a version of Lewis's "J.A.J." featuring Larry Coryell that was recorded by Joe Boles. The band's keyboardist Terry Afdem explained, "We used to go down to the Birdland to hear Dave Lewis. He used to play this tune and wrote it out for me once—showed me the changes to it. We'd play it five times a night and everybody'd go nuts! Played it three or four months, and then recorded it because of the response to it."

With that single, the Dynamics had finally hit their stride. They'd produced a seminal Northwest teen-R&B classic that earned them a regional radio hit. A half decade later, *Hit Parader* magazine praised "J.A.J.," saying the record was "quite possibly [the] finest, subtlest instrumental single to come out of the whole scene." The Bolo disc's flipside, "At the Mardi Gras"—a tribute to the joint on Madison—wasn't too shabby either.

"We were excited about it," Afdem enthused. "'J.A.J.' sold a lot of records and put us right on top. It got Coryell through the University of Washington. By 1962–63, we had a different sound than when we started. Now we were into a Dave Lewis–type sound. A lot more blues. We were really into the Dave Lewis sound. We really liked it."

It was through the connections their Black part-time singer, Tiny Tony, had with Wilmer Morgan that the Dynamics—who, let's recall, also had a Black drummer, Ron Woods—first got their chance to play for the

Birdland's after-hours crowd. They were received well, and the Dynamics celebrated with another tribute single on Bolo, "Doin' the Birdland."

Birdland was cool—and even three decades later, Ron Woods's bandmate Larry Coryell went so far as to identify the venue as playing a key role in the emergence of the whole scene. "It was a hip, sophisticated type of R&B," said Coryell:

> I thought that the youth scene was very vigorous and that the type of music the local bands were playing for the kids was a higher, more sophisticated type of rock and R&B than they might be getting in other regions. That's for sure. . . . It's funny—*something* happened here, that's the thing. Something happened here that *didn't* happen anywhere else. Something happened that allowed this community to develop in a different way in terms of our approach to music and it wasn't as polite. Or it wasn't as easy. It was a small scene. That's how I got to know all the other guitar players. It's *Birdland*!

The year of 1962 saw Wilmer Morgan hiring the Pulsations to play every other weekend (rotating with the Nitesounds) for a ten-month stretch, and Gordy Lockhard offered a glimpse into the nightlife action there: "We were an all-white group in an all-Black club. We fell into that Black music thing early on—we were early adopters. Our singer—Darling Judy—she was a cute little thing. But kinda wild. Like, she'd have her nipples stickin' over the top of her outfit. And the Black guys would go 'Oweee baby!' [*laughter*] There was more dirty dancin' there than I could ever hope to imagine."

But just because whites were now welcome to play on the Birdland's bandstand or attend shows didn't mean rude behavior was going to be accepted. The Continentals' drummer Don Stevenson explained:

> That was a great period of time actually. But I remember we played there and, seriously, there'd be fights. And one time, this big guy that lived up above me—he was like a football guy—and he and his wife came down. And everybody down there used to do "The Pony." And they'd all do it together, and you'd look out there and this whole place would be just throbbing up and down. And they'd raise their hands and then put 'em down, and raise their hands and put 'em down. And when they were doin' that dance—I mean, it was like hypnotic. It was really funky and this guy started goin'

out there and dancin' like some kinda, you know, redneck idiot. And [*laughter*] it was just like piranhas with blood: they just took that guy apart. It was terrible. Yeah, it could be a bad place. I was there one night when a lady had a baby up in the balcony while we were playin'. I had people gettin' punched into my drum set. But it seemed to me that the main issue at that point was, like, the music kind of like made a bond among the people. And you just had to be cool and you were respected and accepted. It was a wonderful place to be.

Such violence was certainly *not* the norm at the Birdland. But Seattle cops were known for keeping an eye on the place and, to no great surprise, sometimes *they* were the problem. For years, there were a couple well-known white cops who regularly patrolled the Madison beat and made trouble for locals. But this was nothing new in the CD, where people knew the score about the police and how they did their job. As an example, there was the time that Oscar Holden Sr. came strolling home from a late-night gig and got roughed up by cops, who were enforcing an unofficial "sunset" rule that Blacks shouldn't be anywhere near downtown after dark. Or the time his son Ron—who had married a white Queen Anne High School girl—had their apartment raided by police who claimed to have received a call reporting nefarious activities there.

Holden's older brother Dave commented on the reality back then: "In those days there was a lot of freedom—but *scared* freedom. In those days, every policeman had to be 6'3" or more. They used to walk the beat in the Central District, every street." Like East Madison, and Birdland in particular. That's where Dave Lewis's drummer, Don Mallory, got cornered. He'd previously gotten a girl pregnant and served some time in lockup. But even after he was back on the scene the cops kept after him—even pulling him off the bandstand mid-performance one night to arrest him for late child support payments. But their larger purpose seemed to be to shame him in front of his community.

Still, sometimes the services provided by police were necessary and welcome. Gordy Lockhard has recalled one traumatic night at the Birdland when the Pulsations were performing: "We were up onstage playin' away and we heard two shots ring out— BANG! BANG!—and a murder went down." Unbelievably, even after *that* the music and dancing continued, all while the police came and did their business without even shutting the crime scene down for the night. That incident certainly demonstrated fortitude and dedication by musicians who subscribed to the old circus troupe ethos that "the show must go on."

And the Birdland *did* go on—along the way serving as the catalyst of a form of rockin' teen-R&B that would come to be known as the Northwest Sound. ★

CHAPTER 22

WORLD'S FAIR TWIST

Seattle's 1962 World's Fair happened thanks to a cabal of boosterish Seattle businessmen who pitched the idea to the Washington State Legislature back in 1957. The hook was that in addition to stimulating business activity in the whole area and raising the city's international profile, the Fair would also involve a major urban redevelopment scheme that would see an entire campus of new buildings erected on a large parcel of underused downtown land that would come to be known as the Seattle Center.

The proposed theme of this Century 21 Exposition (the Fair's official name) would be celebrating the promises of science and a high-tech future—a concept perfectly in step with the giddiest side of the Space Race mindset prevalent during this period. Futuristic razzle-dazzle was highlighted by the architectural design of such iconographic new additions to the landscape as the Space Needle and the Monorail. Relentless optimism marked the Fair's whole zeitgeist, and the opening ceremonies kicked off at high noon on April 21, 1962, with President John F. Kennedy chirping "Let the Fair begin."

The six-month-long Exposition certainly drew plenty of tourists to town—Fair officials tallied over ten million attendees. In expectation of such crowds, a number of new nightclubs had been opened, including jazz rooms like the Penthouse and the Pink Pussycat where Billy Tolles performed, a country joint called the Golden Apple, the Peppermint Lounge, and Pat O'Day's new teen club the Party Line.

There was also, of course, Dave's Fifth Avenue, which happened to be located just across Denny Way from the new fairgrounds. The Dave Lewis Trio had been playing there for about six months when, in March 1962, the Frantics returned home from California (with a new bassist, Jeno Landis) and reclaimed their old gig. When the Fair opened on April

21, the club began drawing SRO crowds of tourists nightly. Lewis moved his trio over to the Tiki Tavern in the CD where he also had crowds, though mainly locals. Meanwhile, Little Bill (bass), Joe Johansen (guitar), and Dickey Enfield (drums) formed a blues trio that played way downtown at the Town House throughout the Fair season.

The Statics were another band that did well throughout the Fair—not only did they hold down a regular gig at the Peppermint Lounge, which was located within walking distance of the fairgrounds, but the band was also hired to perform at a series of outdoor evening dances at the Fair itself. Exposition management was reluctant to book rock 'n' roll bands; however, reacting to growing criticism that not much youth-oriented music had been scheduled, they launched a free dance series. The first Saturday-evening dance took place on July 28, and each week thereafter that the crowds grew larger and more unruly.

Though various steps were taken to increase security at later dances, it was the nature of the bands being hired (and the type of audience they drew) that became an issue. At the end of August, the Fair's assistant vice president wrote a memo to his team asking "Will you be sure that the selection of the orchestra is one which minimizes the attraction of 'birdland' customers?" Toward that end, AFM Local 76 sent over a list of bands "who are fully prepared and competent" to play the dances. It included the Viceroys, Frantics, Dynamics, Galaxies, Regents, Watchmen, Continentals, Counts, Pulsations, El Caminos, Sharps, and Rogues.

Funny then, how a good half of those mostly white groups were Birdland veterans, as were the Statics. The latter's public profile had peaked with the July release of their new Bolo Records single "Hey, Mrs. Jones" which was a sly R&B vocal duet between Tiny Tony and Merrilee that had originally been cut by Bobby Stevens and the Checkmates, a notable Black combo who'd worked the Northwest's military base circuit.

Although neither KJR nor KOL gave the disc any support, the little R&B station KZAM loved it, retail sales skyrocketed, and the tune became a region-wide classic. However, Tom and Ellen Ogilvy couldn't share the excitement of this sweet success with their old friend and partner Joe Boles, as he, at age fifty-eight, suffered a fatal heart attack in his home on July 19, 1962. His death stunned the music community, and his absence left a void in the region's music biz. A big chapter in Northwest history had come to a close.

The Fair itself kicked off with the World's Fair Opening Twist Party, which managed to sell out four shows over two days. Held at the Orpheum Theatre and organized by longtime Seattle events promoters Northwest Releasing, the show featured Pat O'Day as emcee, and "The Twist"–era stars Joey Dee and the Starliters, Chubby Checker, Dee Dee Sharp, and the Dovells. These events opened up O'Day's eyes to the promise of going beyond teen dances and into the realm of big-time concert production.

But even prior to the Fair's opening, O'Day had already taken steps to profit from the impending tourist invasion. Back in late 1961, he arranged to have Joe Boles record the Wailers one night at the Spanish Castle. The goal was to release the recordings on what would be the Etiquette label's first LP, *The Fabulous Wailers at the Castle*, released in time to sell to locals and tourists. Etiquette would presumably profit from album sales and O'Day would make his haul at the Castle's box office.

O'Day borrowed some old radio gear—about six broadcast microphones, a broadcast console, and a couple of Ampex single-track tape recorders—and he and Boles sat next to the stage mixing the Wailers' performance down to one track. "When we were finished that night," O'Day would recall, "Robin looked at the whole mess and sez, 'Pat, if you can make anything that people will buy out of all of this, it'll be a miracle!' [*laughter*] Well, then we took the tape down to Commercial Recorders and dubbed it through an old Cinemagraphic equalizer and put a speaker down the hallway and added some additional reverb, and somehow it all came out halfway listenable! [*laughter*]."

The Fabulous Wailers at the Castle was far more than halfway listenable—it was a great record. It perfectly documented the musical changes the Wailers had experienced in the two years since their Golden Crest era. By now, the band was showing off their singers: Rockin' Robin did "Rosalie" and "Since You Been Gone"—an "original" that was really just a knockoff of Ted Taylor's R&B single "Since You're Home"—and Gail Harris sang Ike and Tina Turner's "I Idolize You," and "All I Could Do Was Cry."

But the greater shift in the band's overall sound was in its instrumentation. Instead of all the chronic chording of the Wailers' early stuff (remember, with John Greek aboard, they'd featured two guitarists and no bass), they now had Buck Ormsby's bass providing a solid bottom. Furthermore, Kent Morrill was now playing a Hammond M-3 organ instead of a piano, which multiplied their oomph factor considerably.

The Wailers' music was getting better, and their business—Etiquette Records—was excelling. Sales of *The Fabulous Wailers at the Castle* album and Rockin' Robin's "Louie Louie" single had brought in enough capital that the label was able to open an office and hire staff. Etiquette was experiencing such success that it began expanding operations by releasing discs for other local talents including the Marshans, the Bootmen, the Rooks, the Galaxies, and the Sonics.

Etiquette also commissioned a local graphic designer (John L. Vlahovich of Tacoma's Vlahovich Design Associates) to design the cover for its next album, *Wailers! Wailers Everywhere*. It was Vlahovich who brought aboard a photographer who'd done his wedding photos, Jini Dellaccio. She took on shooting album covers for the Wailers and the Sonics, becoming the go-to photographer for countless Northwest bands.

Meanwhile, the Wailers' lineup had shifted once again. Buck Ormsby and Mark Marush had been clashing over business decisions. After an epic fistfight Marush exited, and the band grabbed Ron Gardner from the Bootmen (who responded by adding Marush). Gardner had already been a longtime fan of the Wailers and much later gave them credit as instigators of the *Tacoma*-based version of the Northwest Sound. "There *was* a Seattle Northwest Sound," posited Gardner. "Like the Dynamics. The Frantics. You know, with a couple horns. That kind of sound. And that was a little bit different sound than what the Wailers were playing. But I would have to say that the most influential person was Rich Dangel. He was really innovative. He really was the sound. He and John Greek really got the thing started. They played these chunky guitar riffs. And they would just chunk along. It was just its own kind of sound! I mean, 'Roadrunner'! Chunk-a-chunk, chunk-a-chunk. . . . I mean, Hendrix even copped some Wailers things."

"People like Rich Dangel, Joe Johansen, and Larry Coryell had sought out all the old blues masters," said Jimmy Hanna, "and by '59, '60, '61 these guys had learned distortion. They'd experimented with the guitar to the point where they were getting fuzztone and all this type of thing. At a much earlier date than the Memphis people, et cetera. That's where a lot of Jimmy Hendrix's intensity comes from. He'd heard these guys. He was a good student—[he] took that and went even further."

Dangel was discovering records that no one in the Wailers' circle had been aware of—especially the instrumental discs by the great Texas bluesman Freddie King. The sound of those tunes was now influencing the band's new original instrumentals—"Wailers' House Party," "Shivers," "Zig Zag," and "Soul-Long"—which revealed a far bluesier strain than their earlier rock 'n' roll. This evolution was partially a result of the band's tours in California. In addition to the accumulated performance experience they now had, the Wailers had also been exposed to some new sources of musical inspiration. Rich Dangel recalled exactly how he'd stumbled across the music of King:

> As we were driving in Northern California somewhere, and pickin' up radio stations from who-knows-where—I heard the tune "San-Ho-Zay." And it was, "Who is that!?" I mean, I couldn't figure it out 'cause they never said who it was and I think the radio reception finally faded out. So, just from the recollection I had heard from those few minutes, eventually I found the Freddie King record. There was a store down in Tacoma that featured mostly Black artists and we'd go there and pick up all kinds of stuff. And we finally found the Freddie King stuff—and he became my idol at the time. So, I tried to cop his licks. I wasn't real successful, but I tried! [*laughter*] But then I'd go down to the Evergreen Ballroom and watch him play.

Dangel took those records and woodshedded with them until he'd developed a newfound fluidity. King's intensely biting lead attack, chunky rhythmic style, and an extraordinary sense of melody impressed Dangel greatly. And because Dangel was the most admired guitarist on the Sea-Tac scene, his harder blues sound started to take root in the Northwest's musical lexicon—King's classic instrumentals like "San-Ho-Zay," "Stumble," and "Hide Away" became regional teen dance standards—and the next phase of the Northwest Sound was being defined.

That summer of '62—while the World's Fair was underway—saw the emergence of another significant local rock 'n' roll band: the Viceroys. The group's road to success, however, would be a long and rocky one. Their main obstacle was the fact that they struggled to attract any attention from the one guy who controlled the region's teen dance market: KJR radio's program director, Pat O'Day.

The upside was that KJR's underdog rival, KAYO, took the band under its wing and provided them with some support. "Big Daddy" Dave Clark was then ruling the KAYO roost, and the station's staff included other popular DJs like Lee Perkins, Lan Roberts, and Danny Holiday—

each of whom were actively trying to carve out a slice of the teen dance pie for themselves.

Holiday, in particular, began promoting lots of dances with the Viceroys. It could have been because he liked the band's music, but their founding guitarist, Jim Valley, suspected a more fundamental reason: "We were no big deal—but: we were *affordable*. And there weren't *that* many bands around yet." A big deal or not, the band showed promise and had an interesting backstory. Their saga began with Valley, a North End guitarist who'd been in the Moonlighters, a school band that played pop standards. But in 1957 he saw the Four Frantics: "The first time I ever saw a rock 'n' roll band, I was in the ninth grade and it was our talent show in junior high school and the Four Frantics came in from the high school. They just excited us. You know, I loved rock 'n' roll—but I didn't know kids *like us* could play it!"

The following year, while Valley was attending Shoreline High, he got to talking with a Sheridan Beach neighborhood pal, Billy Stull (who had already been a founding guitarist of the Dynamics). These two joined forces with a sax player and drummer and formed Vince Valley and the Chain Gang, whose first gig was at a junior high sock hop intermission at the Lake City Recreation Center in the summer of '58.

Before long they were renamed Vince Valley and the Viceroys, and by '59 the group added Al Berry (piano) and became the Viceroys. After doing a few house parties, the guys scored their first paying gig that spring, which earned them a whopping sixty bucks. Later that year, Bud Potter (bass) joined, sax man Fred Rucker left, and a Roosevelt High kid named Mike Rogers jumped in. Rogers's first combo, the Appeals, had actually recorded a couple of instrumental originals—"Thunderbolt" and "Cloudy Sky"—with Kearney Barton at Northwest Recorders in a bid to get signed by Dolton Records. But after failing to achieve that goal, the band folded.

Now the Viceroys figured they, too, were ready to record. That came about when the owner of the Lynnwood Rollaway skating rink liked their sound and hired the band to cut a radio jingle that could be used for advertising. Jim Valley cranked out a quickie instrumental called "Rocket," which the band cut over at Commercial Recorders. "It went 'badababa baba di-badada'—it basically sounded like 'Walk—Don't Run,'" Valley remembered. "But anyway, the kids picked up on it and wanted us to play 'Rocket' a lot."

The Viceroys' first actual record was "I Love a Girl" backed with "My Only Love," which was recorded at Fred Rasmussen's home studio. The A-side featured Valley singing, the B-side featured Stull, and the backing vocals were provided by the Gallahads. The record was pressed by a fly-by-night vanity label, Dream Records, which charged the band a fee up front and a bit later delivered fifty copies of their new single.

Eventually Stull and their drummer both dropped out, the ace percussionist Fred Zeufeldt joined, and the Viceroys began doing dances with Jimmy Pipkin of the Gallahads on vocals. Later the band worked with Aaron Stewart—the singer who had earlier replaced Ron Holden in the Playboys. Early on, the Viceroys did a lot of gigs for Seattle's "society circuit"—elite parties at places like the Washington Athletic Club, the Seattle Tennis Club, and various yachting and country clubs. The band's resulting "nice guy" image played a key role at a momentous juncture in Seattle rock history.

It occurred during that period after Jerry Lee Lewis had jumped up on the house piano up at Parker's Ballroom, danced around a bit, and managed to scratch the instrument's shiny finish. The incident had led to Parker's banning any rock 'n' roll dances. But, by late 1960, the Viceroys were struggling to move up in the scene and wanted to score some bigger gigs. So, in went sweet Jim Valley who convinced Parker's management to give the Viceroys a shot. Luckily, that evening went on without any trouble, and rock 'n' roll was back to stay at the venue.

Then, with another year and a half of experience under their belts, the Viceroys landed a plum gig. They were hired to perform daily for two months on a new KTNT-TV show called *Deck Dance*, hosted by their pal, KAYO's "Big Daddy" Dave Clark. *Deck Dance* was broadcast live from the deck of a seven-hundred-foot luxury liner, the *Dominion Monarch*, which was docked at the downtown waterfront along Elliott Bay, where it served as a floating tourist hotel throughout the Fair.

The exposure from this gig proved invaluable for the band, as *Deck Dance* brought the Viceroys' music into countless homes. One result was that a song they debuted on the show was getting a tremendous response from fans that began calling and writing KTNT asking if it was available as a record. "Granny's Pad" was a piano-based instrumental that Al Berry had written *in* and then named *after* the place where he was able to practice the piano: his grandmother's house. The song was an extremely catchy teen-R&B number built on a simple but addictive riff, Rogers's sax blatting, Zeufeldt's highly syncopated drumming, and the periodic gang shouting of the tune's title: "Granny's Pad!"

The song's moment to shine had arrived and the Viceroys needed to record it. They reached out to Tom Ogilvy for help, but with Joe Boles now gone he had to choose a different studio to work in. So, he took the band back over to Fred Rasmussen's. Once recorded and issued by Bolo Records, KZAM jumped on the single and KOL and KAYO followed shortly thereafter. KJR, however, remained slow to embrace the tune, even as it became a big enough local success that in February '63 Ogilvy was able to cut a national distribution deal with Dot Records. In March, *Billboard* noted the record as a "Regional Breakout Single," a phrase that indicated serious hope for impending national status.

Finally, in early April, Pat O'Day came around and decided to try the record on the Battle of the New Sounds segment of his afternoon show. Well, surprise! After area teens had phoned in their votes and the dust had settled, "Granny's Pad" was the clear victor and KJR was basically stuck with it. Evidently still not all that enthusiastic, KJR managed to list it on their Fab 50 chart as "Grandmothers Pad." O'Day at least pitched in by trying to tie the song in with comedic bits involving one of his on-air voice characters: Granny Peters, an endearingly befuddled old gal who was perpetually phoning in to KJR and raising havoc on the air.

"Granny's Pad" went Top 10 all over the Northwest and captured the top sales position for fourteen straight weeks at Seattle's biggest retail shop, the Ware House of Music. It remains a mystery how Dot fumbled their promotion of it. Though the song didn't break out nationwide, the Viceroys had become one of Seattle's most in-demand dance bands and did well with a couple of follow-up singles: "Goin' Back to Granny's" and "Granny's Medley" (which included "Granny's Pad," "Louie Louie," the "KJR Theme," and "Goin' Back to Granny's"). ★

CHAPTER *23*

THE O'DAY EMPIRE

The Pacific Northwest's teen universe had come a long way in the dozen years since Wally Nelskog and Billy Tolles were promoting their early dances. By the early 1960s it had grown from innocent high school gymnasium sock hops, to all-city PTA affairs, to a sizeable commercial industry. And while plenty of radio DJs and other entrepreneurs had contributed their energy to all this growth, it was KJR's Pat O'Day who successfully corralled the action and had come to dominate the scene in Washington—just as Ed Dougherty's agency, EJD Enterprises, did around Salem, and Pat Mason's Far West Amusements and Seaside Artists Service did around much of the rest of Oregon. In each case, the promoters contracted with various venues and therefore controlled *which* bands got *what* gigs, *where*, and *when*.

"The number of dances I was running grew and grew," O'Day reflected:

> As a result, by 1962 the Northwest had the strongest dance circuit in the country. Why? I would like to think well-operated dances—and the ability to bring in good talent. It made dancing a more important pastime for teenagers in the Northwest than it was any-place else. It was the quantity and caliber of the dances that made them so important. . . . An important part of that "quality" was the emcee of the dance: the guy who would throw records out and rap with the kids. Things got to the point where I was emceeing six dances a week by myself. My regular Saturday-night procedure was to hit both the Sheridan Park Hall in Bremerton and the Crescent Ballroom in Tacoma. I would do Sheridan Park for the first intermission, then go to Tacoma for the second. Then I would settle up the box office and then head back to Bremerton to settle up that box

office. And then head home. I was driving forty thousand miles a year. I enjoyed it but I finally had to decide if I was in radio or in the dance business. My first love, though, was in broadcasting.

In 1962, O'Day served as both KJR's afternoon DJ and its program director—a dual gig that earned him a healthy $12,000 annual salary (almost $115,000 in today' dollars). But his increasingly high profile in the community also provided a formidable advantage over any dance-promotion competitors—so much so that his dance business bolstered his income with an additional $50,000 per year (almost $480,000 in today's dollars).

KJR would serve as a megaphone, broadcasting weekly dance advertisements (that O'Day paid for) along with countless (unpaid) on-air mentions of upcoming dances that DJs could slip in when spinning local bands' records. By this time, KJR was heading into its true glory days, with O'Day assembling an incredible crew of zany on-air personalities who provided listeners with KJR's Fab 50 playlist, spiced up with all sorts of platter chatter, frantic antics, and hilarious hijinks. KJR's "Good Guys" team came to include such wild men as Robert O. Smith, "Superjock" Larry Lujack, Jerry Kaye, Buzz Barr, and the morning maniac Lan Roberts. These DJs developed a whole cast of on-air voice characters—including Wonder Mother, Dr. Snow, Fernaldo the Security Chicken, and O'Day's aforementioned Granny Peters—that often served as devices to inject all sorts of lunacy into mic breaks.

KJR's popular formula slayed other local Top 40 stations in the ratings wars. O'Day's station was solidifying its regional dominance in a way that was virtually unheard of back then and unimaginable today. Indeed, for a solid decade it would not be uncommon for KJR to capture as much as 37 percent of the market, leaving the remainder for its competitors to fight over. By comparison, in today's glutted radio market any local station would be overjoyed to hold a share equivalent to a tenth of that.

O'Day's power at KJR was complete: he could pick which records got played and favor which local bands he found easiest to work with on his dance circuit. Sometimes those two factors intersected, sometimes they didn't. This reality left some local combos feeling shunted—but for O'Day it was just business. And his entrepreneurial activities were about to go into hyperdrive when O'Day entered the concert-production business with a new partner: KJR's popular evening DJ Dick Curtis.

It was in 1963 that O'Day made his bold move, broaching the idea with Curtis about a potential partnership. They came to terms and quickly formed a new company, called "Pat O'Day and Dick Curtis Present," that was based out of a small apartment and equipped merely with a typewriter and an answering machine. However, the duo's superiors at KJR did make one thing clear: there was to be no mingling of station business with their new concert business. Because of FCC regulations O'Day and Curtis would have to be scrupulous about paying for any on-air advertising. When the time came to produce a concert together at the Seattle Center Opera House, the duo faced multiple challenges and a steep learning curve. "Pat and I made a good combination," said Curtis. "I was always a detail guy, Pat was crammed full of ideas. . . . He was never one to let details get in his way so I was assigned to handle the business side. It was all so new. Ticketing, this included ticket agencies, ticket printing, and scaling of the facility; deciding how much each seat would cost. The responsibility of the Seattle Center personnel, including off-duty police, stagehands, ushers, was shared by the two of us."

Their first concerts together occurred on March 3, 1963, at the Opera House—a posh venue of three thousand seats. The two shows were billed as the 1963 All Star Revue, headlined by Frankie Valli and the Four Seasons and Roy Orbison with the Frantics and Wailers (with Gail Harris) opening. Two separate shows drew sold-out crowds, O'Day and Curtis pocketed some good coin, and their new firm had a successful launch. Their next big Opera House concert was on September 29, 1963: the Hit Parade of Stars show featured the Beach Boys and Little Stevie Wonder with the Viceroys and the Wailers (with Gail Harris) opening. Again it was a sellout, and the future looked bright.

"We went on to produce many of those types of shows with national headliners appearing along with several local acts," Curtis remembered. "The 1964 All Star Revue, the 1964 Summer Spectacular, and eventually moving over to the Seattle Center Coliseum with the 1965 Summer Spectacular. Everything we touched was turning to gold."

O'Day and Curtis's annual multiday events at the Coliseum soon became popularly known as Teen Fairs. These extravaganzas would feature acts both local and national, multiple stages, fashion shows, teen-oriented product booths, food and soda pop options, and Battle of the Bands contests. Because of these, many younger local bands got their first experiences performing on big stages for large crowds. In

1965, the contestants were recorded by Kearney Barton, and Jerry Dennon released two volumes of his *Battle of the Bands* albums, which sold well locally.

That same year, Curtis proposed that he and O'Day expand their operation by adding a third partner, a successful independent dance promoter from Wenatchee named Terry Bassett. According to the new arrangement, incorporated as Pat O'Day and Associates, O'Day would lead the concert production end while Curtis and Bassett would focus on the lucrative weekly teen dance biz.

Meanwhile, Jerry Dennon—having worked in California for Era Records and then fulfilled his obligatory military service—returned home in September 1962 and persuaded Seattle's local Columbia Records distributor, Craig Corporation, to compete with his old employer, C&C. They formed a new enterprise, Independent Record Sales, which went on to help break a number of hit records. Among those was the Tijuana Brass's debut single, "The Lonely Bull," issued by the fledgling LA-based A&M label.

Dennon was also intent on resurrecting his defunct Jerden label; however, not having the funds to finance any new recording sessions, he resorted to digging into a box of old tapes by a band whose sessions remained unissued when the label had collapsed back in 1960. Thus, the second Jerden era commenced with the release of singles by "Jockey John" Stone, Bobby Wayne, Dennon's erstwhile partner Bonnie Guitar, and the now-defunct Checkers. That band's end finally came about when Joe Johansen replaced the Frantics' founding guitarist Ron Peterson, who had moved to attend college in Bellingham. The Frantics had also just added a new drummer, Jon Keliehor, and carried on with a rejuvenated sound and a sense of broadened horizons as they began making forays into the nightclub scene down in California.

But none of these Jerden singles sparked much excitement. Dennon was going to have to beat the bushes and find some fresh acts. That's when he crossed paths with Dave Lewis, who had revamped his Trio by adding Joe Johansen on guitar and the Frank Roberts Trio's supremely tasteful drummer, Dickey Enfield. The Trio had already entered Joe Boles's studio and independently recorded two versions of Lewis's instrumental: "David's Mood, Part 2" and "David's Mood, Part 3." Pleased that Lewis already had these tunes on tape, Dennon offered the guys a contract. Once pressed as a single, "David's Mood, Part 2" became an instant hit on KZAM, after which KJR also began pushing it. Dennon reached out to A&M Records, which agreed to license the song for national distribution; during that summer of '63, Dave Lewis *finally* had his first big radio hit.

One detail overlooked in all the excitement was that Lewis was still under contract to Seafair Records, since he had signed an exclusive deal with Tom and Ellen Ogilvy back in late 1961. However, the Ogilvys chose to stand down and not disrupt Lewis's success with any sort of legal battle with Dennon. Instead, they just watched in disbelief as Dennon replayed his prior theft of another of their contracted acts, Billy Saint, and quietly carried on with the other talents on their roster.

It was in the spring of '63 that Dennon took Lewis's trio into Audio Recording. At the time, as mentioned above, KJR was hyping their air staff as the "Good Guys"; in an effort to win the station's support, Dennon got A&M to release one of the Trio's new instrumental tunes with the title "The Good Guys Theme." That scheme, however, apparently failed to excite KJR: after only a few days, the single was withdrawn from the market.

Meanwhile, one KJR Good Guy DJ, Lan Roberts—who had a gift for coining inane buzzwords—had improvised some on-air tomfoolery about how any listener who sent him a postcard would receive a "little green thing with a duck on it" by return mail. Lo and behold, within days KJR was reportedly swamped with three thousand letters. Now Roberts had to make good on his promise. He promptly bought a bolt of green cloth, cut it into randomly shaped pieces, stamped them with the inked image of a duck, and mailed them out. In other words, just another normal week at KJR came to a close.

Dennon had A&M quickly rerelease "The Good Guys Theme" single under a new title: "Little Green Thing." This time Roberts responded by inviting the Dave Lewis Trio—who were back working nightly at Dave's Fifth Avenue—onto his show, where he debuted the record and even presented the musicians with their very own duck-stamped memento.

In short order, both "David's Mood, Part 2" and "Little Green Thing" became sizeable radio hits. The latter tune was even spotlighted on *American Bandstand,* with Dick Clark introducing the record in this manner by saying, "There's a new sound coming out of Seattle. It's a big, fat, rich sound, and the man behind it is Dave Lewis."

A&M followed up by issuing the *Little Green Thing* album—which included original instrumentals like "Lip Service" that featured Johansen's finest guitar work yet and became a best seller across the region. Johansen's hook-laden, string-bending riffage was a thing of elegant and understated beauty. "He played differently than anybody," Little Bill recounted many years later. "His playing was real sparse and simple. But what he played *counted*."

The significance of the Trio's album didn't escape the notice of one particular journalism student over at the University of Washington. Larry Coryell later noted in a *UW Daily* essay that "the impact of the album was astounding—Lewis became the most copied group in town." His Combo had been the town's top tastemaker for years, and now his Trio was defining the sound of the scene. Both "David's Mood, Part 2" and "Little Green Thing" entered the canon of standards required of nearly every Northwest teen band around. Jerry Dennon had finally launched a couple of moneymaking radio hits. But he wouldn't rest until he scored even bigger successes. ★

CHAPTER *24*

DOIN' THE SEASIDE

Portland's history with big-beat music was rich. As in Seattle, Portland's early R&B scene was an outgrowth of a vibrant jazz community that traced back to the 1920s. By the 1950s, the town had its share of Black doo-wop groups like the Monterays and combos like Chuck Moore and the All-Stars. Toward the end of that decade, the action picked up when two local radio stations—KISN and KGON—locked themselves into a battle for the hearts of the town's teenagers.

It was 1958 when a radio DJ named Dick Novak began producing rock 'n' roll dances. Then, the following year, he joined with the pioneering Vancouver, BC, DJ, Red Robinson—who just happened to be roommates with a local record distributor, Jerry Dennon—as a cohost for KGW-TV's new *Portland Bandstand* teen dance show.

That same year saw KISN launch as a Top 40 station with the exciting DJ "Tiger" Tom Murphy leading the way. But the fun really picked up in September 1962, when the venerable KGON announced their switch to the Top 40 format and the start of their *Saturday Night Dancing Party* show, broadcast live from the D Street Corral. The competition between the two stations fueled a musical war in the summer of 1963 involving two local bands: the recently reactivated Paul Revere and the Raiders and a younger band, the Kingsmen, led by a guitarist named Jack Ely.

At the age of eleven, Ely had switched from piano to guitar after seeing Elvis Presley perform on TV. Armed with his thirteen-dollar Stella bought at Woolworths, Ely learned three chords and set out to become a star by mimicking his idol. In the 1950s, Portland's two main papers, the *Oregonian* and the *Portland Journal*, each had variety troupes that performed around town, and Ely joined the former's stage band, the Oregonaires. Meanwhile, a pal from his church, Lynn Easton, played drums in the Journal Juniors. One night in 1958, that group was short their guitarist so Ely was asked to fill in for their show at the Benson Hotel.

That's when the two boys got to chatting and broached the topic of working together. Within months, Easton brought in a high school mate, Mike Mitchell, to add lead guitar and they became a trio. Then, four or five months later—when school started in September 1958—Easton and Mitchell spotted Bob Nordby playing upright bass with the David Douglas High School band at an assembly. Asked to join their combo, Nordby was hesitant because his family was quite religious and already had an active family string band. Nonetheless, he was enticed to at least come have a listen.

"So, he showed up with his bass and a bow," Ely laughingly recalled, "and we said, [*laughter*] 'The bow's *got* to go!' But he'd never played with his fingers before. He didn't know if he could do it. So, it took him a while—and some real sore fingers—but finally he started getting the hang of it. And so, then we were a foursome. Then we decided we needed a name."

That's about when they learned that a local nightclub group—George Sinko and the Kingsmen—were set to perform their final week before disbanding. The thought occurred that perhaps that group would agree to let their new band take over the name. Easton's mother promptly went to the downtown club and Sinko told her the boys' new combo was welcome to it.

Soon thereafter, Easton whose day job was setting up product displays for a food brokerage firm, Fenimore Pacific—struck a deal: in exchange for a new PA system and a Volkswagen van, the Kingsmen would perform one or two Saturdays a month at various supermarkets around town. And with that fine start, the Kingsmen began building up their repertoire and landing other modest gigs as well, including at Red Cross benefit events and malt shops.

It was in 1962 that the Kingsmen got their best booking yet: a big fashion show at Portland's Paramount Theater where they opened for the Ventures, who also made a live appearance on KGON's *Saturday Night Dancing Party* while in town. Like young bands across America, the Kingsmen had already incorporated a few of the Ventures' hits into their set lists. It was one hell of an exciting show, girls screamed, and the two bands rocked their hardest. Ely had fond memories of hanging out backstage and learning a few technical pointers about electric guitars, tunings, and strings from the Ventures.

"They were big stars by then," Mike Mitchell recalled, "and it was just a real thrill for us to even be there you know 'cause they were the real guitar players. And so for us guitar players it was a real thrill. You know, there really wasn't anything in the way of lead guitar—except the Ventures. The Ventures were it. I mean, there was Duane Eddy and some of those kinda things but there really wasn't anything else—except for the country guys. Now, 'Rock around the Clock' and that kinda stuff—and Chuck Berry—that's *different* than what the local guys played."

The Kingsmen reached the point of wanting to cut their very own record. They decided to record an "original" called "Peter Gunn Rock." In truth, the tune was a knockoff of the Wailers' "Gunnin' for Peter," which had been a knockoff of Henry Mancini's theme for the popular TV detective show *Peter Gunn*. Only a handful of acetate discs were cut, but the Kingsmen managed to get a copy into the jukebox at Douglas High School's cafeteria.

Back in the early sixties, each of Portland's nine high schools supported one designated rock 'n' roll band—and just as the Kingsmen were based out of Douglas High, the one at Franklin High was the Royal Notes. That band's pianist, Don Gallucci, had started playing at age six, studying boogie-woogie techniques with a Black neighbor, and then developed a keen appreciation for the Wailers, whom he saw a few times in 1960 and '61 at Portland's popular D Street Corral.

According to Don Gallucci, "The way it started was I had become a Wailers fan from like age ten or eleven. I mean, I could play every note on *The Wailers at the Castle* album. And I would go when they were performing when I was like twelve years old. I would just sit in front of Rich Dangel's amp or Kent Morrill's Leslie [speaker]."

As 1962 rolled along, the Royal Notes began introducing area teens to the fresh sounds emanating from Seattle and Tacoma. Gallucci continued: "I started teaching them what you would call 'Northwest music.' Like Wailers- or Dave Lewis–type stuff. Anything like that. And so, in about three months we became the number 2 band in the city. And Lynn Easton, who was the leader of the Kingsmen, came to me one day and said, 'We want you to come teach us how to play this new music.' That's how it started. It was like a business deal. He went and did a corporate raid!"

After one rehearsal during which Gallucci tutored the guys, he was invited to join the Kingsmen. His move broke an unwritten taboo: musicians were not supposed to abandon their high school's band to join another high school's band. For that infraction, the diminutive "Lil' Don" Gallucci was threatened with a beating by some toughs in Franklin's cafeteria. But the potential rewards for joining Portland's top high school rock 'n' roll group were too great to resist. Initially the Kingsmen scored some gigs playing short sets at sock hops where local radio DJ's mainly spun records for the dancers.

"What happened in those days was," Mike Mitchell explained, "the disc jockeys used to go out and emcee teen dances all over town. And different jocks would have different dances that they would promote during their shift. And our guy was Tom Murphy at KISN. Tom would have a dance goin' and he'd say, 'Well, why don't you guys come out? I think we can pay ya about fifty bucks to come out and play for a bit.' And fifty bucks was pretty good spending money in high school back in those days."

It was in 1962 that media accounts reported how Bob Eubanks had opened a string of Cinnamon Cinder teen clubs around Southern California. This concept of dance clubs targeted specifically toward teenagers would also pop up all across the Northwest: Seattle's Party Line, Tacoma's Red Carpet, Spokane's Village Teen Club, Boise's Teen Canteen, Billings's Teen Disc Club, Yakima's Walk In Club, the Tork in Eugene, the Wave roller rink in Cannon Beach, Springfield's Cascade Club, Seaside's Pypo Club, and Portland's Town Mart and the Headless Horseman.

That same year also saw the reemergence of Paul Revere. After serving out his term working at Oregon's Dammasch Hospital, he was rejoined by Mark Lindsay and the duo reconstituted a new Raiders from scratch—this time in Portland. During the period when the Raiders had been defunct, a new nonprofit teen club, the Headless Horseman, had been launched. Two of the owners were enterprising young musicians named Mike "Smitty" Smith (guitar) and Ross Allemang (bass) who also played in the house band, Gentleman Jim and the Horsemen (who had originally formed back in 1961 as veterans of the Royal Notes).

It was October 1962 when Lindsay jumped into Revere's snazzy black and white '58 Chrysler convertible. They cruised around town scouting for potential new bandmates at local dances. When they arrived at the Headless Horsemen, Revere couldn't gain entry because he was over twenty-one, so he stayed in the car while Lindsay went in alone.

"So, we were playing," Smitty recalled:

and he came up and he was leaning over the stage looking real close at my guitar playing. . . . When we finished the song, Mark said he was there with a guy named Paul Revere who was in the record business. I hadn'l heard of him, but we got together. Revere wanted to put a band together and he wanted me to play lead guitar for the group—but I declined because I only knew a few songs. We were sittin' out in the car and I said, "Well, I can't play guitar but I'll get you a guitar player."

Smitty recommended another Portland guitarist, Steve West, and Revere hired him along with Allemang on bass. Meanwhile, Smitty was brought aboard as their new drummer: "I had a set of drums and the first time we got together it sounded good and I knew that it was gonna go places, and so did everybody else. I was excited that first moment we sat down and played."

The new Raiders—Revere, Lindsay, Smitty, Allemang, and West—gigged until January '63, when Allemang dropped out and was replaced by Dick Walker, who'd come over from Boise's Hitchhikers. As the guys reconstituted their band, Lindsay made a commitment to himself—*this* time everything would be a full-on, pedal-to-the-metal, gonna-make-it-to-the-top effort: "I made a deal with myself that every night that we played I'd do something different, whether it was hanging from the rafters and singing upside down or walking to the men's room and singing while relieving myself at the same time. Whatever it was, I wanted to create a buzz and get this talk going that we were the craziest, wildest band that ever happened. And it worked."

Revere was all in: "We were unlike any group at that time. . . . Originally we had to be flashy because we weren't that great musically. Mark would jump on the piano and scream, yell, and kick. We were nasty, bizarre, and the rowdiest, rockingest, craziest group that ever set foot on a stage. We were animals. We had the worst reputation in the Northwest. We were known for being naughty and it worked."

While Revere began marketing himself as "The Last Madman of Rock 'n' Roll," Lindsay—with his doe eyes and distinctive dark ponytail—was now on the path to becoming a first-tier heartthrob with his picture on the cover of hundreds of teen-dream magazines.

Meanwhile, a KISN DJ named Ken Chase had noticed the raging success at the Headless Horseman and plunged into the dance biz by opening his own teen club, the Chase, in a former Prohibition-era speakeasy just outside of Portland in Milwaukee. Chase began booking the Kingsmen at his weekly dances, and he soon decided they would draw bigger crowds if he could advertise them as the "*Recording Artists*: The Kingsmen." But that meant that the band needed a commercially released record. The tune the band had in mind was the one they'd first heard the previous summer at a teen dance gig out on the Pacific coast at the Pypo Club in Seaside, Oregon's beachfront promenade.

The odd name of the Pypo Club would prove to have been selected quite appropriately as "pypo" is old maritime slang for a drunken sailor—and beer definitely played a role in this story. For a century already, Seaside had drawn hordes of vacationing families from Portland during the summertime—but now, on Labor Day weekend of 1962, the beachside town was particularly overrun with party-hardy youths.

On Saturday, September 1, legions of beered-up youths began roaming the streets, getting loud and unruly, and the police tried to intervene after two drunken louts started a fistfight in the middle of the street. As the *Eugene Register-Guard* would later describe the incident, "Police moved in to quell the disturbance and suddenly found themselves surrounded by 300 to 400 unruly youths." A sheriff's department reservist, aided by a few citizens, managed to "help the police officers escape. Then the situation got worse. Rocks and bottles, some full, were thrown. . . . Store fronts were damaged, windows broken, cars vandalized." The riot lasted seven hours, 125 arrests were made, thirteen people were hospitalized, and the action didn't wind down until about 2:00 a.m.

On Sunday, the rowdiness continued roiling, and by late afternoon, when the Wailers arrived to set up their gear for a dance at Seaside's roller rink, kids were jumping on tourists' cars and continuing to create general havoc downtown. Soon after the dance began, everyone could hear an increasingly loud ruckus outside. That's about when the police arrived and announced that the dance was cancelled—a curious decision that caused the couple hundred dancers inside to be herded outside into the melee.

In the meantime, local dance promoter Pat Mason suggested to Seaside's police chief that he allow the Wailers to set up their gear on the Pypo Club's second-story balcony and play a free outdoor beach dance to draw the wild kids out of the downtown core. The plan worked, and thusly did the band save the day. As *The Oregonian* put it, "In another 30 minutes thoughts of rioting and window-smashing were forgotten among the strains of 'Tall Cool One.'" In the end, and after performing for four hours—including a marathon rendition of "Louie Louie"—a hat was passed around and the Wailers raked in enough dough to finance their next record, the foot-stompin' instrumental single "Doin' the Seaside." ★

CHAPTER 25

A TALE OF TWO LOUIES

Seaside Oregon's Pypo Club was fast becoming a notorious summertime destination in the Northwest—and thus a favored place to gig for local bands. Among them were the Beachcombers, Counts, Furies, Gentlemen Wild, Moguls, Sonics, Squires, James Henry and the Olympics, and Paul Revere and the Raiders, who got pulled into an effort to quell rioting teens in Seaside during a repeat of the previous summer's incidents. In the meantime, it was the Kingsmen who also made a bit rock 'n' roll history there.

Back in 1962, the Kingsmen had played a Saturday-night dance at the Pypo Club and then returned there the following day to pack up their gear. Hanging out inside was a gaggle of local teens busily pumping nickels into the jukebox and dancing. Strange thing was, the kids were only playing one record over and over, as if mesmerized by it. The song? "Louie Louie" by Rockin' Robin and the Wailers.

It was obvious that the kids in Seaside loved the band and their "Louie Louie" single was clearly addictive. The Kingsmen knew they just had to get their hands on a copy of that year-old Etiquette disc—a record that, while a major radio hit around Seattle and Tacoma, hadn't spread into Oregon.

Once back home in Portland, the boys discovered that Rockin' Robin's single wasn't in stock in any of the usual downtown record shops. But then Jack Ely thought of trying Eager Beaver's Bop City shop over in the traditionally Black Albina District in Northeast Portland. "Bop City had the single so I took it home," said Ely:

Anyway, when we got to rehearsal no one else had been able to find the record. And so, because I thought everybody else was gonna have the record, I didn't bring my copy with me. So I said, "Look, this song's real easy. I'll show it to ya." But instead of teaching it to 'em: 1-2-3-4, 1-2, 1-2-3-4—like the Wailers had done it—I erroneously taught 'em: 1-2-3, 1-2, 1-2-3. . . . So, then we started playing the song and it had the same effect when we played it as it did on the jukebox at the Pypo Club.

"Louie Louie," as one writer would later observe, "is a testament to the power of catchy riffs and raw sloppiness. For years, it existed as a sort of telephone game. A band would hear the song, play it back from memory. . . . Then another band would hear *that* version and record their own take on it. On and on it went."

Ely's faulty recollection of the song's rhythmic pulse transformed the riff. Speeding up the tempo in the process, the change emphasized the addictive drop-off feel at the end of each phrase. Gone was the Wailers' ploddingly hypnotic tempo, gospel-like backing vocals, and blatting sax—instead, the Kingsmen just bashed and crashed their way through the poor song.

Meanwhile, Gentleman Jim and the Horsemen were now in such demand around Oregon that Paul Revere and the Raiders were offered the opportunity to share house-band status at the Headless Horsemen teen club (the bands alternated weeks). It was at about this point that KISN had established its dominance in Portland's Top 40 rock market and recruited DJ Ben Tracy from Seattle. Tracy happened to bring along his copy of Rockin' Robin and the Wailers' "Louie Louie" single, which is how it finally made its way to Portland's radio market. Such exposure helped it to become *the* song at teen dances in Oregon in much the same way as it had up in Washington.

"The first time I heard 'Louie Louie,' the record was brought to me by a kid in Portland," Revere would recall:

We were playing up in the Headless Horseman and this one kid was always bringin' me records. You know, off-the-wall stuff that he had in his record collection. Usually he'd come up with stuff that I liked and we'd learn it. He said, "Have you ever heard of 'Louie Louie'?" And I said, "No, I don't think so." And so he played me this record—it was the Wailers' version—and I went, "Wow, that's hot. I love that!" I was *always* a Wailers fan. You know, I loved "Tall Cool One" and all those old songs that they had. I thought that was great.

All the Raiders revered the Wailers. They'd even paid tribute by recording their own versions of the Wailers' "Tall Cool One" and "Road Runner" for Gardena Records, an exceedingly rare instance of a label issuing covers of *both* sides of another act's previously released single.

"It took about two minutes to learn 'Louie Louie'—it was three chords," said Revere laughingly:

> Any idiot could learn it. Well, we played it at a dance that night and the crowd loved it. And so we played it a couple times. Then after intermission we decided to play a longer version. I think we played for about five minutes straight. Anyway, it had the magic of the perfect beat to dance to at the time. I mean, it's the epitome of a great rock 'n' roll song. It's just a standard that will last for eternity. Those three chords will never die—not as long as I'm around anyway. You can't possibly not like the beat, or feel, of "Louie Louie," if dancing was in your bones at all. And so, it got to be a song that we played regularly—at least twice a night—at every dance that we played.

That's about when KISN DJ Roger Hart got involved in throwing dances and concerts, and his success inspired other KISN DJs to follow suit. By early 1963, Hart had moved over to the competition, KGON, and KISN hired Ken Chase as program director. Meanwhile, "Louie Louie" had become so hot that Hart called on the Wailers.

"The first local group I ever hired was the Wailers," Hart would recall. "Brought them down and they were such a success. It was like, 'Wow, I hafta find another group!' And then I stumbled onto the Raiders who were looking for work. They were people just like anyone else— with day jobs—and Paul needed to get some exposure, and we hit it off and I became their manager."

The Raiders' first big dance with Hart was held at Vancouver, Washington's teen club, the Trapadero Ballroom, on March 30, 1963. With Hart pushing the dance on his radio show, broadcast across the Columbia River from Portland, it was a fine start to a new partnership. But things slowed down momentarily when Hart accepted a new DJ job at

Salem's KGAY for three months. Meanwhile, over in Portland the Kingsmen made their move.

"By this time we were the house band at the Chase and Ken Chase was signed on as our manager," said Ely. "I mean, who *else* was better for a manager than the program director for the local rock station? *And* one who owned a teen club and could give you steady work? So anyway, after I had been hounding Ken Chase to let us record 'Louie Louie' for I don't know how long, one Friday night he said, 'It's now time. It's time to record "Louie, Louie." Let's do it tomorrow.'"

Chase had made a 10:00 a.m. appointment for April 6, 1963, with Bob Lindahl, the owner and engineer at Portland's old radio jingle studio Northwestern Inc. at 411 SW Thirteenth Avenue. Although Northwestern was far from state of the art, Lindahl had a three-track mono quarter-inch tape recorder and a smattering of microphones. Problem was, Lindahl had little experience recording rock 'n' roll. He was used to dealing with mature musicians and professional ad agency suits. While recording radio jingles everyone present would typically be focused on achieving a known goal—and everyone respected Lindahl's authority behind the mixing console. This was an altogether different situation.

"So, we get down there and he sets our gear up in a circle around the room," Ely remembered:

> He had an old ribbon mic on the bass drum and one other mic on the snare. He had a mic in front of each amplifier. Gallucci had a Hohner electric piano running through a Sears Alamo amp that no matter how quiet it was, it was still distorted. And I was playing a Fender Jazzmaster through a Fender Super amp. . . . [Lindahl] took a Telefunken microphone and hung it from a soundstage boom right up near the ceiling. He stood me in the center of the circle under the microphone and had me lean back and sing up towards that microphone. It was more like yelling than singing, 'cause I was trying to be heard over all the instruments.

Another issue was that Ely had a mouthful of dental braces, which didn't help his enunciation skills as a singer. But the elephant in the room was Ken Chase, who seemed not all that concerned about the quality of the recordings they were trying to make. This effort was intended to be quick and simple. Chase figured that a recording budget of fifty dollars would provide plenty of time for the Kingsmen to record two songs—"Louie Louie" and Ely and Gallucci's new instrumental "Haunted Castle." But they would have to rush the whole process in order to accomplish that.

"Ken sat in the control booth with the engineer," Ely recalled. "Well, he said, 'OK start playing the song.' We started into 'Louie Louie' and we'd gotten probably sixty bars into the song and he said, 'Stop, stop!'"

"The first time we heard the playback we all winced," Don Gallucci reminisced. "And—because our fifty bucks is goin' fast—Ken says, 'You know, the kids don't really care about the lyrics. They just like the music.' And he sez to the engineer, 'Turn down the voice.' And the engineer—who hates rock 'n' roll, of course, because it's a jingle studio where they cut things like [sings] 'Buy Your Buick'—he says, 'Mister, see that dial? That's where it's always been. That's where its gonna stay.'"

"We could see there was this huge argument going on in the control room," Ely continued, "and suddenly Ken pushed the engineer out of the booth and shut the door. And he must have locked it cause the guy couldn't get back in. And then Ken's voice came back on the monitors and said, 'OK, from the top.'"

"Well," Gallucci added, "first we said, 'Jack, back off the mic.' But he kept crowding it. So, finally in desperation, we raised the boom so he couldn't reach it."

"So we thought that we were just kinda runnin' through the song again, you know?" Ely recalled:

> We had no idea that second time was going to be the take. We ran the song all the way through and he said, "That's it. Pack it up. We've got it. Sounds great." We were all pretty skeptical but we did like we were told, and then went into a listening room, an office where they had a speaker, and listened to it played back and we were all moaning, 'Oh God, that's *horrible*. That's the worst thing I've ever heard in my life. That sounds like crap." But Ken was all elated—he thought it sounded *wonderful*.

Whether it was "crap" or "wonderful" remains a matter of personal taste. What is not debatable is that the Kingsmen's chaotic version—with its clubfooted drumbeat, insane cymbal crashes, cheesy keyboard figures, lead guitar spazz-out / solo, as well as Ely's famously slurred vocals—was *rock 'n' roll*. And that appraisal doesn't even factor in the recording's most magical moment: the famously fluffed third verse, when Ely loses his bearings and comes in a few bars too early. After bleating "Me see," Ely drops out, waiting until the boys come back around again, and then whelps, "Me see Jamaica moon above." Considered in toto, this whole mess is one of the sloppiest two minutes and forty-two seconds of garage-rock genius ever captured on magnetic tape.

"That sloppiness," as Tom Briehan would point out, "while unintentional, is the magic of 'Louie Louie.' The riff is simple enough that it imprints itself on your brain the first time you hear it. . . . The whole thing is just elementally *fun*. It's not the kind of song that carefully constructs what it wants to say. It's a giggly, horny adrenaline rush, a beautiful stupid frenzy."

Yet, that is not how the song had originated. It began with a Black R&B musician writing a song using a fake Caribbean patois. That recording led to some white boys in Tacoma cooking up their version, which subtracted some nuance and added a stomp beat. That inspired this less-experienced Portland combo to take a shot at it, with the result that "the song mutated backwards and became something quite different from the original through some kind of neanderthalization process."

"Each new version of the song is looser and sloppier than the last," Briehan continued, "as if the song could only achieve true perfection when it became an absolute fucking mess. The shittiness was the appeal." But for the moment, someone needed to come up with some long green. The band had thought Chase would be paying for the session he booked, but now he pressured the boys to pony up the fifty bucks. Short of cash, Lynn Easton's mom ponied up and they all agreed to reimburse her ASAP.

Meanwhile, Paul Revere and the Raiders and their manager were also becoming convinced that "Louie Louie" had a magical effect on their dance crowds. "One night," Revere recalled, "Roger Hart noticed how the kids reacted whenever we did 'Louie Louie.' It was just the perfect dance song! And he says, 'You know, I think you ought to rerecord that.' And I said, 'Hey, no problem. You got the money, I got the time.' So we went into Northwestern one night. I think they charged thirty dollars an hour to record in there, so I sez, 'Roger, you got thirty bucks—we'll cut a couple of songs.'"

While recording on that night of April 13, 1963, Bob Lindahl made a comment that Mark Lindsay long remembered: how odd it was that the Raiders were cutting the very same tune that another group, the Kingsmen, had cut just a week prior. While it is true that these two rivals each ended up recording the same song in the same studio with the same engineer within days of each other, their renditions of "Louie Louie" were vastly different. If the Kingsmen's take was unbridled anarchy that showcased Ely's muffled vocals, the Raiders' version offered a driving beat that chugged along behind Lindsay's grunting sax lines and rabble-rousing incitement for dancers to "Stomp, shout, and work it on out!" After a two-hour session with Lindahl that cost them fifty-seven dollars, the Raiders now had "Louie Louie" and "Night Train" in the can.

It was right about then that Ken Chase began airing the Kingsmen's tape on KISN and Roger Hart began spinning an acetate "instant disc" of the Raiders' recording on KGAY. Meanwhile, Hart set about forming his own label, Sande Records, and arranged to have Gardena Records quickly press and ship a thousand singles. At the same time, Chase struck a deal with an old pal Jerry Dennon, whose Jerden label was actively issuing singles by local artists.

"Obviously, I wanted Ken to be happy with me," Dennon recalled. "If I can do Ken a favor, he'll be a little more receptive to playing some of my records. So, when he said, 'I've got a club and this house-band called the Kingsmen—and if you could help do a record on them, you know, we could guarantee airplay on it,' et cetera, et cetera . . . well, we cut a deal."

The Kingsmen's debut single arrived in May. "So, about two weeks went by," said Ely, "and suddenly there was a box of records and we were givin' 'em to all our relatives and friends and everybody. And we were also calling all our classmates—everybody we knew—'cause Ken needed some credibility in order to play our song on the radio. Even though he was program director, he had to answer to the general manager. So, after school, from three o'clock on, all our friends were callin' the radio station saying 'Play "Louie Louie" by the Kingsmen.'"

Meanwhile, Roger Hart had started to distribute and promote the Raiders' new Sande single all down the West Coast. One day, he received a call from Richard Vaughn—owner of the little Los Angeles–based Arvee Records—who said he liked the Raiders' "Louie Louie" and might want to license it for national distribution. Hart knew that Arvee had successfully scored hits for groups like the Olympics and the Marathons, so this was exciting. But just then, a second call came through from Dave Kapralik, the New York–based A&R man at Columbia Records. Hart put Vaughan on hold, took the call by Kapralik, and the neophyte band manager was stunned to hear a contract offer tendered by the world's greatest label.

The choice was an easy one for Hart: Columbia had the clout to launch hits and build careers. The only downside—which became apparent soon enough—was that the label's management had achieved their enviable success with classical, country, and pop rosters. Indeed, their hottest properties going into 1963 were Steve Lawrence's number 1 hit "Go Away Little Girl" and the top-selling LP of '63, *Days of Wine and Roses* by Andy Williams.

Columbia had largely missed the boat on rock 'n' roll. Because label head Mitch Miller famously despised the music, Columbia had only dabbled with it, issuing a smattering of singles such as Buzz Clifford's "Baby Sittin' Boogie" and Dion Di Mucci's "Ruby Baby" plus a few instrumental rockers like "Pink Socks" and "Rolling Wheels" by Spokane's Runabouts.

In mid-'63 Columbia course corrected and decided they were interested in this crazy band from Portland. Meanwhile, Portland's underdog station, KGON, hired Roger Hart to help them compete with their rival, KISN. But now the Raiders had vanished. Paul Revere had developed some concerns about his business holdings back in Idaho and decided that further investment opportunities might await him there.

Idaho's teen scene had come a long way since Revere's early days there with the Downbeats. By 1963, a local TV station had begun airing a sock hop show called *Teen Telehop*, and two of the show's regular dancers were Drake Levin and Phil Volk. The latter had also been playing guitar in a local band called the Fabulous Chancellors who'd gigged at Boise's Teen Canteen. With the recent demise of that venue, Revere decided to open his own teen dance club, the Crazy Horse. He found a suitable building and then bullied the Raiders into relocating to Idaho for the summer. The move caused Steve West to drop out. He was replaced by Dick Walker's old Hitchhikers bandmate Charlie Coe (guitar), and the Raiders began daily rehearsals at the Crazy Horse.

That's when Hart raced over to Idaho, found Revere, and broke the good news about Columbia. But before Revere could drag the Raiders back to Portland, he needed to find a replacement for the Crazy Horse's house-band position. Luckily he spied a folksy group, the Sir Winston Trio—Volk (rhythm guitar), Levin (lead guitar), and Michael "Doc" Holiday (bass)—on *Teen Telehop* and advised them that if they could find a drummer he'd hire them. They did and were soon rocking out under a new name, the Surfers. "The Ventures, of course, were our big influence," Phil Volk testified. "Me and Drake cut our teeth on the Ventures. That's how we'd learned how to play guitar—listening to Ventures songs like 'Walk—Don't Run' and 'Perfidia.' We'd learn the rhythm and the lead and take turns playing 'em."

Once back in Portland, Revere and Hart signed a contract with Columbia on May 23. The label fronted the band $4,000 and promised to reissue their "Louie Louie" and give it a nationwide push. Two weeks later, on June 11, the Raiders' "Louie Louie" moved up from Hart's small-time Sande label to the big leagues. Beyond that, Columbia allowed Hart to release, on Sande, a show he'd already recorded at the D Street Corral as the *Paul Revere and the Raiders* album. It included cover versions of songs by Bill Haley, Hank Ballard, and Bill Doggett and was released in a limited, five-hundred-disc pressing in late 1963.

The album verifies that at this point the Raiders were, as Lindsay himself would admit decades later, a "bunch of white-bread kids from the Northwest doing their best to sound black. But we were honest. We were doing what we could, the best we could. A crowd can smell when somebody's faking it. . . . We were playing those songs as best we could with all the enthusiasm we could muster."

That Sande album also featured an original song with the perplexing title "Crisco." The tune itself was OK, but the rumors swirling around sparked an unusually uproarious reaction from the band's young fans. It seems word had gotten around that the handsome, virile young men in the Raiders were fond of private after-show gatherings that featured the use of Crisco shortening—a cooking product made from cottonseed oil that had been processed into a lard-like substance used commonly for baking and frying. But at these fabled Crisco parties, it was purportedly slathered onto naked nubiles who then conducted a slippery wrestling exhibition on plastic tarps that had been spread out on whatever motel room floor. The Raiders understandably reveled in this naughtiness—even going so far as to travel with a giant-sized mock-up can of Crisco they'd drag onstage as a prop; when Mark Lindsay would suddenly pop out, this act whipped their hormone-crazed teenaged audience into a frenzy.

Meanwhile, the Battle of Two Louies had commenced in Portland, with Hart and KGON pushing the Raiders' version, while across town Chase and KISN were hyping the Kingsmen's—each station simply favoring the particular band tied to their respective employee's personal business interests. The battlefield shifted when KGON hired Chase away from KISN. As their new program director, he could have sacked the Raiders' single outright; instead, he started easing the Kingsmen's into rotation. But toward summer's end, it appeared the duel might finally just be losing steam. The Kingsmen's Jerden single had only sold about six hundred copies. In contrast, all the Raiders' original thousand Sande label copies had sold, as had plenty more on the subsequent Columbia rerelease. But neither single could be considered a national hit, and both seemed to be fizzling out.

Then, amid all this, the Kingsmen received a blow from within their ranks. It was on August 16, 1963, that Lynn Easton surprised his bandmates with an announcement: henceforth he would be the Kingsmen's new front man and singer. The guys had long known that Easton had an ego: awhile back he had taken to drumming in a dark suit, which made him stand out from his bandmates, who all wore matching striped sports coats; then, too—inspired by Mark Lindsay's excellent honking— he had also taken up playing the sax. In short, he was obviously chomping to do something more than sitting back behind the drums.

So, now his plan was clear: he wanted Ely to switch positions, taking up the drums so that Easton could take the spotlight. The band was aghast and rebelled. That's when Easton raised the stakes by informing his mates that he and his mother had registered the band's name as a trademark that the pair owned. "So," Ely recalled Easton barking, "the name 'The Kingsmen' is registered to *me* with my mom as cosigner, and you'll damn well do what I want. It's *my* band." And with that, Ely told Easton off using some choice words, and he and bassist Bob Nordby tore their gear down and split, never to play with the Kingsmen again.

But the Raiders had also begun experiencing their own personnel upheaval. It was on Labor Day weekend that both Charlie Coe and Dick Walker quit—Coe to attend college, Walker due to health issues. That's when two of Boise's Sir Winston Trio were recruited: Drake Levin (guitar) and Michael "Doc" Holiday (bass).

In the fall of '63 two more significant events occurred. One was that the fun-loving Revere happened by a costume rental shop and a colonial-era soldier uniform displayed on a mannequin sparked his zany imagination. He rented a set of five outfits for a dance later that night, the gambit was a total hit with their audience, and from then on, the Raiders had a trademark look: matching long coats, white tights, knee-high black leather boots, and tricorne hats.

The second important development was that Columbia—which was now promoting the Raiders with this slogan "The Wildest Sound for Miles Around"—finally got the band's "Louie Louie" to break in a number of West Coast radio markets. It shot to number 1 in San Francisco and then looked like it was going to spread across California. Back in Seattle, Jerry Dennon knew instinctively that Jerden's only chance against Columbia's superior might was to engineer a smash on the East Coast. And that's exactly what he pulled off.

"How we broke the record," Dennon later revealed, "is a distributor friend of mine in Boston, basically he laughed at me, too. But he said, 'To me it's a bunch of junk. But if you think you got a hit, you send me two hundred records for free and we can get them on the Black station here. The DJ owns a record store and I just have to spiff him two hundred records that he can put in his store. Believe me, we'll get airplay, OK?' And that was the only time I participated in payola in my life."

It was October when that Boston DJ, Jimmy "Early Bird" Byrd, came through with airplay on WILD-AM. But mere hours later, the Boston market's major pop station, WMEX, jumped in and their star DJ, Arnie "Woo Woo" Ginsburg, showcased the Kingsmen's "Louie Louie" during his popular Worst Record of the Week segment. Hey, any publicity is good publicity, right? Sure enough, Boston's teens had discriminating taste enough to recognize the song's genius. "They were getting incredible demand for this thing," Dennon recalled with amazement. "We were having to airship pressings from LA to Boston. Thank God, I guess, for payola and two hundred free records or we would never have gotten it on the air."

Long story short, the New York–based R&B label Wand Records took notice and hammered out a quick deal with Dennon. Wand rushed fresh pressings into the marketplace and within the week twenty-one thousand copies were reportedly sold in Boston alone. The October 19 issue of *Billboard* touted the record as a "regional breakout" disc to be watched. Meanwhile, the war continued between Wand and Columbia. Wand was showing its agility in the marketplace, while Columbia's expertise and clout was proving useless when it came to the Raiders' teen R&B. Columbia was too old-fashioned and slow for this new market. Even with their "Louie Louie" getting a good head start on Wand, Columbia failed to follow through with any promotional oomph.

"The Raiders *did* beat us in some of the Western markets," Dennon admitted, "because they'd had months ahead of us. There *again*, I don't think Columbia knew what they had. The other thing is that Wand was a hot, little, mostly Black–oriented label and they knew how to merchandize, market, and run. They just beat the socks off Columbia. Columbia was used to doing it their way, very deliberately. Johnny Mathis, Andy Williams, et cetera. And Wand just killed 'em. They took it and ran with it."

"Columbia *blew* it!" bellowed Revere decades later:

Columbia was *not* pushing this record. They did *not* believe in it. And that gave Wand Records a little time to get a foothold and so the Kingsmen's version started getting airplay in the eastern part of the United States. So, it was kind of a battle there for a while to see who was going to make it. But Wand was an R&B label and they were very hip to which rock stations and what R&B stations to get to play this song. And they immediately got airplay—whereas Columbia, I don't think they even had a *list* of rock 'n' roll stations to take the record to! So, we ended up kinda getting lost in the shuffle.

This shuffling was first documented in the November 2 issue of *Billboard*, when the Kingsmen's "Louie Louie" was listed as "bubbling under" the Hot 100 chart at number 127 while the Raiders' single appeared merely as a "regional breakout" from the Los Angeles area. Still, at this point Lynn Easton knew he had to reactivate the Kingsmen— *this* time with himself out front. He quit college, recruited Norm Sundholm (bass) and Gary Abbott (drums), and began rehearsals.

"Sometime in November," Jack Ely recalled sadly, "I was at the Chase hanging out and Ken told me about it being on the charts. So, I immediately went out and got a copy of *Billboard* at this newsstand downtown." Ely just about fainted when he saw the six-month-old recording now charting—and his first reaction was a noble one: to try and bury the hatchet with Easton. "So, what happened was," Don Gallucci recalled, "we were at a rehearsal—this is after it hit—and Jack comes into the rehearsal and says, 'Lynn! It's like our dream come true! We made it! I want back in the group.' And Lynn said, 'You quit. You're never getting in.'"

By the next week their single was up to number 83 while the Raiders were at number 108. Making the most of this ongoing success, Jerry Dennon and Ken Chase plotted to have the band cut an entire album for Wand. The Chase was reserved for the nights of November 15 and 16 and arrangements made to have them recorded live before a hometown crowd. To beef up their sound—because Jack Ely's rhythm guitar parts would be absent—Don Gallucci rented a Hammond organ along with a large Leslie loudspeaker for the gigs.

On the fifteenth, a sold-out crowd showed up—including an admittedly beer-fueled Ely, who displayed just enough belligerence that the doorman refused him entry. The two gigs resulted in recordings that would constitute *The Kingsmen in Person Featuring Louie, Louie*—an LP that Wand slated for a pre-Christmas rush release. Following those dates, the latest *Billboard* pop chart showed that the Kingsmen had vaulted up to number 58 and the Raiders had fallen by the wayside. David had beaten Goliath. The little Wand label had outhustled Columbia.

Two weeks later the Kingsmen's single was riding high in *Billboard*'s Top 10, and by early December it had climbed to the number 3 slot in both *Billboard* and *Cash Box*. The *Oregonian* noted, "There has been some astute speculation in this most speculative industry that 'Louie, Louie' may well be rated Number One next week." It then quoted the band's ecstatic new front man: "'That shows you what a crazy business music can be,' marveled Easton. 'We recorded the song last May [*sic*]. It sold maybe 600 copies. Then it just laid low. We figured, "Well, so we dropped a bomb." The experience was worth the trouble.'"

When *Billboard* listed the single at number 2 on December 14, concert and television opportunities poured in. America's top talent-booking firm, the William Morris Agency, jumped in with a ten-day tour offer which—once Ken Chase was squeezed out—the band accepted. The tour started in Boulder, Colorado, and from there headed to Chicago. "I remember driving into Chicago," Gallucci recollected, "and the sun's going down and we picked up a New York radio station. And the guy's saying 'Here it is, the number 1 record in the country, "Louie Louie."'"

With "Louie Louie" atop the *Cash Box* charts and resting at number 2 on *Billboard*, the Kingsmen's debut tour wound its way through various midwestern towns and then back to Oregon. Stressed out, the band broke up again. For his part, Don Gallucci—who was still a junior at

Franklin High—had to bow out when his parents forbade any more touring and pushed him to finish his schooling. Easton, however, was now fixated on stardom, and he replaced Gary Abbott with a new drummer, Dick Peterson, whom he'd spotted performing with Lanny Hunt and the Majestics at the 1963 KISN Battle of the Bands. To replace Gallucci, they searched high and low, finally finding an amiable keyboardist in Barry Curtis, who had played in a few obscure Yakima combos, including the Klassics.

Curtis recalled Lynn Easton contacting him in January 1964 with the offer to join and head out on the band's second tour. "You *bet* I'll do it!'" exclaimed Curtis. "I mean, *yeah*! That was the ticket out. I just jumped at that chance. I went to Portland, had no audition. We rehearsed for about three days and hit the road." Who needs rehearsals when every band played the same songs anyway? "I'd already played 'Louie Louie' hundreds or thousands of times, maybe, before I'd ever even heard of the Kingsmen."

Curtis was thrilled at the opportunity and excited about this new trajectory that his region's signature sound was taking: "The Northwest Sound had never really gotten out of the Northwest—with the exception of some early Wailers tunes—prior to this. And it was a totally new sound. It was an unusual sound. I thought, anyway. It just caught on and became tremendously successful." By this point, the Kingsmen had revamped themselves enough times—and having added a sax and switched from piano to organ—that they closely mirrored their forebears, the Wailers.

Meanwhile, it was a couple months earlier that fate had intervened for the Raiders, when their newly hired tour manager—Pat Mason from Seaside—showed that he still had a knack for arranging the right gigs at the right venues at the right times. It just so happened that he booked the Raiders to play a large teen dance in Salem, Oregon, on the very night that Dick Clark and his troupe of touring hit singers—the so-called Caravan of Stars—rolled their buses into town to present their extravaganza.

"They had ten big rock stars, and about fifty people showed up at their concert," Revere gloated. "They couldn't figure it out, until someone told them everyone was across town watching us. Out of curiosity, one of Clark's reps checked out our gig—we were packed! We had 5,000 people standing on each other's shoulders going crazy for our show. It was mind-boggling seeing guys in three-corner hats, playing upside-down, setting their amps on fire, busting things up and making terrible noises. The rep reported the bizarre event to Dick, who said, 'Sounds like they're *visual*.'"

Dick Clark was planning a new teen dance program and was keeping an eye out for promising new talents. "Mainly it was rumors," Clark stated:

> At first, that is. In coffee houses and in the studios, people I respected would nudge me and tell me about this impressive group with the way-out uniforms. . . . So I . . . asked around Hollywood and show-business circles, and by mid-winter 1964, it seemed clear that Paul Revere and the Raiders were most certainly "happening." They had no hit record, which was unusual because all the important groups seemed able to produce a hit of sorts. But I wasn't prepared to discard the group simply because there was no chart action. . . . In January 1965, I took a chance and called the group in for an audition. I was overwhelmed by their showmanship—-and their fresh, outgoing appeal. . . . This was what I needed for the pilot of a television show which had germinated in my mind some-time earlier.

Turns out that Clark had stumbled onto just the right act: Paul Revere and the Raiders were about to become the house band on ABC-TV's *Where the Action Is*, appearing on TV every afternoon five days a week.

Meanwhile, up in Seattle, the action was at Kearney Barton's studio, where the Kingsmen were recording more tunes. By now, Wand had moved six hundred thousand units of "Louie Louie" and the song had also shot to number 1 in England. Thus it was that on January 14, 1964, a *Seattle Post-Intelligencer* reporter cornered the band outside the studio and informed them that their hit song was in the news—not for its commercial success, but instead because it had been condemned as obscene by the Indiana governor Matthew Welsh and banned from radio play. James J. McManus, press secretary to the governor, said the words were "indistinct but plain if you listen carefully."

Although momentarily stunned, the guys started recalling that they'd been hearing rumors that some youthful fans were spreading about some "dirty" lyrics in their recording. The following day the newspaper reported, "A Portland musical quintet making a recording in

Seattle last night found themselves the center of a controversy in which the governor of Indiana charged [that] their top selling record, 'Louie, Louie,' was 'in questionable taste.' The core of the charge was that one set of words are heard when the record is played at normal speed while another version emerges when the record is played slower." Easton "emphatically denied the group had made two versions of the number," saying, "We took the original lyrics as written and recorded by Richard Berry several years ago and reproduced them faithfully for our record." That they did—but in all fairness, Jack Ely's mumbled and slurred vocalizations were, and remain, so indecipherable anyone can imagine *anything* is contained in them.

The rest of this oft-told tale is well known: Welsh's attack was followed by the National Association of Broadcasters' commitment to investigate, and the FCC and the Department of Justice were apprised of the situation, leading to the US Postal Service, FBI head J. Edgar Hoover, and US attorney general Robert F. Kennedy getting involved. FBI agents tracked down the Kingsmen, including the unemployed Jack Ely, for interviews, along with Richard Berry and Jerry Dennon. Over in New York, the G-men visited Florence Greenberg, the head of Wand Records, to talk about the brewing scandal.

"'Louie Louie.' That's the shame of my life," Greenberg laughed as she recalled. "Also the most lucrative thing in my life. I didn't like it one bit. Don't ask me why. It was just lousy. Bob Silverman, my distributor, forced me into taking it. . . . It was a sloppy record done in a garage [*sic*]. . . . It was so shocking to me when they banned it. It was just an old song about a sailor! The FBI came to my studio. I swear. They sat there all day listening to Kingsmen's tapes. They never found nothing."

No one did. Even while numerous conservative communities across America were rallying to have the song banned locally, the FCC's investigative report concluded that all the charges made against the Kingsmen's record were meritless: "As a matter of fact, we found the record to be unintelligible at any speed we played it"—which, in and of itself, is a towering, if backhanded, compliment for a rock 'n' roll song.

Meanwhile, the Kingsmen were on a roll, touring with the Beach Boys and seemingly appearing on national TV every week. It was torture for Jack Ely, sitting on the sidelines, to see his old group on *Shindig, Shivaree, Hullabaloo*, the *Murray the K Show*, and eventually *Where the Action Is*. The cumulative result of all the exposure it received—both positive and negative—was that the Kingsmen's "Louie Louie" would saturate the market, sell upward of twelve million copies, and be established as key bit of the garage band canon.

Among rock players and fans, the song's title alone was shorthand for a tune so absurdly sloppy and epically uncomplicated that any simpleton could play it. Rock historian Jerry Hopkins wrote that the Kingsmen's "Louie Louie" "was so basic, so popular and so uninspired, it joined the slang of rock, as in 'I used to be in a Louie-Louie band, before I knew how to play or sing.'"

Even Lynn Easton—whose televised skills at lip-syncing to Jack Ely's original vocal recording weren't stellar—had to admit the serendipity behind the hit: "I would love to say it was a masterpiece of marketing, planning, careful and skillful craftsmanship. But it was blind-ass luck. Something lined up for us at that moment." ★

CHAPTER 26

HERE THEY COME

The "British Invasion" of '64 commenced with a vanguard assault spear-headed by those four loveable mop-tops from Liverpool, the Beatles. In Seattle, there had been an early warning sign as far back as May 1963 when an odd-sounding pop number—their second US single, "From Me to You"—aired on KJR a few times before slipping off the Fab 50 chart due to a lack of audience response.

But as the year progressed and more news of the Beatles' phenome-nal rise in popularity in England traveled stateside, America's teens grew increasingly interested. After the Beatles made their game-changing American television debut via the *Ed Sullivan Show* on Sunday evening, February 9, 1964, everything changed. A whole new world of British pop music, Carnaby Street fashion, screaming teenyboppers, and all things Beatles burst wide open. Suddenly zillions of American kids—even those who'd not been big fans of rock 'n' roll music prior—were swept up in the Anglophilic-mania that resulted in the arrival of legions of other long-haired Brit bands, storming our shores and dominating our television and radio programming.

Meanwhile, most American record companies—excluding Capitol Records—sat stunned, not knowing what to do next. Capitol executives—alert to new trends in part because they'd already experienced great commercial success guiding the Beach Boys while that band spear-headed California's surf rock craze since 1962—had fortuitously signed a deal with the Beatles' British label, Parlophone Records, giving them the rights to market the promising British band's songs in America.

But Capitol's rival, Columbia, had to have been desperate by this point. Its signing of Paul Revere and the Raiders back in mid-1963 hadn't paid off, and the bigwigs upstairs surely calculated that band hadn't done enough to earn their keep. Even after the Kingsmen had routed the Raiders, the latter just couldn't give it a rest: Revere and his troops persuaded Columbia to issue a "Louie Louie"–related song as their next volley. The Raiders seemingly wanted to fight an old battle instead of devising a new strategy. They'd somehow gotten the nutty idea that perhaps Richard Berry had another, *similar* tune that they could take to the battlefield.

So, the Raiders set out on a recon mission to a bowling alley lounge in Watts where Berry was gigging. They watched a set of his band's tunes and then introduced themselves as fans, explained their circumstances, and begged him to supply them with another bit of musical ammo. Unimpressed by their outreach, Berry asked why they just didn't take a stab with another of his old tunes, "Have Love, Will Travel"—which, in truth, was itself a knockoff of his "Louie Louie." The Raiders' front man, Mark Lindsay, felt slighted by Berry's attitude and that very night crafted his own pissy musical response: "Louie—Go Home."

"Louie—Go Home" / "Have Love, Will Travel" was released and promptly disappeared into the void to Columbia's ongoing chagrin. So, it must have seemed serendipitous to Columbia when the label learned that their rock band, Paul Revere and the Raiders, had accepted the offer to be regulars on Dick Clark's daily *Where the Action Is* ABC-TV show. This was a priceless opportunity: to be the first rock band to enjoy such wide exposure for two full years! (though the show wouldn't begin airing until 1965).

Columbia had been disappointed with the performance of the band's last few singles—silly stabs at dance-fad fodder like "The Swim"— but now it had a plan for pushing their upcoming album, *Here They Come*, epitomized by the LP's liner note provided by their manager, Roger Hart: "In 1964, the British invaded America all over again. . . . Since history seemingly repeats itself, the United States is now marshaling its forces to protect the American Way of Music. Among the staunch defenders are five swingin' gentlemen known as Paul Revere & The Raiders."

"Tiger" Tom Murphy, the band's friendly DJ up at KISN in Portland, also picked up this theme in his liner notes for the 1966 *In the Beginning* release. Shrouded in the fog of war, he imagined that the Raiders had somehow conquered the Beatles: "Paul Revere began a modern day ride to the top. . . . This Paul Revere rides a piano and has nothing in common with the ancient P.R. other than they both fought the British and won. . . . With the advent of this modern day militia, and growing attention, it may be any day now that the legendary Paul Revere invades England. This Pied Piper from Portland . . . and his Musical Minutemen seem headed once again to prove a nemesis to the British."

Well, not quite. Even though the Raiders could hardly be described as having routed the Beatles or the Rolling Stones, even *Time* magazine chimed in with a prediction of potential victory: "Paul . . . and the colonially clad quintet may make whole regiments of fans waver from their British alignments." In truth, there was room in the hearts of rock 'n' roll fans for the music of the Beatles, Stones, Raiders, and countless other bands simultaneously.

Here They Come was released on May 24, 1965—a month before the Raiders performed on the debut episode of *Where the Action Is*—and the album charted for forty-five weeks on *Billboard*, peaking at number 71. But the best was yet to come. ★

CHAPTER *27*

THE SOUL OF
THE NORTHWEST

The Northwest's rock 'n' roll sounds continued to evolve with the times, so by the mid-1960s local bands were composing songs that were more soulful and complex. Moreover, many players were now coming of age, so the possibility of escaping the grind of scattershot teen dance gigs and for longer-term nightclub residencies loomed as an attractive step up in the biz.

In addition to the obvious advantages of having regular employment via "extended engagements" at certain venues—plus not having to set up and break down gear every night—there was also the allure of the adult nightlife they hadn't yet experienced. But playing in smoky downtown nightclubs called for a different musical approach. The bands that would survive this process shifted toward a jazzier/bluesier bag. This change was likely as much a result of the advancing skills of the players as it was a function of the different new venues in which they were playing.

This drive to emphasize the jazz elements of their sounds led many previously guitar- or piano-oriented bands to employ electric organs and horns. Dave Lewis's switch from piano to a Hammond B-3 organ in 1963 had made a big impact locally. In his wake, many of the region's prominent bands—the Wailers, Frantics, Viceroys, Kingsmen, Beachcombers, Paul Revere and the Raiders, Don and the Goodtimes, and Merrilee Rush—upgraded their sounds with rich organ chords. Meanwhile, a few organ-based trios, led by Johnny King, Corky Ryan, and Sarge West, were emerging in town. Even Little Bill resurfaced on the nightclub scene in 1963 playing bass and leading a new Bluenotes trio that featured Buck England on a Hammond B-3. Later, in the late '70s, he and Joe Johansen led a trio holding down a steady blues gig at the Mint restaurant at Seattle's Pike Place Market. In subsequent decades, he became established as the grand old statesman of the Northwest blues scene.

For their part, the Kingsmen took to recording Dave Lewis's organ-driven songs every chance they got. "I was the organ player in the Kingsmen," said Barry Curtis, "and I liked Dave Lewis very much at that time—as did we all—and so it was easy enough for us to record Dave Lewis songs. We'd put out singles and often times the flipside of whatever the single was would be a Dave Lewis instrumental tune."

That this employment of keyboards in rock 'n' roll was not common practice elsewhere—setting aside a few stellar examples like Memphis's Bill Black Combo and Booker T and the MGs—is confirmed by Mike Mitchell, Barry Curtis, and Dick Peterson of the Kingsmen, a band that had toured widely throughout the 1960s and saw the best local bands from every regional scene. "We were basically influenced by R&B rock," said Peterson. "The Northwest area of Seattle, Tacoma, and Portland seemed to espouse this type of music, whereas everybody else was doing surf instrumentals and Bobby Rydell stuff." "I think we were such a success—maybe not so much here on the West Coast but elsewhere," said Curtis, "because, there was a great kind of lag in American music. There was surf music—which had just about had its day. The novelty of it was wearing off. . . . [But] when we took our equipment out into Iowa, say, and we'd set up my Hammond organ people were sure we would be playing hymns! They had no concept what a Hammond organ did in a rock 'n' roll band. Until they heard it. And then they saw what it was."

Asked back in 1976 what the "Northwest Sound" was, Curtis said, "Well, Hammond organs were used in Northwest rock 'n' roll music. And also, heavy bass and a really excellent solid drummer. That rhythm and blues rhythmic base that is really solid, always has been, and always will be, a part of Northwest music. And Rich Dangel and players like that—with that Freddie King influence."

According to Little Bill, "at one time there were two sounds in the Northwest: The Frantics, Wailers, and all those groups with the guitars. Then there was the sound that we had—and the Playboys had: the horn sound." Although the use of multiple reed and/or brass instruments was one of the defining characteristics of the Northwest Sound, there were countless R&B bands across America that included a saxophone in their lineups. But the most impactful bands in this region happened to be the ones who used multiple horns—including the Dave Lewis Combo, the Doug Robinson Combo, Clayton Watson and the Silhouettes, Little Bill and the Bluenotes, Ron Holden and the Thunderbirds, the Velvetones, the Playboys, Fabulous Chancellors, Counts, Imperials, Nitesounds, Elegants, and Dynamics.

It was back in 1963 that the Dynamics had upped their game by adding ace trumpeter Mark Doubleday, who had been discovered by Larry Coryell at a jazz jam session. Coupling the trumpet with Jeff Afdem's sax helped them score a region-wide hit with 1963's "Genevieve," which KAYO broke after KJR rejected it. But KJR came around with heavy airplay for 1964's "Busybody" and 1965's "Leavin' Here."

In short, the Dynamics embodied the peak form of the classic horn-driven Northwest band. At the time, this funky/jazzy sound did not guarantee that their records would be embraced by local radio. Even the best bands would struggle to win much support from local stations. One notable exception was that little FM station in Seattle's Central District, KZAM, which came through on numerous occasions when KJR and KOL couldn't muster any interest in rockin' R&B records.

One of the hot local bands KZAM helped out was Seattle's Nitesounds. Formed in 1963 at Franklin High, the band boasted a fine horn duo—Jim Walters on trumpet and the Velvetones' former sax man Luther Rabb—and landed a steady gig downtown at the Tolo House. The Nitesounds' original instrumental "Get Clean" was issued as a single by Seafair Records, only to be ignored by every local station except KZAM.

Unfortunately for local fans of soul and R&B, KZAM's days were numbered; when it abruptly closed its doors in January 1964, a big hole was left on the radio dial. Luckily, in December 1964 a new station, KYAC—"The Soul of the Northwest"—emerged at 1407 East Madison Street, retained KZAM's popular DJ Bob Summerrise, and hired Quincy's brother Lloyd Jones as staff engineer.

KYAC picked up the slack after KZAM's demise in offering support to local R&B acts. One of those was a young band, the Living End, featuring a sax, trumpet, and Hammond B-3 organ played by Gordon DeWitty. The blind son of a preacher, DeWitty was a musically gifted Black kid who had been raised on church music. He had also been DJing at KZAM since back in 1962 when he was only twelve years old. When the Living End's Bolo Records single "Jumpin' at the Lion's Gate" came out in 1966, KYAC provided airtime. The station also supported the Boss Four, a band formed by Jimmy Pipkin, the original leader of the Gallahads and drummer who had replaced George Griffin in the Dave Lewis Combo. Pipkin had recruited two members of the Velvetones, Anthony Atherton (tenor sax) and Pernell Alexander (guitar), along with Butch Snipes (bass) from the Sharps. When Lewis left the Birdland, the Boss Four became the house band. Their recording for Camelot Records, a dance-fad tune called "Walkin' the Duck," shot to the top of the charts with the help of the band's new manager, Chuck Cunningham, who happened to be a DJ at KYAC.

KYAC would prove helpful to several other local teen-R&B bands, including the Counts, another of Seattle's mostly white bands that had earned their stripes onstage at the Birdland. The band had been founded back in 1959 by several Ballard High School kids, including Dan Olason (guitar), and by '62 they were drawing good crowds on Seattle's North End teen dance circuit. Soon the band began working with a few different Black singers, among them Tiny Tony and Billy Burns, and in 1964 the Counts added their guitarist's younger brother, Bill Olason (organ).

By this point, the band had developed a tight, horn-driven sound, as heard on their original instrumental "Turn On Song," which had been wildly popular at local dances. The Counts wanted to get a recording contract and contacted Golden Crest label head Clark Galehouse, who came to Seattle and set about auditioning various acts in one of the Olympic Hotel's ballrooms. After Galehouse passed on the Counts, the Olasons' father mentioned that he had a local music-biz connection who might be able to help. Andy Huffine ran an independent record distributing company at 3131 Western Avenue and liked the idea of forming his own label. After the Counts had a successful recording session with Kearney Barton, Huffine proceeded to form Sea Crest Records and a single was issued early that summer.

The band had figured their ace in the hole was the fact that their acting manager was KJR DJ Lan Roberts. However, Roberts gave the disc one listen and told them to forget it: the song was "*way* too R&B for O'Day." Luckily, KYAC and a few other local stations embraced "Turn On Song," and the resultant airplay helped the single become a regional best seller and one of the definitive classics of the Northwest's teen-R&B

years. The Counts went on to record several more great instrumentals, including renditions of Dave Lewis's "And Then I Cried" and "Feel Alright." In November '64, Sea Crest issued a single of the Counts doing Richard Berry's "Have Love, Will Travel," which featured vocals by the Gallahads.

That same year brought upheaval to many established bands. The Viceroys—with new bassist Gary Snyder—recorded their *Granny's Pad* album, a regional hit for Bolo Records in the spring. But three months later, Snyder split to join the Dynamics; when Al Berry bowed out, Mike Rogers switched from sax to a Hammond B-3 organ in order to cover the bass lines. When the Viceroys then hired Kim Eggars (sax), the band became an organ-driven quartet.

The next big change came after the Viceroys were booked to play down at the Pypo Club in Seaside. They'd been told to expect as many as eight hundred kids in attendance, but only about eighty showed up. Problem was, Paul Revere and the Raiders were gigging nearby and had drawn nearly everyone to their dance. The good news was that a month later, the Viceroys were hired to open for the Raiders at a Spanish Castle dance—and the double billing was a great success. Jim Valley was floored by the Raiders' manic stage show. When he met up with Revere backstage, Valley blurted out, "If you ever need a guitar player, give me a call." Valley couldn't have known, but that call would come two years later.

Meanwhile, the Dynamics were in peak form and had become one of the most respected bands on the scene. And Larry Coryell had become a star attraction in his own right. "By early 1963 people were coming to watch us just to see Coryell play," admitted keyboardist Terry Afdem. "When we [originally] got him we heard that he was good, but it wasn't until after he came with us that we realized how really great he was."

On the Dynamics' off nights, Coryell stayed active by trying to play real jazz sitting in at various spots around town, including the top downtown jazz venue, the Penthouse at 701 First Avenue, where he was able to jam with guitar icons like Wes Montgomery and Grant Green. Still, he wasn't yet comfortable in that milieu: "I was having a hard time at the jam sessions 'cause I really couldn't get in sync with the rhythm, the jazz rhythm, I just couldn't get it. I can't really remember too much, except that I was a scared kid. And I'd never been around so many Black people before."

Coryell would also describe in hindsight—using regrettable but then common terminology—the goal that he, his bandmates, and their peers had: "The bands I worked with had a more sophisticated, city-Negro outlook . . . the music bordered on jazz, and we always felt that if only we were good enough, we'd play jazz. . . . We felt that the only way to play in our style was to be Negroes. So we hung around with Negroes, talked like Negroes, and finally we acted like them and tried to play like them."

It was May of 1964 when Coryell finally split from the Dynamics in order to join Chuck Mahaffay and the Individuals, a popular jazz combo that worked six nights a week. "When Larry left it did hurt the band," Jimmy Hanna explained, "because he was a phenomenal guitar player. He really set the trend in the city and all over, as far as what's expected for a guitar player. The guitar player was the arranger—people came to hear the guitar player play solos. There were few on par with Larry. Our crowd was full of musicians. Musicians coming to see us—mostly to see Larry, Ron Woods, and Mark Doubleday. We were kind of a *musicians' band* at that point."

Coryell's growth as a player was astonishing during this period; after gigging and recording with Mahaffay, he went on to form the Larry Coryell Trio with Sarge West (Hammond B-3) and Dean Hodges (drums). The band held down a steady gig at the Embers nightclub, a hotspot that was soon drawing touring stars to jam including Howard Roberts and Randy Brecker.

With Coryell gone, the Dynamics replaced him with a fine new guitarist, Harry Wilson, who had played in a few Bellevue bands like the Valiants and the Fabulous Casuals. After recording a set of songs at a dance up at Parker's Ballroom, Bolo Records' *The Dynamics with Jimmy Hanna* album was issued in September '64. That debut album—which featured Coryell's work on one side and Wilson's on the other—became an instant local best seller.

The Wailers had also been navigating personnel changes. First, Rockin' Robin left temporarily to serve for a few months in the Marine Corp Reserve in Pendleton, Oregon. Then Gail Harris left and began singing with the Capris. When sax man Mark Marush subsequently exited, the band nabbed Ron Gardner from the Bootmen, who responded by adding Marush. Soon after that, Rich Dangel quit to join the Rooks, and the Wailers replaced him with Neil Andersson from the

Bootmen. Along the way, Rockin' Robin informed the Wailers that he was moving on to study chemistry at the University of Oregon. Later, in 1966, the Wailers would invite him to a recording session in Los Angeles, and the resultant single, "You Don't Love Me" backed with "You Weren't Using Your Head," would be their final Etiquette Records release. In 1967, he moved to San Francisco and on December 21 of that year lost his life as a passenger in a tragic car wreck.

It was a sad and abrupt ending, and Rockin' Robin would miss out on much over the next years. But by this point the Northwest Sound was established, and the records produced by the area's top bands were influencing one another and reinforcing that sound.

Meanwhile, the Kingsmen were enjoying their glory days, constantly touring, recording, appearing on TV, and doing shows with the likes of the Rolling Stones, Kinks, Zombies, Righteous Brothers, and many other stars. From 1964 into 1965, the Kingsmen also released a string of *Billboard* chart hits: "Little Latin Lupe Lu" (number 46), "Death of an Angel" (number 42), "The Climb" (number 65), "Annie Fanny" (number 47), and "The Jolly Green Giant" (number 4).

In the spring of 1964, the Kingsmen's founding keyboardist, Don Gallucci, resurfaced with a new combo, the Goodtimes, which included Pierre "Pete" Ouellette (a fine guitarist who'd briefly played with Paul Revere and the Raiders in mid-1963), Dave Childs (bass), and two members of another local band, the Invaders: Don McKinney (sax) and Bob Holden (drums).

McKinney had roots in this music:

> I'd started out in jazz and R&B. Period. Just funky, nitty-gritty stuff. [Bob] Holden and I had worked in a twelve-piece, racially mixed group before. It was straight R&B. We did James Brown. We did the Mar-Keys. We had four horns and five instruments and five black singers. We used to do revues for strictly Black audiences. . . . So, we came out sounding really funky just because we had less of a white orientation musically. I used to go to after-hours places on Sundays where I'd be like the only white guy there. That's pretty much where I got my stuff.

Now the question was, who could be the Goodtimes' singer? "We decided that we needed a singer," said bassist Dave Childs, "because none of us could sing at the time. Don Gallucci had worked with Jack Ely in the Kingsmen, and Ely was a logical choice. Gallucci thought he had the potential of being a really good singer."

Alas, Ely didn't fit in, so his stint with the Goodtimes proved brief. Other changes were happening as well: Pete Ouellette was soon replaced by Ron Overman (guitar) from the Gems. And then a young promoter named Mike Zalk popped up and offered to manage the band. His first actions, however, were ethically dubious. "A couple of times he put us on the road as 'The Kingsmen,'" confessed Don Gallucci. "Or the '*Original* Kingsmen.' He thought he could say that because I was in the group. So, we went out—just like they have five Ink Spots all traveling all over the country. Right? I remember Don McKinney's principles were just so violated. He couldn't stand it. But we needed the money [*laughter*]."

After that bit of chicanery, the guys settled on an amended name—Don and the Goodtimes—with Zalk devising their look and image. The Goodtimes were decked out in black tuxedos and top hats and photographed before a swanky Rolls-Royce, Gallucci would mount the stage hoisting a gigantic prop champagne bottle, and the band even bought a Cadillac as their band car. Gallucci—who was still attending school—liked the fact that when the Goodtimes picked him up at school his classmates all were wowed by the Caddy's arrival.

Inspired as they were by Paul Revere and the Raiders' raucous stage show, the Goodtimes assembled a similarly action-packed act and teen-R&B set list copped, to a great extent, from the repertoires of that band as well as those of the Dave Lewis Trio, the Kingsmen, and the Wailers. "It was a mixture, I would say, of rhythm and blues and white soul," said Ron Overman. "But it was just done in such a way that it caught on later. The bass was always so heavy. Where[as] on records in other parts of the country you wouldn't hear it so much. Always here in the Northwest, that was a selling point."

The Goodtimes made their live debut at the Chase teen club and after only a few performances scored a record contract with Jerry Dennon. For their first session, the Goodtimes chose to lay down the Counts' "Turn On Song," and their new take on the tune was hot enough that Dennon was able to cut a deal with Wand Records, which made the band labelmates with the Kingsmen. Though the single didn't do much outside of Portland radio, it showed enough promise that Wand issued a second one—this time a rendition of Big Jay McNeely's "There Is Something on Your Mind."

It was in March 1964 that an increasingly desperate Jack Ely—who found himself working as a door-to-door vacuum cleaner salesman—received a call from the Raiders' regional promoter, Pat Mason, who informed him that he'd heard that the Kingsmen were having all sorts of problems on the road. Booking agents were getting reports that people were noticing that the Kingsmen's current singer—Lynn Easton—didn't sound *anything* like the voice on "Louie Louie."

Ken Chase chimed in with the suggestion that Ely should record another "Louie Louie"–type song and try to carve into Easton's band's momentum. Ely agreed and recruited Portland's Squires to work with him. After playing a few dances, they entered Northwestern Studios and recorded "Love That Louie." Scoring a deal with RCA proved easy enough, but the single sank like a stone.

Along the way Ely began booking some gigs as Jack Ely and the Kingsmen, which prompted a lawsuit from his old band. News coverage of the battle reported that "the Kingsmen claimed that people who had never seen them before were paying to see Ely thinking that his group was the original Kingsmen. So they brought Ely to court and won." Defeated, Ely could only lash out and question the skills of his former band: "I can't tell you how sorry I was to lose the court case and it took some time to get over it. But I had to accept the fact. My one consolation is that a name is a name. It only means what you make it mean. It's alright to have a name you like, but if you are not a good group then it doesn't stand for very much."

Vengeance has its measure of pleasure, but what to do now? How about starting over with another group with the rather pointed name of the *Courtmen*? Connections were made with New York's Bang Records, which hired a local public relations firm to promote Bang's new signing. The introductory press release read, in part, "They come from the Pacific Northwest . . . wild and wooly Westerners out to have a good time and not be very subdued about it. . . . On stage, they are only slightly less than certifiably insane. . . . They play . . . like this is the last song they're ever going to sing. They give the impression that they are going to take off under their own power and circle the earth. They say that they have a typical Northwest sound which they describe as 'gutsy rock.'"

Bang charged ahead, releasing the Courtmen's first single, a familiar number called "Louie Louie '66." Alas, by this late date, "Louie Louie" wasn't exactly a fresh idea in the broader pop culture and the disc met little success. Ely gave his final musical commentary on the whole mess by having Bang issue one last single—a cover of the Raiders' "Louie—Go Home." Alas, Ely was just never able to get the big break he wanted so badly.

Instead, the poor guy was conscripted by the military and shipped off to Vietnam. Once back home, he sank into depression and eventually slipped into heroin addiction. Later, Ely made efforts to rise above, playing bass with a series of hippie-era groups including Phleobus Union, Thanx, and the Portland Zoo Electric Band. He kicked his heroin habit by voluntarily spending a week laced by friends into a straitjacket and locked in a garage. He also worked some interesting studio gigs in Hollywood—"I was the bass player on one of Prince's first sessions. Only he wasn't calling himself 'Prince' then. He was an arrogant little asshole and we couldn't wait to get out of there"—before returning home and training horses on his Oregon farm.

Meanwhile, another band going through some big changes was the Statics. Most members of the group were satisfied with their steady gig as the house band at the BFD teen-R&B club down near Burien. But by August 1965, Neil and Merrilee Rush sensed a shift in their audience and wanted to move toward a more rock sound. As a result, they formed a new band that would push her into the spotlight: Merrilee Rush and the Turnabouts. In no time, the group became regional stars, and Jerry Dennon stepped up with a Jerden Records contract. However, they declined the opportunity and instead formed their own labels, Merrilyn and Ru-Ro Records, which released some tunes—like "Party Song" and "Tell Me the Truth"—which proved too hot for KJR. Little could KJR have imagined what unprecedented form rock 'n' roll would be taking in the years ahead. ★

CHAPTER 28

HERE ARE THE SONICS

The Northwest Sound had been codified by a few bands who retained a debt to instrumental jazz traditions. It had a certain level of sophistication to it: tight horn charts, keyboard fills, and snappy drumbeats. But a new generation of bands was coming along with their own ideas about which direction this music should progress to—or regress from.

The new trajectory would emphasize bludgeoning guitar riffs, squalling sax runs, and pounding drumbeats. And the prime instigators of this aural revolution actually honored their forebears' accomplishments, but just naturally ratcheted the music's intensity up by going lowdown. Their savage musical approach would soon prove to have an outsized influence as it directly inspired many of those same forebears, including Paul Revere and the Raiders, the Wailers, the Kingsmen, and Don and the Goodtimes.

If anybody had thought the earlier Northwest bands had employed a "garage-rock" aesthetic, they needed to brace themselves for what was about to be unleashed by the Sonics. The origins of this fabled band involved two brothers who grew up in Bremerton, Larry and Andy Parypa, both of whom had been impressed early on by Tacoma's Wailers and their exciting appearance on the *Dick Clark Show* in July of '59. "I was thrilled to watch them on [the *Dick Clark Show*]," enthused Andy Parypa. "'Tall Cool One' was number 17 on *Billboard* magazine's top 100 at the time. The first time I heard them live I felt a huge overdose of adrenalin shoot through my body. I was hooked and my grades went to shit!"

The Parypas' band began in 1960 when Andy's younger twin brothers, Larry (guitar) and Jerry (sax), began holding weekend jams in their parents' living room, hacking away at their version of Rockin' Robin and the Wailers' "Louie Louie." A few junior high pals joined in, but as Andy would later recall, "They were all of a kind of equal ability—which basically meant zero. They were learning together." Before long, a Black sax player named Tony Mabin came aboard and turned the guys on to his collection of Ray Charles and other R&B records. Like most every other Northwest band, the band also drew inspiration from the Wailers and the emerging Northwest Sound.

"I honestly thought the Northwest Sound was the Wailers," Larry Parypa admitted. "Rich Dangel influenced guitar playing so much. His licks. All of the guitar players emulated and copied Rich. All the drummers thought that Mike Burk was a gift of God. And Kent Morrill, for singing, was the greatest thing since sliced bread. So, everybody copied the Wailers. And they pretty much set a pace and a pattern for Northwest rock. Every band of that time was in some way affected by the Wailers. That was the beginning of rock 'n' roll."

Before long Andy bought a bass guitar and began studying how to play it: "I pretty much learned to play bass from listening to Ventures albums. I remember getting that *Walk—Don't Run* album and tuning my bass to the same key as that record and learning to play it." Andy joined the band, while brother Jerry dropped out.

As the boys began pondering playing some gigs, they found inspiration for their name in the ear-shattering sonic booms of US Air Force fighter jets breaking the sound barrier at nearby McChord Field. It was December of 1961 when the Sonics won an audition for an upcoming dance at their Clover Park High School, which led to another show at Lakewood Terrace. Next came self-promoted dance gigs at St. Mary's Parish Hall in Lakewood, the Lake City Community Club, the Tacoma Community Hall, and a few CYO dances in Tacoma and Bremerton.

Over this period, their overall sound began toughening up. "We were getting more of a meaner sound," said Larry:

> Things like Johnny and the Hurricanes, Bill Doggett, Bill Black's Combo, Link Wray and the Wraymen—things like that. We knew the Wailers' stuff. We knew some of the Frantics tunes, and some of the Dynamics tunes. About this time in '62, a teenage club called the Gaslight opened down on Pacific Avenue here in Tacoma. We auditioned for that job and got it. We played there—it must have

been six months. Two nights a week. While we were there we got extremely popular for this area. So much so, that we got notions in our head about "beating" the Wailers. We were going to get the Wailers. Surpass them. That was a major goal.

It was at a dance at Tacoma's newest teen nightclub, the Red Carpet, that the Parypa brothers first saw the Searchers play and were impressed by their pianist-singer Gerry Roslie. Later in 1963, while attending a Wailers dance at the Crescent Ballroom, they crossed paths with Roslie and invited him to audition with their band. "Before I got in the Sonics," said Gerry Roslie, "they were what I considered—and what most musicians in Tacoma considered—one of the better local groups. Of course, they were doing a lot of Wailers material, and the style was copied after the Wailers. Because the Wailers were really good. The Wailers' sound was what everybody was trying to get, at least in Tacoma, and generally around the Northwest. The Sonics were up and coming and I thought it was really an honor that they would even call me up."

Soon after, two of Roslie's buddies, Rob Lind (sax) and Bob Bennett (drums), joined the Sonics. And perhaps *too* soon after getting acquainted, they took on their first gig together. "My first job with the Sonics was at a fraternity at UPS [University of Puget Sound] and we stunk," confessed Rob Lind. "We had just met each other and somebody said, 'Hey, I think we can go down there and play for this fraternity.' We went down there. We'd never played together. But we all knew the same songs because we had been playing the same songs in different bands! So that's before we started practicing. A noncommissioned officers club at Fort Lewis was the second time we played together. They never asked us back because we were too loud."

As time went by the Sonics got tighter as a unit, but they never considered getting quieter. Even later, when they played dances at Perl's Ballroom in Bremerton, the Sonics boomed. "When we would play there, which we usually did about once a month," Andy recalled, "it would be packed to the rafters with dancers, and we would be playing as loud as we could. We could always count on Perl's wife to walk by the bandstand at least a dozen times a night holding a sign that she always kept in the back room that said, 'YOU ARE TOO DAMN LOUD!'"

Maybe. But their set-list selections were perfect, comprising lots of Wailers tunes—"Shanghaied," "Wailin'," "High Wall," "Wailers House

Party," and "Dirty Robber"—along with R&B classics like Bill Doggett's "Honky Tonk" and "Leaps and Bounds," James Brown's "Please, Please, Please," and the Phil Upchurch Combo's "You Can't Sit Down."

As the Sonics' reputation grew, better gigs followed at venues like the Midland Hall, the Crescent Ballroom, the Tacoma Armory, the Lakewood Knights of Columbus Hall, and Olympia's Capitol Skateland. For a while, they played so frequently at the Red Carpet that they were practically considered the house band.

And that's about when Roslie brought in a new original song, "Do the Witch." He'd penned it in the hopes that it might spark the next big dance craze like "Do the Monkey" or "(Do the) Mash Potatoes." By 1964, the options for recording in the area were still limited. Joe Boles's studio gear had all been sold off, Fred Rasmussen's Acme Sound was inactive, and Kearney Barton was preparing to move his Audio Recording from Denny Way to new digs at 2227 Fifth Avenue. The option they went with was Commercial Recorders, a studio largely used for cutting radio jingles rather than rock bands. Befuddled by the technical challenges of recording these punks, Commercial's audio engineers argued with Etiquette Records head Buck Ormsby about how to best mike the band's instruments, how to capture their loud sound without distortion, everything!

Ormsby's repeated instructions were simple: let me set up the microphones, ignore the red-lining audio meters, forget about audio bleed from the various microphones, roll the tape, let's cut a hit! The session yielded two songs, "The Witch" and a cover of Little Richard's "Keep A' Knock'in," and afterward the Sonics spent the thirty-mile drive back home bickering. The *only* area of agreement was that they'd produced nothing but crap. It took about two months for the singles to arrive, at which point the band was invited to come up to Etiquette's warehouse and get some copies. With records in hand, the guys drove home and had their first listen—to a man, they were appalled. To their ears, it didn't sound as good as it had back at the studio. And it certainly didn't sound as good as the Wailers' records. They thought that "Keep A' Knock'in" was OK, but "The Witch" was just too sloppy.

By October, Etiquette began distributing the single to various local radio stations. However, because of the record's maniacal sound, Seattle's major stations—KJR, KOL, and KING—didn't even respond to the label's outreach. It looked like the Sonics' big hopes for "Keep A'

Knock'in" were failing to materialize, and *nobody* felt that "The Witch" held much promise.

But Etiquette did manage to get the single placed in the jukebox at the Red Carpet, where the kids started pumping nickels in to hear "The Witch" every time the band took their breaks. Weeks later, as Halloween approached, somebody at Seattle's tiny KTW station thought it would be funny to air "The Witch" as a holiday gimmick. The station then began receiving a shit ton of phone requests to play it again.

It was on December 25, 1964, that "The Witch" made its debut on KJR's Fab 50 chart at number 26—based on the disc's retail sales figures. For the band, hearing it broadcast by the state's most powerful station was a major thrill. The first five hundred copies of the record sold out and Etiquette ordered a second batch. Days went by and the song was up at KJR's number 6 slot. Who could guess how high this record might climb?

Andy had an interesting memory to share: "Years later O'Day told me that sales-wise it was easily number 1 for a long time, but they never charted it higher than number 2. Because their station format was that the number 1 song would get played at all hours of the day and night— whereas I never ever heard 'The Witch' till after three o'clock in the afternoon."

Pat O'Day knew that "The Witch" was not the type of music any typical homemaker would want to hear during the day, but after teenagers were cut loose from school the song roared out of transistor radios all across the region. "If our records sound distorted," Andy happily admitted, "it's because they are. My brother was always fooling around with the amps. They were always overdriven. Or he was disconnecting the speakers and poking a hole in them with an icepick. That's how we ended up sounding like a trainwreck."

Yes, a runaway train barreling toward musical catastrophe that sounded utterly magical to the ears of young rock 'n' roll fans. And if you ever got a chance to see the band in action, you would definitely not be disappointed, for the Sonics had developed a stage show to match their hit's ferocity.

Larry saw where this was all heading: "That's when we really started going wild: sweating on stage, jumping around, standing on our amplifiers, laying on our backs, being really loud, and just a dirty rotten group. . . . To be *different* from all the other bands. They were still doing steps and being dressed real nice. We'd just go out there and jump up and down on our amps, and people liked it."

"I never suffered from any illusion of the Sonics being a great musical band," Andy said. "I always knew we sucked. But at the same time I always knew that we had a certain something that nobody else had and that certain somethin' was the fact that we could get on it, and jump on it, and just flat plaster people to the wall."

The Sonics were invited to appear on KTNT-TV's weekly *Teen Time* program, Tacoma radio DJs Tom Coleman and Glenn Brooke began booking the band at some well-advertised dances, and soon they were playing the area's biggest venues including Perl's Ballroom in Bremerton, the Evergreen Ballroom, and, now that Pat O'Day had belatedly embraced the band, even the Spanish Castle.

On January 1, 1965, O'Day hired the Sonics (along with the Kingsmen, Dynamics, and Viceroys) to open a concert at the Coliseum headlined by the Beach Boys. A few months later, they were hired to open for the Righteous Brothers, Kinks, and Sam the Sham. But the most legendary such gig was the Spring Spectacular in 1966, when the Sonics backed up the New York bad-girl vocal group the Shangri-Las, who were reportedly snotty and unappreciative.

Meanwhile, "The Witch" had begun moving thousands of units and Etiquette Records saw they were sending sizable royalty checks to the copyright holder of the disc's B-side, Little Richard's "Keep A' Knockin'." That's when they informed the Sonics that they needed to head back to the studio and cut an original song that could be substituted on future pressings of the single.

Heading up to Kearney Barton's studio in Seattle, the band cut another masterpiece from the demented teenage mind of Gerry Roslie. Inspired by Alfred Hitchcock's haunting 1960 horror epic *Psycho*, Roslie wrote a song by that title which featured more crazy screaming and thunderous rocking. This new B-side also began climbing the local charts and the Sonics were suddenly a two-hit band. They now drew crowds of excitable kids to dances across the state—and left a trail of chaos and controversy in their wake.

One night, they were hired to open at a dance in Yakima that was being promoted to celebrate the release of a new single by a local band, Danny and the Seniors. The gig was held at the Parker Heights neighborhood grange hall. Hours prior to the doors opening, large numbers of teens had gathered, and the town's fire department noted that the crowd looked to be way over the hall's legal capacity. It was a hot summer night, the place was jammed, and the Sonics had just kicked off their opening song, "Leaps and Bounds," when the fire chief flipped the building's power switch, sending the room into darkness, and barked out commands for everyone to break it up and go home.

Instead, the young rock 'n' roll fans spilled out into the streets of Yakima, rioting and vandalizing as they went. The Sonics fled to their dressing room and began packing up their gear, but the unrest continued. The Washington State Patrol arrived quickly, but that just escalated matters. One patrolman was knocked to the ground by a young tough while another ran off with the officer's hat. Some rioters overturned the hall's Coke machine and pried the bottles free, while others heaved chairs through the front windows. Danny and the Seniors' big night was ruined and they disappeared into history, while the last anyone saw of the Sonics in Yakima were their vehicle's taillights speeding off into the dark.

With massive regional sales of almost thirty thousand units, "The Witch" backed with "Psycho" started to attract industry attention. The first to call Etiquette was Al Schmidt, a big-time producer at RCA, who said he'd noticed the strong chart action over on KJR. He also expressed an interest in working with the band *if* the single could perform beyond the Northwest. Sure enough, "The Witch" did just that when, following KJR's lead, stations in Vallejo, San Jose, Orlando, Pittsburgh, and Cleveland all began giving the hit heavy airplay. "The Witch" became the best-selling local rock single in Northwest history up to that point.

Etiquette's executives, Buck Ormsby and Kent Morrill, delayed responding to Schmidt while they pondered the situation. But then Columbia Records started circling like a shark. With both RCA and Columbia tipping their hands, Ormsby and Morrill figured that the Sonics were such a hot property that the duo could ride out "The Witch" and catapult Etiquette into a higher profile nationally. In hindsight, Larry Parypa had regrets: "They had a lot of offers to sell the record to major labels and they didn't really take advantage of it. But we were young and naïve. We were told, later, that that was probably the mistake we made. We had some natural follow-up hits to 'The Witch,' which could have made us a lot of money, but they didn't take advantage of it. And we didn't know any better so we kind missed the boat."

Instead of entering the big leagues, the Sonics were shipped out to the sticks beyond Tacoma, where a couple of good ol' country pickers, Bill Wiley and Bill Griffith, had converted a rustic rural storefront into a makeshift recording studio. Etiquette's goal was to have the boys cut enough more songs to fill out an album. *Here Are the Sonics* would include their scorched-earth versions of the Wailers' "Dirty Robber," Little Richard's "Good Golly Miss Molly," and Richard Berry's "Have Love, Will Travel."

The Sonics were nothing less than gazillion-watt shock therapy—an unforeseen amping up of the Northwest's established rock 'n' roll traditions. Plenty of the songs they played were the same ones many other local bands included in their repertoires—but in the Sonics' hands, they had an extreme musical menace about them which would prove to be utterly contagious. ★

CHAPTER 29

THE NORTHWEST SOUND

Where the Action Is—Dick Clark's new daily afternoon ABC-TV show—hit the air in June 1965 with Paul Revere and the Raiders playing "Louie Louie" on the first episode and Ray Charles's "What'd I Say" on the second. The band was sensational. The winsome boys hammed it up, jumping around, mugging for the cameras, smiling incessantly, being the life of the party.

This timing couldn't have been better for the Raiders. By this point—twenty-five long months since Columbia Records had signed the band—the label *must* have been wondering why they had made that decision. The initial failure of the "Louie Louie" single now seemed like a trend, as the Raiders' follow-up discs—"The Swim" and "Louie—Go Home"—had also sunk like stones.

In addition, the Raiders' lineup always seemed to be in a state of flux. Back in January 1965, "Doc" Holiday had resigned, and once again Revere reached back to Boise to recruit Phil "Fang" Volk, formerly with the Sir Winston Trio, to play bass. Problem was, Volk was now attending the University of Colorado and felt he needed to check with his parents. He sent them a telegram informing them that he was quitting school to join the Raiders. The parents panicked and contacted the dean and other university administrators seeking help, but Volk was already gone, making his debut with Revere at the Pussycat a Go-Go nightclub in Sin City, Las Vegas.

And then began the full summer of appearances on *Action*, where Volk's parents presumably could watch their son goofing off doing improvised slapstick routines with the Raiders daily. Meanwhile, the guys still hadn't scored a hit single. But then came a breakthrough: Mitch Miller was superseded by a new exec at Columbia Records, Clive Davis, and the Raiders started receiving far better promotional support.

It was in September when they debuted on the show a newly penned song called "Steppin' Out." The single began climbing the *Billboard* charts but stalled at number 46. In December, the Los Angeles–based *KRLA Beat* magazine took notice of this underachievement while also noting that the Raiders were excelling in their live shows: "How do Paul Revere and the Raiders persistently draw such huge crowds in their live shows and get so many TV spots without a top selling record? Maybe it's because they put on one of the wildest shows ever seen. The Raiders' performance can only be described as all-out chaos. All five of them have been known to climb all over a stage and everything on it including themselves and their instruments."

The Raiders' stage show might have looked like anarchy in action, but it was actually a tightly choreographed act that was equal parts comedic laff riot and kickass rockin'. In other words, perfect visual fodder for TV. That first year's successful thirteen-week *Action* production had come to an end and Clark was set to move forward with a second season. But that's when the Raiders' management reminded Clark and ABC that their original contract was for exactly *one* season: ABC had inadvertently neglected to pick up the option to renew the contract.

Meanwhile, Etiquette Records took the Sonics into Tacoma's Wiley/ Griffith studio, where they cut some garage-punk gems that would appear on their second album, *The Sonics Boom*, including "Cinderella," "He's Waitin'," "Shot Down" (which, when issued as a single, hit number 15 on KJR), and a killer version of "Louie Louie."

Regarding that latter tried-and-true song, one writer pointed out back in 1973, "Now here you got EVERY SINGLE BAND IN THE COUNTRY, thousands and thousands of 'em doing this song, [and] the Sonics get their hands on it and make it their own." The band put their brutal stamp on the three-chord tune by having the audacity to change the progression—from the standard C–F–G to a far more sinister E–G–A. That same writer continued, "Larry Parypa was far and away the raunchiest guitarist in America in those years, with the ability to take a song like 'Louie Louie' and make the Kingsmen version sound like Freddie and the Dreamers."

He heaped further praise on the Sonics' music: "Rip-snorting, gut clenching, window rattling, dirty white blast furnace rock 'n' roll, the best ever. . . . Jesus Christ, they're heroes for all of us, for every single person that ever insisted that rock 'n' roll's greatest virtue was its inherent stupidity, its utter tastelessness. Not only did these guys understand that, they took stupidity and repetition to whole new levels. . . . Of course there'll be some who say it's just the same song played twelve times and they're right about that, but it's a helluva song!"

No wonder that the Sonics' proto-punk was having an undeniable impact on other musicians. Indeed, numerous Northwest bands— including the Raiders, Wailers, Kingsmen, and Don and the Goodtimes—began rocking out in a tougher manner than they had before. For example, the Raiders' newest Columbia single, "Just Like Me," would be their punkiest record ever: all block chords, titanic drum fills, serpentine, interlocking lead guitars, and vocals by Mark Lindsay that range from sinister to hysterical. The track rocketed up *Billboard*'s charts straight into the Top 20—a new data point that certainly didn't hurt the Raiders' bargaining position with ABC-TV (a contract was successfully negotiated for a second season of *Action*).

Similarly, when the Wailers' new *Out of Our Tree* LP hit the racks in '65, it revealed a tougher overall sound—downplayed were the trusty ol' saxophones and keyboards, and featured were great big gobs of greasy grimy guitars and snotty vocals. Songs like the title track, "Hang Up," and even a new version of "Dirty Robber" came replete with garage-punk screams and buzz-saw guitars.

The Frantics' sound and personnel had also been evolving. Jon Keliehor was brought on as their new drummer, and later Jerry Miller— formerly with Tacoma's Searchers—had replaced Joe Johansen on guitar. The band was still landing lucrative gigs in California, but en route to one in the fall of '65 Keliehor was involved in serious car wreck and hospitalized. Reacting quickly, the Frantics recruited the Continentals' Don Stevenson as a replacement, and the band played on.

Meanwhile, the Viceroys played a gig in 1965 with Don and the Goodtimes as the opening act, and the Viceroys' leader, Jim Valley, was impressed. He found their stage show to be "even crazier" than that of Paul Revere and the Raiders. Backstage he met the Goodtimes' manager, who mentioned that Pete Ouellette was about to exit the band and wondered if Valley knew of any other guitarists who also sang. "I'll let you know" was Valley's response. After a night of tossing and turning, Valley changed his mind, called the Goodtimes up, and volunteered himself.

Valley arrived with a punky new tune, "Little Sally Tease," which became a regional radio hit when Jerden released it as a single in July 1965. The song became so popular locally that the Kingsmen even adopted and recorded it. Don and the Goodtimes were on a roll: Don Gallucci had finally graduated from high school in June and was now free to travel, and great gigs were coming their way, including television appearances on LA-based programs like the *Lloyd Thaxton Show*, *Hollywood Discotheque*, *Ninth Street West*, *Hollywood a Go-Go*, *Hullabaloo*, *Shebang*, and *Malibu U* (with Ricky Nelson) as well as a night headlining at the Whisky a Go-Go on the Sunset Strip.

Meanwhile, the Goodtimes were signed by ABC–Dunhill Records, which reissued "Little Sally Tease" nationwide with a new B-side: a rendition of Dave Lewis's "Little Green Thing." Their drummer, Bob Holden, wrote one of the toughest garage-punk songs of the whole era—"Take a Look at Me." But instead of the Goodtimes recording it, he passed it to Newport, Oregon's Mr. Lucky and the Gamblers, whose 1966 version became a regional hit that was licensed by Dot Records for national distribution. That same year, the Goodtimes were invited to appear numerous times on the second season of ABC-TV's *Action* show. Then, Wand Records released their debut album, *Where the Action Is!!!*, which was a showcase of the Northwest canon of regional garage-band staples, including Big Jay McNeely's "There Is Something on Your Mind," the Sonics' "The Witch," the Counts' "Turn On Song," and the Kingsmen's "Long Green," "Bent Scepter," and "Jolly Green Giant."

Meanwhile, Paul Revere and the Raiders were enjoying a good run of success with a newly toughened-up sound before ultimately bending to the temptation to soften things up to further expand their fan base. Their next single in 1965, "Steppin' Out," was a menacing original stomper that reached *Billboard*'s number 46 slot. And the next single, "Just Like Me," was a classic Northwest-style rocker that had recently been penned by Richard Dey and recorded by his band, the Wilde Knights from Vancouver, Washington. The Raiders loved the song and cut a publishing deal with Dey—a seemingly fishy arrangement that saw the name of the Raiders' manager, Roger Hart, listed with Dey's as a cowriter. Their rendition hit number 11 on *Billboard* and helped *Just Like Us!* go gold.

"Just Like Me" would be the Raiders' grungiest recording ever. Hell, even the single's B-side, "B.F.D.R.F. Blues," was gnarly: its enigmatic title stood for the anti-corporate fightin' words "big fucking deal, rat fuck." Part of the band's newly aggressive sound was due to Revere's new instrument, which helped define the classic garage-rock sound of the day: a compact Vox Continental organ.

For their part, the Kingsmen had scored another hit with a silly novelty song penned by Lynn Easton, "Jolly Green Giant," and then also had their throwaway song "The Krunch" co-opted as an ad for a potato chip firm. But they finally got around to recording something more substantial. Probably their toughest garage rocker of all, "Give Her Lovin'," alas, was unfortunately diminished by being included in the pointless beach romp film *How to Stuff a Wild Bikini* starring Annette Funicello.

Following behind the Sonics, Wailers, and Raiders came a new generation of Northwest bands who also pushed things ahead, releasing their own punky garage classics, including the Bootmen ("Ain't It the Truth Babe"), Paul Bearer and the Hearsemen ("I've Been Thinking"), the Talismen ("She Was Good"), the Dominions ("I Need Her"), and the Live Five's "Hunose."

But just as these garage rockers were popularizing a Sonics-style, punky aesthetic, Columbia Records hatched a new plan for the Raiders. Label executives—who, let's recall, had zero idea what to do with the band in '63 and '64—were now beginning to mold the Raiders into their corporate vision of what rock 'n' roll *should* be. This was just the music industry being, well, *industrial*: making the production process more efficient and dispensing with superfluous personnel, with the result being far less edgy music. In short, this unfolding process was a rock version of what the noted jazz critic Gunther Schuller once described as the "creepy tentacles of commercialism."

In practice, the result, musically, was less pounding and screaming, and more playing cleanly and singing harmonies; less recording of regional favorites, and more renditions of pop confections—even some admittedly great ones!—as penned by professional songsmiths. Management is typically attracted to the raw talent of an artist—and how the act had developed a local following of fans—but cannot resist trying to mold the act to increase its appeal to a broader audience.

So, it was now time for Mark Lindsay to finally tuck his sax back in its case—he wouldn't be needing it any longer. One writer even posited that this neutering of the Raiders was a sort of experiment, proving that all sorts of other scruffy bands could be reformed: "Paul Revere and the Raiders appeared to be their model. There was a sweetening of the Vox organ–led garage band style, substituting a coy winsomeness for the psychotic machismo of that style's early pioneers."

If there was one person who thoroughly approved of this taming of the Raiders, it was Dick Clark, who had long been making his living on the periphery of rock 'n' roll but never seemed to actually *like* the real goods. So, with all sorts of musical revolutions now swirling—the Beatles going arty, the Rolling Stones penning increasingly heavy tunes, Cream pushing the blues forward, and most *everybody* beginning to dabble in psychedelia—leave it to Clark to lavish praise on Paul Revere's authoritarian band-management style, keen business sense, and singular focus on commercial success: "Paul himself was clearly a solid, sensible young man with an iron grip on the group's direction. He had no boring, complicated 'hang-ups' about labels of images or eccentric musical values and had decided . . . that they were to be a first-class, professional, middle-of-the-road rock team who would give full-blooded, full-value entertainment to the fans."

If he were aware of it, Clark would surely have enjoyed the fact that when the Raiders formed their own music production company it was called TAM Enterprises—named for their targeted revenue stream, Teen-Age Money. But the band's youthful audience never knew about the "B.F.D.R.F. Blues" or TAM, because the promotional effort for the Raiders' actively pushed the goofy, fun-lovin', slapstick aspect of their TV appearances. As one writer noted, "Though undeniably marketed for the teenybopper audience, the group's history as a pre-Beatles show band paid off musically throughout their teen idol career."

It was in March 1966 that Revere made his next hiring decision. He finally called Don and the Goodtimes' guitarist, Jim Valley, which Valley had been longing for since 1964. Revere explained that Drake "Kid" Levin was leaving to join the National Guard—a common way for guys at the time to sidestep joining the army and escape having to go fight in the jungles of Vietnam. The military was also sniffing around, looking to grab Phil Volk as well.

The Vietnam War drained talent from countless American bands during this period. In an effort to retain Levin, the Raiders had even contacted the military's Special Services department to volunteer to play shows for the troops via the USO. But the war affected people in other ways as well. On the evening of April 10, when the Raiders were waiting to go onstage at the Coliseum in Lubbock, Texas, two police officers appeared backstage and said they had a telegram to deliver to Phil Volk. Some folks may have worried it was his draft notice, but the news was even worse: the telegram informed him that Volk's brother had just been killed in Vietnam.

Levin left the band shortly thereafter and Revere recruited Jim Valley. As the newest Raider, Valley joined Mark, "Smitty," "Fang," and "Uncle Paul" and was bestowed the nickname "Harpo" because the boss man thought he looked like that particular member of the Marx Brothers comedy troupe. One other notable member of the Raiders' posse was their roadie, Mark Amans, on whom Revere bestowed the nickname of "Hoss" because the hulking ex-jock looked like the Hoss Cartwright character on the *Bonanza* TV show. It was Amans's 2010 memoir *Where the Action Was* that finally revealed stories about the band's groupies, recreational drugs, all-night parties, road life, and hangovers. Amans also rated which American towns offered the best groupie action, with Seattle coming in third behind Atlanta and Chicago.

Endless fun doubtlessly awaited Valley as a Raider, because the band was one of America's top live acts, right up there with the Young Rascals and Mitch Ryder and the Detroit Wheels. They would be featured in countless editions of teenyhopper-oriented publications, including *Tiger Beat, Teen,* and *16*. In addition, over the next few years the Raiders would set an industry record by making over seven hundred appearances on TV, including such popular programs as *Where the Action Is, American Bandstand, Hullabaloo, Shebang,* the *Tonight Show, Ninth Street West, Hollywood a Go-Go, Upbeat,* the *Lloyd Thaxton Show, Hollywood Palace,* the *Milton Berle Show,* the *Smothers Brother Comedy Hour,* and even *Batman,* where they performed for the villainous Penguin.

Two months after Valley joined the group, Columbia released their next album, *Midnite Ride,* which included two timeless rockers: "Kicks" and "(I'm Not Your) Steppin' Stone." "Kicks" had been penned by veteran Brill Building pop composers Cynthia Weil and Barry Mann specifically for the Animals; however, legend holds that their singer, Eric Burdon, had rejected the song because of the lyrics' uncool antidrug message. The Raiders' version entered the charts in March '66 and peaked at number 4 in *Billboard* and number 3 in *Cash Box.* Another proven hitmaking duo, Tommy Boyce and Bobby Hart, contributed the other great rocker, "(I'm Not Your) Steppin' Stone," to the Raiders, only to see the Monkees swoop in, latch onto the tune, and score the hit. The Raiders' next rockin' single, Weil and Mann's "Hungry," broke out in June, charted for eleven weeks, and peaked at number 6 in *Billboard*. Those hits were soon followed by a couple more: namely, "The Great Airplane Strike" (number 20) and "Good Thing" (number 6).

And *this* is how corporate machinations transformed the Raiders from a towering regional band who had always displayed their Northwest roots proudly into something, well, *different*. Although this late-stage commercial success by the Raiders was good for them, it wasn't necessarily all that great for their original dance-crowd fans. One thing is for certain, though: they sure didn't sound like a Northwest band any longer. And from this point on, the Raiders' records would shift to a more generic pop aesthetic and generally rock less.

Indeed, by the time the Raiders scored their first and only number 1 hit—"Indian Reservation"—there were negligible remnants of their rowdy teen-R&B origins. This somber, overproduced chart-topper features over-the-top orchestral overdubs and funereal church organ lines. In essence, it was unfun *and* unfunky. Still, the tune was more substantial than the rootless pop fluff that would follow—'70s smiley-face dreck like "Country Wine," "Song Seller," and "Love Music."

As it happened, and with sad symmetry, Don and the Goodtimes were following in the Raiders' footsteps. While appearing regularly on big-time TV shows like *American Bandstand*, the *Joey Bishop Show*, and even the *Dating Game*, they also moved up to Columbia Records' subsidiary label, Epic, and would finally score a couple of national hits. But this was achieved by watering down their original, ballsy sound to a bland, "sunshine pop" aesthetic, as evinced such saccharin hits as the painfully Beach Boys–esque "I Could Be So Good to You" (number 56) and "Happy and Me" (number 98). Sure, they were successful, but it came at the cost of their rock 'n' roll street cred. In hindsight, the band's bassist, Ron Overman, pondered the dilemma they'd faced: "The Northwest should have been the biggest music in the country because it really had a lot of groups and different sounds. It really was developing something where other areas weren't developing at all. California was always kind of rinky-dinky, surf, et cetera. California came up with big things—and a lot of people made money—but the

Northwest just kind of sat up here, because the right people didn't do anything with it. Now music is more or less blended, but at one time the Northwest did have a sound."

So, while the Raiders and Goodtimes were having the rootsy Northwest sound—with all its old R&B elements—siphoned away by their producers, arrangers, and professional session players, the Kingsmen were now experiencing an opposite sort of issue. Unlike Columbia and Epic, Wand Records didn't want to overly polish and neuter their band. Rather, while the Kingsmen had been actively trying to expand their artistry and use their advancing knowledge of studio techniques, their label sought more of the same ol' same ol' from them. "They were a Manhattan record label who didn't really understand the intricacies of Northwest music such as we did," a frustrated Barry Curtis once noted. "And no matter *what* we would try to do over several subsequent years of recording, the people in New York would take these different tunes and remaster them to try and get the same horrid, raunchy recording quality that 'Louie Louie' had. Which is a dichotomy really: they'd take us into expensive sophisticated studios and try to get the sound that 'Louie Louie' had—which was recorded on a mono machine in a garage [*sic*] in Portland. So, you know, it was a defeating thing ultimately."

Then there is the case of the Viceroys. Invited to appear on *Where the Action Is* in August of '66, the band opted to lip-synch their last Bolo single—a catchy original tune called "That Sound"—from the deck of the RMS *Queen Mary* ocean liner which was docked in Long Beach, California. Well, someone at Columbia Records was impressed enough to sign the Viceroys to a contract. But that's when the pressure began to make a new recording of "That Sound"—this time with psychedelic/pop elements added, all-new lyrics, and the new trendy, druggy title of "Out of My Mind." More than that, the band's name was changed to the *Surprise Package*.

It was *Hit Parader* magazine that published the epitaph of the once great Wailers, who by 1966 had slid down the slippery slope of generic commercialism: "The new Wailers have . . . cast aside their jazz-tinged Northwestern ways and become an American Standard group, enjoyable but without any real distinguishing qualities. Be that as it may, their old sound got around quite a bit in the 1960s, and in fact it could be argued that a great chunk of Southern California's vaunted surf instrumental sound is borrowed right off that first Wailers album."

The Dynamics, too, had lost their distinctive edge. By late 1966, the Afdem brothers and Harry Wilson had added some new players and recast themselves as the Springfield Rifle. Jerry Dennon arranged for them to go to Hollywood's Gold Star Studios, where the legendary pop producer Stan Ross did his thing. The result was "100 or Two," a Jerden single which became a moderate regional hit even though—or maybe *because*—it boasted bubblegum orchestration that made the boys sound more like the Mamas and Papas than the old Dynamics.

"To be popular," Wilson told one reporter, "a hit record has to have the commercial sound. It can't be too complicated, and it has to have a sort of *even* sound." Terry Afdem added, "If a band is going to make it, it's got to get away from the Northwest sound, which is sort of unprofessional." And sure enough, with their newly professional, uncomplicated, commercial, and "even" sound, the Springfield Rifle had moved on from the R&B-informed "Northwest sound" of their past. Over the next five years, the band—now led by saxophonist Jeff Afdem (who had switched to flute)—released a series of soft, rhythmless pop ballads that some regional radio stations embraced, but the tunes didn't exactly drive crowds to the dance floor. Once Afdem took charge, his band took the next logical step—as the Springfield *Flute*!—and the transformation into easy listening music was complete.

Interestingly, it was their onetime bandmate Larry Coryell who, while back as a journalism student at the University of Washington, had penned an essay for the *UW Daily* that explained why Northwest bands had originally forged their own rock aesthetic: "Tonight's presentation of local Blues groups is a good indication of their tendency to ignore musical fads and crazes that permeate the nation's pop market. The Seattle bands have, by and large, stuck to the blues and have turned a deaf ear toward the Beatles, the Beach Boys, and Al Hirt. Hence, Seattle bands like Dave Lewis and the Dynamics have developed original and natural styles of playing that are welcome alternatives to the pop music that is packaged and peddled by Madison Avenue and shoved down the ears of gullible subteens as 'music of today.'"

Alas, that local focus on "original and natural styles of playing"— the region's formerly wild and wooly Northwest Sound—was fading out, making way for more corporate-approved forms. Instrumentals were now out of favor and vocal harmonies were in. Honking saxes and whooshing organs were old school and guitar solos were bustin' loose.

Brit rock, folk rock, and the first murmurings of Haight-Ashbury's psychedelic sounds were all the rage. Time had marched forward and the heyday of the classic Northwest Sound was drawing to a close.

Who better to sum these matters up than one of the art form's architects, Little Bill Engelhart? "The 'Northwest Sound'? There *was* one—it grew up." But questions remained. Had the region's pioneering rockers truly contributed all they could? Or might there be one more triumphant chapter in that generation's saga? ★

CHAPTER *30*

WEST COAST SEATTLE BOY

The rock 'n' roll landscape in the Pacific Northwest was evolving rapidly by the mid-1960s. The old sock hop days of "The Twist" were a distant memory. The subsequent tsunami of California surf rock had already ebbed. The early British Invasion pop was evolving into a more complex art form, and the once earnest folk rock movement began evincing a psychedelic aesthetic.

Then, in late 1966, a comet-like talent named "Jimi" Hendrix burst across the musical universe and overnight became the rock 'n' roll galaxy's brightest star. The twenty-four-year-old's utterly compelling sounds were an otherworldly blend of unprecedented electronic effects, cutting-edge studio trickery, mumbly acid-inspired lyrics, and mind-blowing psychedelic electric guitar playing like no one had ever heard before.

Hendrix's songs had a uniquely bluesy depth to them. But it sure wasn't typical Mississippi Delta blues, or Chicago blues, or Texas blues, or British blues. Instead, it seemed to emanate from some mysterious and uncharted place that critics were unable to identify. They couldn't quite fathom *where* in the world his sound's roots were planted.

Having left Seattle for basic training at Fort Ord in May of 1961, by November PFC James Marshall Hendrix had been stationed with the Army Airborne at Fort Campbell, Kentucky. In July of '62 he was discharged:

> One morning I found myself standing outside the gates at Fort
> Campbell, on the Tennessee-Kentucky border with my duffle bag

and three or four hundred dollars in my pocket. I was going to go back to Seattle, which was a long way away, but there was this girl there I was kinda hung up on. Then I thought I'd just look in at Clarksville, which was near; stay there the night and go home the next morning. That's what I did. . . . I went in this jazz joint and had a drink, liked it, and stayed. I came out of that place with sixteen dollars left, and it takes a lot more than that to get from Tennessee to Seattle. All I can do, I thought, is get a guitar and try to find work here.

His story from there on is well known: within a couple months Hendrix had formed a band with an army buddy bassist named Billy Cox, and they began working on Nashville's R&B scene. Then came Hendrix's days of crisscrossing the nation, gigging with various R&B combos on the "chitlin' circuit." It was around 1963 when he began touring with his boyhood hero Little Richard, and then came work with Canada's Bobby Taylor and the Vancouvers, Ike and Tina Turner, the Isley Brothers, and Joey Dee and the Starliters.

Settled in New York, Hendrix got involved in some recording sessions in 1965, leaning on tunes he'd learned during his formative Seattle years. Among them were Big Jay McNeely's "There Is Something on Your Mind," Ray Charles's "What'd I Say," and Freddie King's "San-Ho-Zay." That same year, Hendrix was rehired by Little Richard, and Vee-Jay Records released their recording of "I Don't Know What You've Got but It's Got Me."

In 1966, Hendrix caught the attention of visiting British rockers, among them the Animals' bassist, Chas Chandler, who whisked him off to London, where he was introduced as "Jimi Hendrix." A trio was formed around him—the Jimi Hendrix Experience—that quickly scored a couple of radio hits ("Hey Joe" and "Purple Haze") and then made a triumphal performance stateside at the 1967 Monterey Pop Festival. The *Are You Experienced* album was released in August, to be followed in December by *Axis: Bold as Love*, which included "Spanish Castle Magic," a song that caught the attention of everybody in the Northwest.

Of that particular song, the veteran *Rolling Stone* writer Dave Marsh would note, "Once you know the legend of the . . . Castle and the facts of Jimi's attendance there, the lyrics of his 'Spanish Castle Magic' seem haunted by homesick nostalgia. 'It's very far away, it takes about half a day / To get there, if we travel by my ah . . . dragonfly,' he sings, in the voice of a kid stranded a couple of continents from home.'"

It was in June of 1967 that Hendrix's managers accepted an offer from Pat O'Day's new Concerts West event production company, and from then on, that firm handled all the band's concert bookings—including the four "homecoming" shows the Experience played in Seattle between 1968 and 1970. Along the way, Hendrix and O'Day formed a friendship, while Concerts West grew to be the biggest concert production company in the world. O'Day once recalled a memorable conversation he and Hendrix had on September 13, 1968, backstage at the Alameda Coliseum: "We talked about the Wailers, and about some of the people that he thought had great promise. Jimi *loved* the Checkers. And the Frantics. And the Dynamics. And Little Bill and the Bluenotes. And Dave Lewis. He *loved* his roots! He loved his roots and that was all on his mind. He would play me some things that he had written when he was still in Seattle. You know, he didn't just happen. He didn't create this because of his English experience or his club experiences. It was all there from the very beginning."

While touring through Seattle in September 1968, Hendrix reunited with his boyhood bandmate Pernell Alexander, who had, like Hendrix, also worked on the road as guitarist for Little Richard. By 1968, Alexander and Butch Snipes (formerly of the Boss Four) formed Juggernaut, and Hendrix spent some time hanging out at their jam pad, listened to them rehearse, and even dedicated "Hey Joe" to the band from the Seattle Center Coliseum stage that night. According to Juggernaut's keyboardist, Dan Bonow, Hendrix even left them with parting words of support: he "gave us his new phone numbers and told us to hang on, he was getting to a place where he could help. Jimi told us: 'Don't sign *anything* 'til I get in touch.' We took it as a cryptic warning-promise of at least news coming from inside the industry." Alas, the band never heard from Hendrix again, and no recording deal would ever materialize.

Other interesting interactions would occur with notable Seattle music scene figures, including the Dynamics' guitarist Larry Coryell and drummer Ron Woods, and the Velvetones' Luther Rabb and Butch Snipes. Larry Coryell played jazz locally until August of 1965, when he realized he needed new challenges. But he was shy and still lacking self-esteem. "I had such a low opinion of myself," Coryell openly confessed, "that when people suggested that I move to New York, I thought it was some kinda joke. They said, 'There's no more you can do here.' They said, 'You've reached the top.' I had a Gibson Super 400, two amplifiers, and some clothes and a dog—and I decided to move to New York. . . . I was totally intimidated by the musicianship. Completely. I mean, here were the players of my dreams. It was unbelievable."

On September 3 Coryell arrived in New York, where he quickly made a name for himself in the elite jazz world. Indeed, he would go on to be acknowledged as a pioneer of the jazz-rock genre after he and fellow former Checker Mike Mandel formed the Eleventh House. Over time, Coryell would garner critical acclaim: *Rolling Stone* would reference him as the "young messiah" of jazz; noted critic Robert Christgau raved, "Coryell was a revelation—a guitarist of unmatched facility and melodic inventiveness who wasn't afraid to wail"; and *Vintage Guitar* magazine deemed him the "Patriarch of Prog" and the "Father of Fusion."

But back in 1968, he wasn't nearly as famous as Hendrix, the star who had been admiring his playing back in the old days. When Coryell's career was on the rise but Hendrix was ruling the rock world, Coryell looked him up in New York: "I came to his hotel, we were hanging out, and we talked about, you know, Dave Lewis and the good blues scene in Seattle. We talked about some of the music we both learned by living in Seattle—like 'Come On' by Earl King. And right after that conversation he went into the studio and recorded that song."

In addition, soon after that conversation the two proceeded to jam together at the Scene nightclub on June 22, 1968. Interestingly, Hendrix opted to play bass that night so he could watch Coryell's outstanding technique. Two months later, on August 27, Hendrix did record "Come On," which was issued on his third album, *Electric Ladyland*. One of Hendrix's old bandmates in the Rocking Kings, Terry Johnson, retained a memory for many years about the importance of that song—which was commonly referred to as "Come On (Let the Good Times Roll)"—to them as boys: "One of our favorite songs was 'Let The Good Times Roll'— because it had a really neat guitar part in there where Jimmy could do the lead, and I could come in and do the background. Later on I heard that song ['Come On'] on one of his albums. And I couldn't help but think it was like a tribute to when we were young kids playing that song."

In 1969, Hendrix reconnected with Ron Woods, who since leaving the Dynamics had been drumming with the Buddy Miles Express. Hendrix invited Woods to attend a recording session in New York, where they recorded a new song, "Room Full of Mirrors." Hendrix also reconnected with his former sax-playing Velvetones bandmate Luther Rabb, who'd formed a funky new band, Ballin'jack, in Seattle—a dual-horn outfit that Rabb proudly admitted was inspired by the Dave Lewis Combo. "[Jimi] had decided that he was going to produce Ballin'jack's next record," remembered Rabb. "We were going to record it at [Hendrix's own studio in New York] Electric Ladyland. We started to formulate ideas. . . . It was getting to be pretty serious business."

The old bandmates were able to catch up a bit when Ballin'jack was hired to open for Hendrix on a string of national concert dates between April and June 1970. Story goes that Hendrix thought Ballin'jack was the funkiest opening act he'd yet taken on tour, hence his offer to produce their next album. On July 26, 1970, Hendrix returned to Seattle to perform at Seattle's venerable outdoor ballpark, Sick's Stadium—the same venue where he'd seen Elvis Presley play back in 1957. The following morning, he flew to Hawaii, where his band played a concert on Maui, before returning to England. James Marshall Hendrix died in London at age twenty-seven three weeks later, on September 18, 1970. Seattle's music community came together on January 22, 1971, for a three-day Jimi Hendrix Memorial Concert tribute jam at the Eagles Auditorium. Among the thirty local groups to perform was Cameo, a funk band that included Terry Johnson (Hammond B-3 organ) and Hendrix's cousin Eddy Hall (guitar).

Although it sometimes seemed like Seattle had forgotten their own native son, Hendrix never forgot his hometown. Indeed, it was later discovered that among his personal songwriting notebooks were handwritten scribblings including the phrase "West Coast Seattle Boy"—an intriguing clue regarding Hendrix's own personal sense of identity and his view of the place where he'd first learned about music. Luther Rabb once noted, "We were isolated in Seattle. . . . We were doing things that were unique. There was a lot of jazz with a funky kind of rock thing with the guitar and bass. Seattle had the dual sax, and we used the jungle beat. . . . It was a syncopated rhythm. A cool thing because it could go with a lot of songs, and people could dance to it. . . . Rhythm here in Seattle was a heavy sound. We used to call it a 'kicking sound.' The Seattle jungle beat made people move."

Seattle musicians of Hendrix's generation and beyond knew they were following the trails that had been blazed by musical giants. Gordon

DeWitty was another Seattle kid who came up through the ranks and went on to great success. Playing his Hammond organ, he had gigged with the George Griffin Trio, the Soul Deacons, and the Living End before being recruited into Bobby Womack's band in Los Angeles in 1967 on the recommendation of the band's guitarist, Pernell Alexander.

From there DeWitty went into studio work with Earth, Wind & Fire and many other notable blues, soul, R&B, rock, and funk stars. But his Seattle roots always served him well: "When you say 'Seattle' everyone relates to Jimi Hendrix, Ray Charles or Quincy Jones, who've made great marks in the business, so it's good to be from here. . . . One of the best things about Seattle is that it's such an integrated area. Everyone's in the melting pot and they're not segregated, so it keeps your information level high, because you're exposed to more things."

This open cultural atmosphere was indeed a "secret" behind the original Northwest Sound—in essence, a melding of fairly sophisticated rude-jazz riffage spiked with garage-rock aggression. Steeped in this whole milieu, Hendrix gifted the world some uniquely beautiful songs. Moreover, he offered his hometown the ultimate compliment of sharing the music community's distinct musical roots with the whole world; his contributions to music ought to be viewed as nothing less than the finest flowering of the Northwest's rockin' R&B traditions. ★

CHAPTER 31

IN HINDSIGHT

It is difficult not to be impressed by the achievements of the Northwest's early R&B and rock 'n' roll pioneers. They created a remarkably sophisticated, jazz-tinged, instrumental-oriented, regional strain of music, which then morphed that into a delightfully crude garage-rock aesthetic that would have a long-lasting impact.

Taking a step back to get the wider picture, though, it is important to remember that while this region had enjoyed a long history of country music and urban jazz scenes, neither of those cultural realms created their own distinct regional sound. It took the emergence of the rockin' teen-R&B scene to do that.

In addition to the many players mentioned in this book, there were plenty more who contributed to the shared sense of a separate and unique world of teenage interaction. And just imagine the odds they'd faced! Young bands had to rely on novice audio engineers with their jerry-built recording studios coupled with inexperienced record companies. Yet they still managed to create music that mattered: records that resonated with the broader public; tunes that became national, and even international, radio hits; Top 40 hits; Top 10 hits; even chart-toppers; songs that have lost none of their original magic over all these decades.

Just consider the sheer number of hits that piled up for the first generation of local groups and singers. Taken as a whole, the Barons, Fleetwoods, Frantics, Bluenotes, Wailers, Gallahads, Ventures, Kingsmen, Paul Revere and the Raiders, Don and the Goodtimes, Chan Romero, Ron Holden, Mark Lindsay, and Merrilee Rush scored more than eighty legit hits throughout their recording careers. And—as we've already seen—that's only half the story, as there were additional local and regional hits by scores of other acts, including Dave Lewis, the Counts, and Tacoma's revered garage-punk pioneers, the Sonics.

Alas, all good things must come to an end, and the initial bursts of creative energy that resulted in the original rockin' R&B mode of the Northwest Sound—which persisted long enough to overlap with the subsequent Sonics-led garage-punk era of the mid-1960s—had to fade. This happened for multiple reasons, including fierce competition from a series of popular musical waves including surf, Brit, folk, and psychedelic rock.

Plenty of the top bands tried to stay relevant by adjusting their look and sound to meet the new demands, but ultimately most of them disbanded. Some players retired, while others built nonmusical careers while remaining weekend warriors gigging in taverns, lounges, or casinos. But the sad fact is that the region's once vibrant musical ecosystem was fading into the past.

By 1969, the whole industrial infrastructure of the old scene had crumbled, and most of the critical components were defunct. The once mighty teen dance circuit had shifted to high school–sponsored events. Several early studios, including Acme and Camelot, had stopped recording local bands—and why not? Regional radio had largely gone corporate and no longer saw the benefit of supporting local acts.

Not to mention that the area's most successful labels had all gone extinct, including Seafair Records, which had issued twenty-plus discs by twenty-five-plus local artists between 1956 and 1965; Dolton, which had issued more than one hundred discs by eighteen local artists between 1959 and 1967; Bolo, which had issued fifty-plus discs by twenty-five-plus local artists between 1960 and 1968; Jerden, which had issued more than one hundred records by around ninety local artists between 1960 and 1969; Etiquette, which had issued more than thirty records by nearly a dozen local artists between 1961 and 1966; and Camelot, which had issued forty-five-plus records by thirty-plus local artists between 1964 and 1967.

The old scene had surely peaked and sputtered out—but all was not lost. The last vestiges of the original Northwest Sound still existed in record collections and the hearts of veteran players. Most of them never lost their fondness for the good old days—and their fans didn't either.

The preservation-phase revival of the Northwest Sound began in 1970. That's when an all-star local band was formed by a group of highly experienced players from the old scene. Jr. Cadillac—which developed into the region's top-drawing rock 'n' roll band throughout subsequent decades—specialized in danceable oldies rock and proudly carried the torch of the Northwest Sound. They regularly played—and even recorded—such key tunes as "There Is Something on Your Mind," "Tall Cool One," "Louie Louie," and "Leavin' Here."

Jr. Cadillac was initially Buck Ormsby (ex-Bluenotes/Wailers), Jim Manolides (ex-Frantics), Bob Hosko (ex-Frantics), Andy Parypa (ex-Sonics), Ned Neltner (ex-Red Coats / Demons / Mark Five), plus, at times, Jeff Beals (ex-Kingsmen) and singers like Tiny Tony and Nancy Claire. Once established, Jr. Cadillac managed to score all the best gigs—they backed Chuck Berry at several shows and opened for other '50s icons including Bo Diddley and John Lee Hooker. The band also opened concerts by Beach Boys, the Kinks, ELO, Ten Years After, Jethro Tull, and Yes. In addition, their gigs regularly attracted touring stars who stopped by to jam. The band also penned new songs and formed their own record label (the Great Northwest Record Co.) in 1971.

The following year their guitarist and front man Ned Neltner decided that the pioneering generation of local rockers deserved a retrospective salute: "Even in '72, I felt that the distance between what had been, and what was, was so enormous. I mean, all of a sudden there were not teen dances at the Spanish Castle and Lake Hills [Roller Rink, in Bellevue] anymore. The music was moving into the taverns and bars, and a lot of the bands that had influenced all of us had disbanded. So I just thought it would be something worthwhile to do. Because even in '72 it felt like an historic idea."

The plan was to hold a big Northwest Rock 'n' Roll Revival concert at Seattle's grand Paramount Theatre. Neltner enlisted Pat O'Day to serve as emcee and got the Rainier Brewery to chip in as well. And thus it was that at 8:00 p.m. on Sunday, May 14, 1972—after a grueling, and beer-fueled, all-day rehearsal session—the biggest names in Northwest rock history reunited for a one-night blowout before a crowd of 1,400 fans. Appearing onstage were Dave Lewis, the Frantics, the Wailers (with Gail Harris), Little Bill, Tiny Tony, the Viceroys, Merrilee Rush, the Kingsmen, and, in their only reunion for the next thirty-five years, the Sonics.

Additional reunion concerts followed over subsequent decades, including the Wailers House Party (with the Wailers [Morrill, Dangle, Ormsby, Gardner, and Burk], Gail Harris, Little Bill, Jr. Cadillac, and emcee Pat O'Day at the Aquarius Tavern in 1979), the Great Northwest Rock and Roll Show (with the Wailers, Little Bill, Gail Harris, Tiny Tony, and Nancy Claire at the Place nightclub in 1980), the Best of Louie Louie show (with Richard Berry, Little Bill, Ron Holden, the Wailers, Kingsmen, Gail Harris, Nancy Claire, and Merrilee Rush at the Tacoma Dome in 1983), the Northwest Rock Reunion (with Dave Lewis, Ron Holden, Tiny Tony, Merrilee Rush, the Fleetwoods, Kingsmen, and Don and the Goodtimes (at the Seattle Center Coliseum in 1984), and the Northwest Legends concert (with Little Bill, the Wailers, Ventures, Dynamics, Viceroys, Merrilee Rush, Kingsmen, and Paul Revere and the Raiders at the grand opening of the Experience Music Project in 2000).

It was sad that the Father of Northwest Rock—Dave Lewis—had passed in back in 1998 and so was unable to see his contributions to the Northwest Sound represented in the *Northwest Passage* exhibit at Seattle's Experience Music Project. Lewis had remained active on the scene. In the early '70s, he formed a great funk group, Back-to-Back, which served as the Mardi Gras Grill's house band while also opening Paramount Theatre concerts for the likes of Earth, Wind & Fire, B.B. King, "Johnny Hammond" Smith, and Graham Central Station. In the 1980s, he'd aimed even higher, forming and conducting his funky Paramount Theater Orchestra. But the Northwest Rock Reunion, produced in '84 by the Bumbershoot Festival, would be the final time Lewis appeared with his peers and acolytes. All those reunion shows offered fans of the Northwest Sound great opportunities to reflect on what had been created here—a scene and a sound that reflected Warren Gill's notion of "local conditions" mentioned at the beginning of this book—and what was slipping away as the past continued its inexorable retreat.

Back in 1976, another of the founding fathers of the Northwest Sound already had this to say about the area's past and his hopes for the future of its legacy. "The music thing that was happening in this area at the time was totally different than anywhere else," Rich Dangel reflected. "It really was. . . . It's a different kind of music that's come out of the Northwest. It's not the same, by any means, as your standard West Coast music. Even the jazz players—they're not like in California. They're not at all like the East Coast. Same with rock 'n' roll. It's got its own quality, which I think should be accepted for what it's worth. And I think it will. It's like a tree growin'—the things that are growin' here musically eventually grow big enough to be noticed on a national level."

Or, in the belated case of the Sonics, on an international level, because that particular band's reputation—based solely on their original

'60s recordings and raving word-of-mouth testimonials—only continued to soar over the decades. So much so that, by 2007, public demand persuaded them to reunite and hit the road. The Sonics roared to life once again and embarked on a decade-plus of international touring, playing before legions of fans, old and new. Upon the release of their 2015 album *This Is the Sonics*, one critic attempted to soothe fans' fears that perhaps the old boys had gone soft over time: "Northwestern rock 'n' roll is a hardy strain. It survived the softening of early '60s pop and the eclecticism of the British Invasion, remaining purest with Tacoma's Sonics, back with their first full new album in nearly 50 years. That time span has spawned no artistic 'growth'; they're still channeling Little Richard with added crunch."

The Sonics' old mentor and original producer, Buck Ormsby, couldn't have been more pleased that the band's unique sound was still generating new fans. "I've never given up the hope and belief that people in the Pacific Northwest have another way of approaching things, that we've got our own way of creating fun, honest and exciting rock 'n' roll."

Along the way, the young Northwest musicians did create a lot of music and fun for their fans—and would later be heralded as pioneers of what became widely admired as a DIY movement. In 1980, one savvy Seattle journalist, George Arthur, tipped his hat in salute to the efforts and accomplishments of Dangel, Ormsby, and their entire generation: "What makes the Northwest scene so interesting in retrospect, apart from the powerhouse rock 'n' roll it spawned, was its unusual independence. . . . In the era which gave birth to the stereotype of the fast-talking manager manipulating naïve, teen-age rock bands, Northwest rockers managed to do it themselves."

A decade later, Dave Marsh echoed that thought: "The teenage rock bands of the Pacific Northwest built a great lost rock 'n' roll scene in those years when the Big Beat wandered in the wilderness and, not only that, without the help of a single Brit, they created one of the first great modern rock scenes, one in which spirit and community were central for both musicians and audiences."

Way back in the beginning, few folks involved in the rock 'n' roll realm dared to dream—and *nobody* could have predicted—what would come to pass. But the pioneering players had blazed a viable trail in the music biz. Then, due to the amazing creativity of many additional individuals, this region went on to earn its rock-solid reputation as an important incubator of original sounds. Dolton Records led the way, followed by Nite Owl, Seafair-Bolo, Jerden, Etiquette, Camelot, and other successful companies. The musical seeds they collectively planted blossomed in spectacular ways. Indeed, during the grunge era, Seattle's Sub Pop Records seemed to actually have achieved their founders' cheeky goal of "world domination"—helping to firmly establish the Pacific Northwest's esteemed status in rockdom. ★

NOTES

Introduction

xii   "there was, and perhaps": Hansen, "Northwest Rock Scene," 44.

xii   "The story of rock 'n' roll": Shipper, *"Explosives,"* 4.

xiii   "All over the country": Barnes, "Sonics: *Explosives*," 39–40.

xiii   "As a tried and true East Coaster": Miller, *History of Northwest Rock.*

xiii   "Not every region of the United States": Shaw, "Northwest Sound."

xiii   "In regions as disparate as Texas": Palao, "Spanish Castle Magic."

xiii   "The Pacific Northwest": Joynson, *Fuzz, Acid and Flowers*, 6.

xiv   "The *thang* in the Northwest": Chris Morris, "Seattle, 30 Years B.G. (Before Grunge)," *Los Angeles Reader*, April 8, 1994.

xiv   "Take a loud, sloppy": Shaw, "Northwest Sound."

xiv   "There's a tradition of": Morrell, *Nirvana and the Sound of Seattle*, 11.

xiv   "The biggest reason Seattle": Marsh, *Louie Louie*, 70–71.

xv   "the rhythm-and-blues-based": Gill, "Region, Agency and Popular Music," 120.

1. Alone in This City

1   "I thought that I had gone": "Seattle to Stardom."

3   "investigate all complaints": Seattle City Ordinance 44785 (Council Bill 3427). Office of the City Clerk (Seattle), March 7, 1923. http://clerk.seattle .gov/~legislativeItems/Ordinances/Ord_44785.pdf.

3   "dances given by responsible": Seattle City Ordinance 44785.

2. Stompin' at the Savoy

6   "I sneaked off with my little": Billy Tolles, interview by Paul de Barros, January 30–31, 1993, notes, in the author's possession.

7   "Frank Waldron would come": Tolles interview.

8   "I got a saxophone": Tolles interview.

8   "So, the music scene": "Seattle to Stardom."

8   "Bumps acted like a father to us": "Seattle to Stardom."

9   "I never *did* figure out": Jones, Q, 47.

10   "On the first of the week": Bumps Blackwell, interview by Roberta Penn, December 5–6, 1983, recording, in the author's possession.

10   "We'd play five nightclubs a night": Amy Wallace, "Quincy Jones Gives Us a Glimpse into the Life of a Musical Legend," *Los Angeles Magazine*, March 14, 2016, www.lamag.com.

11   "With all the good, the bad": Blackwell interview.

12   "I must tell you, I really": Charles and Ritz, *Brother Ray*, 10.

12   "I had my little trio at the Black": Jones, *Q*, 56.

12   "One evening, he asked": Ford, *Ray Charles*, 8.

13   "One night he approached me": Charles and Ritz, *Brother Ray*, 113.

13   "Ray's tone is straight": Sampson, "Maxin Trio: 'Rocking Chair Blues,'" *Spontaneous Lunacy*, March 21, 2019, www.spontaneouslunacy.net.

14   "Seattle's own blind": Lowell Fulson concert ad, *Seattle Times*, October 16, 1951.

3. Billy's Bucket of Blues

15   "When I got home from college": Tolles interview.

16   "The first band I used": Wally Nelskog, interview by Bruce Smith, undated, transcript, NWMA.

17   "That came about": Nelskog interview.

18   "I was already": Tolles interview.

18   "We kicked ass": Tolles interview.

18   "the best scat": de Barros, *Jackson Street after Hours*, 163.

18   "a jumper that defies": *Billboard*, July 4, 1942.

19   "We played riff": Tolles interview.

19   "For a long time, I was a honker": Tolles interview.

19   "When I got back": Tolles interview.

4. Rock 'n' Roll Party

23   "The music scene": Siderius, "Searching for the Sound," 4.

23   "When you get through": Frank Roberts, interview by the author, October 2, 1985, recording and transcript, Northwest Music Archives, Seattle (hereafter cited as NWMA).

23   "There's no genius": Roberts interview.

23   "I went in": Powers and Love, "Frank Roberts," 2.

23   "I remember going": Powers and Love, "Frank Roberts," 2.

24   "That's when my career": Powers and Love, "Frank Roberts," 2.

25   "In 1950, Dave and I were": Barney Hilliard, interview with the author, September 23, 2015, recording and transcript, NWMA.

25   "We put together": Dave Lewis, interview with the author, 1983, recording and transcript, NWMA.

26 "Madison Street was very": George Griffin, interview with the author, September 23, 2015, recording and transcript, NWMA.

26 "Because R&B music": Hilliard interview.

27 "The combo had played all these": Hilliard interview.

27 "decided to challenge": de Barros, *Jackson Street after Hours*, 176.

28 "He was pissed off": Tolles interview.

29 "I said, 'I've been doing this'": Tolles interview.

29 "The police didn't like": Tolles interview.

5. David's Mood

32 "acted in a disorderly manner": "Elvis Lands in Lap of City Council," *Seattle Times*, October 16, 1956.

32 "So, all the other musicians": Hilliard interview.

33 "Well, guess what he": Hilliard interview.

33 "the business side of music": Chris Ott, "Robert 'Bumps' Blackwell (1918–1985)," *Black Past*, www.blackpast.org.

34 "What was playing on the radio": Lewis interview.

34 "To me Birdland was": Griffin interview.

35 "As I recall": Hilliard interview.

35 "At that time, the Century Ballroom": Stokey Wilford, interview with the author, 1985, recording and transcript, NWMA.

37 "I was very poor": Big Jay McNeely, interview with the author, March 18, 1998, video recording, MoPOP, transcript in author's possession.

38 "We recorded our biggest hit": McNeely interview.

6. Teenage Hop

40 "I started out with": Johnny O'Francia, interview with Bruce Smith, undated, recording and transcript, NWMA.

41 "When I first started getting": Rolen "Ron" Holden, interview with the author, September 19, 1985, recording and transcript, NWMA.

41 "We were getting most": Andy Duvall, interview with Bruce Smith, undated, recording and transcript, NWMA.

42 "You guys aren't gonna play": Ron Peterson interview with the author, 1984, recording and transcript, NWMA.

43 "We leaned more towards": O'Francia interview.

43 "Right after we started": Duvall interview.

44 "The Frantics joined": Duvall interview.

7. "Louie Louie" Arrives

46 "It was a Black and white": Little Bill Engelhart, interview with Bruce Smith, undated, recording and transcript, NWMA.

47 "Theo's sister (and Jimmy's girlfriend)": Engelhart, *So Anyway*, 20.

47 "By all logic": Eliot, *Rockonomics*, 54.

48 "That was where the cop": Lassie Aanes, interview with Bruce Smith, undated, recording and transcript, NWMA.

49 "So Robin—being real": Little Bill Engelhart, interview with the author, 1983, recording and transcript, NWMA.

49 "Normally everything": Engelhart, *So Anyway*, 30.

50 "We were green": Engelhart interview with Smith.

50 "We beat the tap dancer": Engelhart interview with Smith.

50 "Hello, this is Bill": Engelhart, *Next Stop*, 22.

8. The Evergreen

53 "It was the greatest": Engelhart interview with the author.

53 "Those Sunday nights": Engelhart, *So Anyway*, 27.

53 "We'd go out": Wright and Wright, "The Wailers," 38.

53 "So, are you a musician?": Engelhart interview with the author.

54 "I was so nervy": Engelhart interview with the author.

54 "The place'd be full": Aanes interview.

55 "One of the groups": Engelhart interview with Smith.

55 "Thrill Jive Addicts": undated newspaper clipping, NWMA.

9. Wailers House Party

58 "I just had": Rich Dangel, interview with the author, 1988, recording and transcript, NWMA.

58 "The Blue Notes were": Tom Geving, interview with Bruce Smith, undated, recording and transcript, NWMA.

59 "The three saxes": Dick Stewart, "Up Close with Buck Ormsby," *Lance Monthly*, August 27, 2005.

59 "The Blue Notes played": Engelhart interview with Smith.

59 "The Wailers were giving": Engelhart interview with the author.

60 "It just got": Buck Mann, interview with Bruce Smith, undated, recording and transcript, NWMA.

60 "The City Council": Engelhart interview with the author.

60 "And so, of *course*": Engelhart interview with the author.

61 "started printing up": Eric Lacitis, "Northwest Rock: A History," *Seattle Post-Intelligencer*, July 29–September 2, 1984 (six-part series).

61   "only sour note": Katherine Hunt, "Tacoma's Rock 'n' Roll 'Wailers' in National Recording Spotlight," *Tacoma Sunday News*, May 3, 1959.

62   "They finally . . . barred the Wailers": Rich Dangel, interview with Mike Feeney, March 25, 1976, KUID-FM, University of Idaho.

62   "There'd be a thousand": Dangel interview with the author.

62   "Hey everybody": Engelhart interview with Smith.

62   "My house was full": Tomashefsky, "Fabulous Wailers," 8–9.

63   "Rock 'n' roll is just catching on": Hunt, "Tacoma's Rock 'n' Roll 'Wailers.'"

63   "There were definite lines": Holden interview.

10. Straight Flush

64   "if balance is not paid in full": document in John Greek's personal collection.

66   "Gretchen and I": Gary Troxel, interview with author, 1985, recording and transcript, NWMA.

66   "I was singing lead": Bristol, "Gretchen Christopher," 10.

67   "Gretchen had this tape": Bob Reisdorff, interview with the author, 1985, recording and transcript, NWMA.

68   "How about . . . oh": Reisdorff interview.

70   "He put the son of a bitch": Jim Manolides, interview with the author, 1984, recording and transcript, NWMA.

70   "*Seattle Bandstand*": undated newspaper clipping, NWMA.

11. Tough Bounce

73   "The Blue Notes were basically": Engelhart interview with the author.

74   "So, we did it": Engelhart interview with the author.

74   "He says, 'Man!'": Aanes interview.

74   "He said, 'Everybody sit down'": Engelhart interview with the author.

74   "The song stayed pretty": Geving interview.

74   "So, Bob Reisdorff": Engelhart interview with the author.

75   "Well, so Joe": Reisdorff interview.

76   "When I told him": Engelhart, *Next Stop*, 105.

76   "There was a lot of": Engelhart interview with the author.

77   "No. Robin's too crazy": Engelhart interview with the author.

77   "He says, 'How do'": Engelhart interview with the author.

78   "Bill had a record": Frank Dutra, interview with Bruce Smith, undated, recording and transcript, NWMA.

78   "The Wailers serve up": undated clipping in John Greek's personal collection.

78   "I am speaking": Barbara Henifin, "Likes 'Bluenotes,'" *Tacoma News Tri-bune*, undated newspaper clipping, NWMA.

80   "They said, 'OK'": Dangel interview with the author.

81   "'So, . . . everybody goes'": Dangel interview with the author.

81   "from day one": Eric Lacitis, "Northwest Rock: A History Part 2—The Wailers," *Seattle Times/Seattle Post-Intelligencer*, August 5, 1984.

81   "primeval Jazz-rock": Hansen, "Northwest Rock Scene," 44.

82   "The Wailers' hit": Hansen, "Northwest Rock Scene," 44.

12. Mr. Blue

83   "At that time": Kearney Barton, interview with the author, 1983, recording and transcript, NWMA. NWMA.

85   "Liberty was the label": Jerry Dennon, interview with the author, December 3, 1988, recording and transcript, NWMA.

85   "We had some wonderful": Dennon interview.

13. Radio DJs and Teen Dances

89   "In 1958, . . . I was with KJR": "Big Daddy" Dave Clark, interview with Bruce Smith, undated, recording and transcript, NWMA.

89   "I think that records": Clark interview.

90   "I went to the people": Clark interview.

90   "Then he looks at Joe": Tom Ogilvy, interview with Bruce Smith, undated, transcript, NWMA.

92   "raucous rock 'n' roll": Pat O'Day, interview with the author, 1988, recording and transcript, NWMA.

92   "the listening public": O'Day interview.

14. Blowing the Blues

94   "That town will eat": Pat Mason, interview with the author, 1985, recording and transcript, NWMA.

95   "I had a small rock band": Robert "Chan" Romero, interview with the author, August 1987, recording and transcript, NWMA.

96   "sparked off the entire movement": Finnis, *Those Oldies but Goodies*.

97   "We started throwing": Duvall interview.

97   "I was singing": Holden interview.

98   "Kearney was doing": Andy Duvall, interview with Bruce Smith, undated, recording and transcript, NWMA.

99   "The guy had": Duvall interview.

100 "We got the call": Anthony "Tiny Tony" Smith, interview with the author, September 5, 1984, recording and transcript, NWMA.

100   "We were on our *own*": Anthony Smith interview.

101   "It was perfect for me": Holden interview.

101   "He says, 'I've got'": Holden interview.

102   "Then in 1961": Jimmy Pipkin, interview with the author, February 5, 1988, recording and transcript, NWMA.

15. Cookies and Coke

104   "It was *rough*": Eric Lacitis, "The Ventures Finally Arrive at the Rock and Roll Hall of Fame," *Seattle Times*, March 10, 2008.

105   "We went to Skip Moore": Don Wilson, interview with the author, circa 1985, recording and transcript, NWMA.

105   "Reisdorff had already": Wilson interview.

105   "My head was so": Dennon interview.

105   "We put it on": O'Day interview.

106   "When Reisdorff called": Wilson interview.

106   "And so, . . . Reisdorff sent it down": Wilson interview.

106   "We went to New York": Bob Bogle, interview with the author, 1988, recording and transcript, NWMA.

107   "The year 1959": Shaw, "Instrumental Groups," 104.

108   "Jim Hammer somehow": Eldon Butler, interview with the author, circa 1980s, recording and transcript, NWMA.

110   "You know, I've seen Dave Lewis": Anthony Smith interview.

110   "too R&B": Ogilvy interview.

111   "We couldn't get the group": Jimmy Hanna, interview with Bruce Smith, undated, recording and transcript, NWMA.

16. I'll Go Crazy

112   "At the end": Dangel, interview with the author, January 24, 1987, recording and transcript, NWMA.

112   "I think he felt": Engelhart interview with the author.

112   "All I can say": Ormsby interview.

113   "He was a very": Kent Morrill, interview with the author, 1988, recording and transcript, NWMA.

113   "I talked to Pat O'Day": Engelhart interview with the author.

113   "'Jockey' John Stone was": O'Day interview.

114   "he *forgot* to pay": O'Day interview.

114   "Let me tell you how much": Joe Johansen, interview with the author, May 15, 1997, recording and transcript, NWMA.

115   "I just always thought": Johansen interview.

115   "I met them at a dance": Nancy Claire, interview with the author, August 7, 1985, recording and transcript, NWMA.

115   "It was Robin": Morrill interview.

115   "Now, the main controversy": John Greek, interview with the author, April 28, 1988, recording and transcript, NWMA.

116   "There was a hardcore thing": Greek interview.

117   "They never got it": George Arthur, "When Rock Rolled Over, the Northwest Kept the Beat," *Seattle Post-Intelligencer*, May 9, 1980.

117   "Everybody in the Northwest": Dangel interview with Feeney.

118   "Topaz had a producer": Engelhart interview with the author.

119   "He was doing certain": Dangel interview with Feeney.

119   "When I saw the Wailers": Jimmy Hanna, interview with the author, 1985, recording and transcript, NWMA.

119   "Fine Blues vocal": undated clipping in John Greek's personal collection.

119   "'Louie Louie' was a song": O'Day interview.

120   "I flew down there *twice*": O'Day interview.

120   "It didn't sound": O'Day interview.

120   "In 1961 I was": Dennon interview.

120   "So the Wailers'": O'Day interview.

17. Like, Long Hair

122   "I had been playing by ear": Doege, *Paul Revere and the Raiders*, 10.

123   "I remember . . . traveling": Skok, "Fabulous Wailers," 6.

123   "We'd rock in the key": Doege, *Paul Revere and the Raiders*, 10.

124   "Covered in flour": "Mark Lindsay (Former Lead Singer of Paul Revere and the Raiders)," Flower Power Cruise, n.d., www.flowerpowercruise.com.

124   "I remember Paul bringing Mark": Doege, *Paul Revere and the Raiders*, 11.

124   "If you ever let Lindsay": "Mark Lindsay."

124   "The Wailers' 'Tall Cool One'": Dominic Priore, "The Tall Cool Tale of Paul Revere and the Raiders: A Conversation with Mark Lindsay and Paul Revere," Sundazed, March 24, 2011, www.sundazed.com.

125   "It wasn't actually": Paul Revere, interview with the author, 1988, recording and transcript, NWMA.

125   "He gave us checks": Doege, *Paul Revere and the Raiders*, 12.

125   "Someone had": Revere interview.

125   "How about Paul Revere": Revere interview.

126   "That's *me* on the *radio!*": Doege, *Paul Revere and the Raiders*, 13.

126   "I actually was inspired": Revere interview.

127 "When he got drafted": Rob LeDonne, "Paul Revere and the Raiders' Mark Lindsay on Meeting Charles Manson, What He Thinks about Tarantino's Film," *Billboard*, August 1, 2019, www.billboard.com.

127 "When I got out": Doege, *Paul Revere and the Raiders*, 15.

18. Swingin' Summer

129 "He sounded just": Mike Mandel, interview with the author, August 20, 1984, recording and transcript, NWMA.

129 "And . . . these guys said": Mandel interview.

130 "a country boy": Elwood, "Larry Coryell," 15.

130 "I was never more": Elwood, "Larry Coryell," 15.

130 "it was the thrill": Larry Coryell, interview with the author, 1984, recording and transcript, NWMA.

130 "The two main": Mike Metko, interview with the author, August 1984, recording and transcript, NWMA.

131 "We *kidnapped* Larry": Mandel interview.

132 "An agent named": Mandel interview.

132 "I remember riding": Mandel interview.

19. The Girl Can't Help It

134 "I remember one time": Ormsby interview.

135 "We were inspired": Dangel interview with the author.

135 "I started singing": Palao, "Spanish Castle Magic," 4.

135 "She was this": Dangel interview with the author.

136 "The Wailers were the band": Mike Mitchell, interview with the author, 1983, recording and transcript, NWMA.

136 "I saw the Frantics": Neil Rush, interview with the author, 1988, recording and transcript, NWMA.

137 "Lynn Vrooman brought": Rush interview.

137 "the Aztecs ground": Rush interview.

137 "We basically had": Merrilee Gunst, interview with the author, March 1987, recording and transcript, NWMA.

138 "At 10:30 that night": Rush interview.

138 "Tony got thrown": Rush interview.

140 "The next thing": Palao, "Spanish Castle Magic," 14.

20. Jimmy's Blues

142 "I was upstairs while the grownups": *Rolling Stone*.

142 "I ran away from home": James, "Wild, Man!"

142 "School wasn't for me": Brown, *Jimi Hendrix*, 21.

143 "We had one room there": Al Hendrix, interview with the author, 1983, video recording, MoPOP, transcript in author's possession.

143 "We were friends": Pernell Alexander, interview with the author, 1983, recording and transcript, NWMA.

143 "My dad danced": Welch, *Hendrix*, 15.

143 "I learned all the riffs": Hendrix, *Starting at Zero*, 20.

143 "The *Grand Ole Opry* used to": Joe Bosso, "Rare Jimi Hendrix Interview: Songwriting, Dylan, Guitar Destruction," *Music Radar*, September 24, 2012, www.musicradar.com.

144 "I learned to play on a guitar": *Beat Instrumental*.

144 "He played the blues": Alexander interview.

145 "I came out to Seattle": Mark Dalton, "L. V. Parr Interview," *Jet City Blues* (blog), October 8, 2005, www.jetcityblues.blogspot.com.

145 "Jimmy Hendrix used to": Dalton, "L. V. Parr Interview."

146 "One of the songs we'd": Willix, *Jimi Hendrix*, 16.

146 "we'd sneak in": Willix, *Jimi Hendrix*, 64.

146 "I formed this group": Brown, *Jimi Hendrix*, 20.

146 "I got a few dollars ahead": Hopkins, *Hit and Run*, 29.

146 "Jimmy and I both started": Alexander interview.

147 "My father was a preacher": Willix, *Jimi Hendrix*, 68.

147 "Oh, *primitive* wasn't the word": Alexander interview.

147 "I remember my first gig": *Melody Maker*.

147 "Well, it was so very hard": *Melody Maker*.

148 "We started messing 'round": Joe Gray, interview with the author, 1983, transcript, NWMA.

148 "My brother Jimmy": Holden interview.

148 "Butch Snipes: he's the one": Alexander interview.

149 "At first we were hesitant": Willix, *Jimi Hendrix*, 76–77.

150 "I *know* how good he was": Terry Johnson, interview with the author, 1993, recording and transcript, NWMA.

150 "We all knew Jimmy was good": Willix, *Jimi Hendrix*, 91.

150 "He used to come into the Carpenters Hall": Holden interview.

151 "Jimmy used to come to Birdland": Lewis interview.

151 "The Dynamics turned him down": Ron Woods, interview with the author, 1983, recording and transcript, NWMA.

152 "There was this disc jockey": Roby, *Black Gold*, 10–11.

21. Doin' the Birdland

154 "It was the *Dave Lewis* sound": Johansen interview.

154 "Dave Lewis was our model": Willix, *Jimi Hendrix*, 44.

154 "back in those days": Butler interview.

155 "I know I have a gift": Willix, *Jimi Hendrix*, 44.

155 "The Dave Lewis Combo": Willix, *Jimi Hendrix*, 73.

155 "I remember playing Birdland": Butler interview.

156 "The first week I arrived": Coryell interview.

156 "It was all African Americans": Gillingham, "Conversation with Larry Coryell," 4.

157 "The first time I saw Dave": Gillingham, "Conversation with Larry Coryell," 4.

157 "And that was so": Claire interview.

158 "Because I only": Lewis interview.

160 "I used to go there to see Dave": Gordy Lockhard, interview with the author, 2004, recording and transcript, NWMA.

160 "We used to go down": Terry Afdem, interview with the author, 1984, recording and transcript, NWMA.

160 "quite possibly [the] finest": Hansen, "Northwest Rock Scene," 45.

160 "We were excited about it": Afdem interview.

161 "It was a hip": Gillingham, "Conversation with Larry Coryell," 4.

161 "We were an all-white": Lockhard interview.

161 "That was a great period": Don Stevenson, interview with the author, 1984, recording and transcript, NWMA.

162 "In those days there was a lot": Heather MacIntosh, "Dave Holden: On Race and Music in Seattle, 1956–1966," HistoryLink, May 25, 2000, www .historylink.org.

162 "We were up onstage": Lockhard interview.

22. The World's Fair Twist

165 "Will you be sure": Lt. D. W. Jessup to Capt. L. J. La Pointe, memo, August 20, 1962, accession 420-001, box 5, Ewen C. Dingwall, Operations and Services Correspondence, Washington State Archives.

165 "who are fully": L. H. Newman, Louis V. Larsen, letter, July 27, 1962, box 272, folder 9-1-25: Saturday Night Teenage Dances, Century 21 Exposition, Special Events Division, General Subject Files, Special Events, Washington State Archives.

166 "When we were finished": O'Day interview.

167 "There *was* a Seattle Northwest": Ron Gardner, interview with Mike Feeney, March 21, 1976, KUID-FM, University of Idaho.

167 "People like Rich Dangel": Hanna interview with Smith.

168 "As we were driving": Dangel interview with the author.

169   "We were no big deal": Jim Valley, interview with the author, 1984, recording and transcript, NWMA.

169   "It went 'badababa'": Valley interview.

23. The O'Day Empire

172   "The number of dances": O'Day interview.

174   "Pat and I made": Curtis, "Me, Myself, and I."

174   "We went on to produce": Curtis , "Me, Myself, and I."

176   "There's a new sound coming": Dave Lewis, interview with the author, April 12, 1989, recording and transcript, NWMA.

177   "He played differently": Doug Clark, "Guitarist Takes Final Bow on Good Note," *Spokesman-Review*, June 10, 1997.

177   "the impact of the album": Larry Coryell, "Why Did the Northwest Have a Different Sound?," *UW Daily*, November 10, 1964.

24. Doin' the Seaside

179   "So, he showed up": Jack Ely, interview with the author, 1989, recording and transcript, NWMA.

180   "They were big stars": Mike Mitchell, interview with the author, 1997, recording and transcript, NWMA.

180   "The way it started": Don Gallucci, interview with the author, January 16, 2021, recording and transcript, NWMA.

180   "I started teaching them": Gallucci interview.

181   "What happened in those days": Mitchell interview.

181   "So, we were playing": Mike "Smitty" Smith, interview with the author, 1989, recording, NWMA.

182   "I had a set of drums": Mike Smith interview.

182   "I made a deal with myself": LeDonne, "Paul Revere and the Raiders' Mark Lindsay on Meeting Charles Manson, What He Thinks about Tarantino's Film."

182   "We were unlike any group": Doege, *Paul Revere and the Raiders*, 16.

183   "Police moved in to quell": "Seaside Still Holds Memories of Riots," *Eugene Register-Guard*, September 7, 1987.

184   "In another 30 minutes": Richard Field, "Music Soothes Beach Riot," *The Oregonian*, September 3, 1962.

25. A Tale of Two Louies

185   "Bop City": Ely interview.

186   "'Louie Louie' . . . is a testament": Tom Breihan, "The Number Ones Bonus Tracks: The Kingsmen's 'Louie Louie,'" *Stereogum*, November 17, 2020, www.stereogum.com.

186   "The first time I heard 'Louie Louie'": Revere interview.

187   "It took about two minutes": Revere interview.

187   "The first local group": Roger Hart, interview with the author, 2001, recording, NWMA.

188   "By this time we were the": Ely interview.

188   "So, we get down there": Ely interview.

189   "Ken sat in the": Ely interview.

189   "The first time we heard": Gallucci interview.

189   "We could see": Ely interview.

189   "Well, . . . first we said": Gallucci interview.

189   "So we thought": Ely interview.

190   "That sloppiness": Breihan, "Number Ones Bonus Tracks."

190   "the song mutated": Peter Jönsson, *Pop Diggers*, October 24, 2018, www.popdiggers.com.

190   "Each new version": Breihan, "Number Ones Bonus Tracks."

190   "One night, . . . Roger Hart noticed": Revere interview.

191   "Obviously, I wanted Ken": Dennon interview.

191   "So, about two weeks": Ely interview.

193   "The Ventures, of course, were": Don Ciccone, "'We Were More the American Stones Than the American Beatles . . .': An Interview with Paul Revere and the Raiders' Mark Lindsay," *Stereo Embers*, n.d., www.stereoembersmagazine.com.

193   "bunch of white-bread kids": Dominic Priore, "The Tall Cool Tale of Paul Revere and the Raiders: A Conversation with Mark Lindsay and Paul Revere," Sundazed, March 24, 2011, www.sundazed.com.

194   "So, . . . the name": Ely interview.

195   "How we broke the record": Dennon interview.

195   "They were getting": Dennon interview.

196   "The Raiders *did* beat us": Dennon interview.

196   "Columbia *blew* it": Revere interview.

196   "Sometime in November": Ely interview.

196   "So, what happened was": Gallucci interview.

197   "There has been some": William Sanderson, "Portland's 'Kingsmen' Score with R-B Record," *Oregonian*, December 11, 1963.

197   "I remember driving into": Gallucci interview.

198   "You *bet* I'll do it!": Barry Curtis, interview with the author, September 28, 1983, recording and transcript, NWMA.

198   "The Northwest Sound had never": Barry Curtis, interview with Mike Feeney, March 26, 1976, KUID-FM, University of Idaho.

198   "They had ten big rock stars": Doege, *Paul Revere and the Raiders*, 23–24.

199   "Mainly it was rumors": Clark, liner notes.

199   "indistinct but plain": "Ind. Gov. Hears 'Obscene' Words on Record," *Seattle Post-Intelligencer*, January 15, 1964.

200   "'Louic Louie.' That's the": Jancik, "Scepter-Wand Records," 11.

200   "As a matter of fact": Sara Hottman, "The Kingsmen's Infamously Innocent 'Louie, Louie' Back in Front of the Feds at Downtown Federal Building," *The Oregonian*, July 25, 2013, www.oregonlive.com.

201   "was so basic": Hopkins, *Rock Story*, 74.

201   "I would love to say": "Laying Down 'Louie, Louie,'" 93.

26. Here They Come

203   "In 1964, the British": Hart, liner notes.

203   "Paul Revere began a modern": Murphy, liner notes.

204   "Paul . . . and the colonially clad": Anonymous, liner notes.

27. The Soul of the Northwest

206   "I was the organ player": Curtis interview with Feeney.

206   "We were basically influenced": Vorda, "The Kingsmen," 32.

206   "I think we were": Dick Peterson, interview with Bruce Smith, undated, recording and transcript, NWMA.

206   "Well, Hammond organs": Curtis interview with Feeney.

206   "at one time there were": Engelhart interview with Smith.

208   "*way* too R&B": Dan Olason, interview with the author, 1984, recording and transcript, NWMA.

209   "If you ever": Valley interview.

209   "By early 1963": Terry Afdem, interview with Bruce Smith, undated, recording and transcript, NWMA.

209   "I was having a hard": Coryell interview.

210   "The bands I worked with": Leonard Feather, "Jazz, Rock Differences Escalate," *Los Angeles Times*, January 28, 1968.

210   "When Larry left": Hanna interview with Smith.

211   "I'd started out in jazz": Don McKinney, interview with Bruce Smith, undated, recording and transcript, NWMA.

211   "We decided that we": Dave Childs, interview with Bruce Smith, undated, recording and transcript, NWMA.

212   "A couple of times": Gallucci interview.

212   "It was a mixture": Ron Overman, interview with Bruce Smith, undated, recording and transcript, NWMA.

213   "the Kingsmen claimed": Gallucci interview.

213   "I can't tell you": "Courtmen vs. Kingsmen," 1.

213 "They come from": "Jack Ely and the Courtmen," press release, n.d., Connie De Nave Public Relations, New York, www.ebay.com.

214 "I was the bass": Ely interview.

28. Here Are the Sonics

215 "I was thrilled to watch": Andy Parypa, email message to the Daily Flash Facebook page, November 3, 2020.

216 "They were all": Parypa email message to the Daily Flash Facebook page.

216 "I honestly thought": Larry Parypa, interview with Mike Feeney, March 21, 1976, KUID-FM, University of Idaho.

216 "I pretty much learned": Andy Parypa, interview with the author, 1987, recording and transcript, NWMA.

216 "We were getting more of a meaner": Larry Parypa, interview with Bruce Smith, undated, transcript, NWMA.

217 "Before I got in": Gerry Roslie, interview with Bruce Smith, undated, transcript, NWMA.

217 "My first job with the Sonics": Rob Lind, interview with Bruce Smith, undated, transcript, NWMA.

217 "When we would play there": Andy Parypa, email message to Pacific Northwest Bands, May 2001, www.pnwbands.com.

219 "Years later O'Day": Parypa interview with the author.

219 "If our records sound distorted": Eric Lacitis, "Northwest Rock: A History," *Seattle Post-Intelligencer*, July 29–September 2, 1984 (six-part series).

219 "That's when we really started": Parypa interview with Smith.

220 "I never suffered": Parypa interview with the author.

221 "They had a lot of offers to sell": Parypa interview with Feeney.

29. The Northwest Sound

224 "How do Paul Revere": *KRLA Beat*.

224 "Now here you got": Shipper, "*Explosives*," 4.

225 "Rip-snorting, gut clenching": Shipper, "*Explosives*," 1.

225 "I'll let you know": Valley interview.

227 "creepy tentacles of commercialism": Ricky Riccardi, "Not a Wonderful World: Why Louie Armstrong Was Hated by So Many," *The Guardian*, December 17, 2020, www.theguardian.com.

228 "Paul Revere and the Raiders appeared": Carducci, *Rock and the Pop Narcotic*, 189.

228 "Paul himself was clearly": Clark, liner notes.

228 "Though undeniably marketed": Margaret Moser, "Paul Revere & the Raiders Featuring Mark Lindsay," *Austin Chronicle*, May 14, 2010, www.austinchronicle.com.

230 "The Northwest should have": Overman interview.

231 "They were a Manhattan": Curtis interview with Mike Feeney.

231 "The new Wailers": Hansen, "Northwest Rock Scene," 51.

232 "To be popular": Marty Loken, "Teen-Gauge: What Ingredients Are Necessary to Make Today's Hit Recording?," *Seattle Times*, March 25, 1967.

232 "If a band is going": Loken, "Teen-Gauge."

232 "Tonight's presentation of local Blues": Larry Coryell, "Why Did the Northwest Have a Different Sound?," *UW Daily*, November 10, 1964.

233 "The 'Northwest Sound'?": Engelhart interview with Smith.

30. West Coast Seattle Boy

234 "One morning I found": Brown, *Jimi Hendrix*, 25.

235 "Once you know": Marsh, *Louie Louie*, 151.

236 "We talked about the Wailers": O'Day interview.

236 "gave us his": Dan Bonow, interview with the author, circa 1990s, recording, NWMA.

236 "I had such a low": Coryell interview.

237 "young messiah": Elwood, "Larry Coryell," 15.

237 "Coryell was a revelation": Christgau, *Any Old Way You Choose It*, 64.

237 "Patriarch of Prog . . . Father of Fusion": Marshall, "Larry Coryell," 60.

237 "I came to his hotel": Coryell interview.

237 "One of our favorite songs": Willix, *Jimi Hendrix*, 17.

238 "[Jimi] had decided that he": Willix, *Jimi Hendrix*, 71.

238 "We were isolated in Seattle": Willix, *Jimi Hendrix*, 46.

239 "When you say 'Seattle'": Patrick MacDonald, "Singer, Songwriter, Producer DeWitty Isn't Famous—Yet," *Seattle Times*, March 23, 1984.

31. In Hindsight

242 "Even in '72": Ned Neltner, interview with the author, May 1, 2012, recording and transcript, NWMA.

243 "The music thing": Dangel interview with Feeney.

244 "Northwestern rock 'n' roll": Barnes, "Sonics: *Explosives*," 39–40.

244 "I've never given up": George Arthur, "When Rock Rolled Over, the Northwest Kept the Beat," *Seattle Post-Intelligencer*, May 9, 1980.

244 "What makes the Northwest": Arthur. "When Rock Rolled Over."

244 "The teenage rock bands": Marsh, *Louie Louie*, 60.

SOURCES

Anonymous. Paul Revere and the Raiders, *Midnight Ride*. Liner notes. Released May 1966. Columbia Records, LP.

Barnes, Ken. "The Sonics: *Explosives*." LP review. *Fusion Magazine*, July 1973.

Beat Instrumental, March 1967.

Billboard, July 4, 1942; March 1963.

Bristol, Mark. "Gretchen Christopher of the Fleetwoods." *Blue Suede News*, Fall 1993.

Brown, Tony. *Jimi Hendrix: A Visual Documentary*. London: Omnibus Press, 1992.

Carducci, Joe. *Rock and the Pop Narcotic*. Chicago: Redoubt Press, 1990.

Charles, Ray, and David Ritz. *Brother Ray: Ray Charles' Own Story*. New York: Warner Books, 1978.

Christgau, Robert. *Any Old Way You Choose It*. New York: Penguin, 1973.

Clark, Dick. Paul Revere and the Raiders, *Just Like Us!* Liner notes. Released 1965. Columbia Records, LP.

"Courtmen vs. Kingsmen: What's in a Name?" *The Beat*, April 30, 1966.

Curtis, Dick. "Me, Myself, and I: We're on the Road Again! A Dick Curtis Memoir." Self-published, 2006.

de Barros, Paul. *Jackson Street after Hours: The Roots of Jazz in Seattle*. Seattle: Sasquatch Books, 1993.

Doege, Claudia M. *Paul Revere and the Raiders: History ReBeats Itself*. Reno, NV: Dia Press, 1985.

Eliot, Marc. *Rockonomics*. New York: Franklin Watts, 1989.

Elwood, Phillip. "Larry Coryell." *Rolling Stone*, May 17, 1969.

Engelhart, Little Bill. *Next Stop: Bakersfield*. Rochester, WA: Graham Printing, 1999.

Engelhart, Little Bill. *So Anyway . . .* Montlake Terrace, WA: Bill Engelhart, 2005.

Feeney, Mike. Miscellaneous musician interviews produced for an unrealized 1976 radio special at KUID-FM, University of Idaho.

Finnis, Rob. *Those Oldies but Goodies*. Liner notes. Compilation released 1982. Ace Records, LP.

Ford, Carin T. *Ray Charles: I Was Born with Music inside Me*. Berkeley Heights, NJ: Enslow Publishers, 2007.

Fricke, David. Paul Revere and the Raiders, *Mojo Workout!* Liner notes. Compilation released 2000. Sundazed Music, CD.

Gill, Warren. "Region, Agency and Popular Music: The Northwest Sound, 1958–1966." *Canadian Geographer* 37, no. 2 (Summer 1993).

Gillingham, Paul. "A Conversation with Larry Coryell." *Journal of Northwest Music* 1, no. 1 (April 1992).

Hansen, Barret. "The Northwest Rock Scene." *Hit Parader*, August 1968.

Hart, Roger. Paul Revere and the Raiders, *Here They Come*. Liner notes. Released 1965. Columbia Records, LP.

Hendrix, Jimi. *Starting at Zero: His Own Story*. Edited by Peter Neal. New York: Bloomsbury, 2014.

Hopkins, Jerry. *Hit and Run: The Jimi Hendrix Story*. New York: Perigee, 1983.

Hopkins, Jerry. *The Rock Story*. New York: Signet, 1970.

James, Dawn. "Wild, Man!" *Rave*, August 1967.

Jancik, Wayne. "Scepter-Wand Records." *Goldmine*, August 21, 1992.

Jones, Quincy. *Q: The Autobiography of Quincy Jones*. New York: Harlem Moon / Broadway Books, 2002.

Joynson, Vernon. *Fuzz, Acid and Flowers*. Telford, UK: Borderline Productions, 1993.

KRLA Beat, December 1965.

"Laying Down 'Louie, Louie.'" *Rolling Stone*, June 24, 2004.

Marsh, Dave. *Louie Louie: The History and Mythology of the World's Most Famous Rock 'n' Roll Song*. New York: Hyperion, 1993.

Marshall, Wolf. "Larry Coryell: Patriarch of Prog, Father of Fusion." *Vintage Guitar*, June 2017.

Melody Maker, February 2, 1969.

Miller, Billy. *The History of Northwest Rock Volume 1*. Liner notes. Compilation released 1976. Great Northwest Music Company, LP.

Morrell, Brad. *Nirvana and the Sound of Seattle*. London: Omnibus Press, 1993.

Museum of Pop Culture (MoPOP), Seattle.

Murphy, Tom. Paul Revere and the Raiders, *In the Beginning*. Liner notes. Released 1966. Jerden Records, LP.

Northwest Music Archives (NWMA), Seattle.

Palao, Alec. "Spanish Castle Magic." The Fabulous Wailers, *At the Castle / & Co.* Liner notes. Compilation released 2003. Big Beat Records, CD.

Potash, Chris. *The Hendrix Companion*. New York: Schirmer Books, 1996.

Powers, Julie, and Shannon Love. "Frank Roberts: The Incredible Wildman on Saxophone." *Real Blues*, December 1999.

Roby, Steven. *Black Gold: The Lost Archives of Jimi Hendrix*. New York: Billboard Books, 2002.

Rolling Stone, March 1968.

"Seattle to Stardom: Quincy, Ernestine & Ray." *PM Northwest*, KOMO-TV, 1983.

Shaw, Greg. "The Instrumental Groups." In *The Rolling Stone Illustrated History of Rock and Roll*, edited by Jim Miller. New York: Random House, 1976.

Shaw, Greg. "The Northwest Sound." *Highs in the Mid Sixties Volume 7: The North-West*. Liner notes. Compilation released 1984. Archive International Productions, LP.

Shipper, Mark. "*Explosives*: The Sonics." LP review. *RPM*, June 1973.

Shipper, Mark. "Five Great Musicians!! Three Great Chords!!" The Sonics, *Explosives*. Liner notes. Compilation released 1974. BuckShot Records, LP.

Siderius, Charles. "Searching for the Sound: Saxophonist Frank Roberts Rocks the Blues." *Applause*, May 1992.

Skok, Neal. "The Fabulous Wailers." *Cryptic Tymes*, December 1987.

Tomashefsky, Michael. "The Fabulous Wailers: A Bridge Too Far." *Blue Suede News*, Spring 1998.

Vorda, Alan. "The Kingsmen." *DISCoveries*, April 1990.

Washington State Archives, Puget Sound Branch, Bellevue.

Welch, Chris. *Hendrix: A Biography*. New York: Flash Books, 1973.

Willix, Mary. *Jimi Hendrix: Voices from Home*. San Diego: Creative Forces Publishing, 1995.

Wright, Alan, and Lisa Wright. "The Wailers," *Cryptic Tymes*, Spring 1994.

INDEX

Louie," 195–97; pop chart, 67; R&B chart, 36, 39, 69; "Steppin' Out," 224, 226, 229; "Tall Cool One," 73, 215; "Walk—Don't Run," 106–7

Birdland (club), 26, 155, 161–62; audience, 34–35; Boss Four, 208; Dave Lewis Band, 32, 35, 41, 96–97, 148, 150, 156, 159, 208; "Doin' the Birdland," 160–61; grand opening show, 24; and Jimi Hendrix, 144–45, 151, 152; influence of, 41, 111, 146, 148, 154–56, 159–60, 165; and *Live at Birdland*, 39

Black and Tan (club), 4, 9, 12, 145

Blackwell, Charlie, 5–6

Blackwell, Robert A. "Bumps," xi, 2, 8, 10, 11, 12, 15, 20–21, 23, 33, 37

Blanchet High School, 108

Bland, Bobby "Blue," 31, 33, 52, 54, 59, 115, 135, 145–46

Blue Comets (band), 66–67

Blue Horizon Records, 104–5, 107

blue laws, 8

Blue Notes (band), 45–47, 53–54, 55, 58; and Battle of the Bands, 62, 63; held dances, 49, and "Louie Louie," 51; name change to Bluenotes, 75; ousted from Tacoma, 60–61; and recording, 72–74; sound of, 59, in talent show, 50

Bluenotes (band), 76, 78, 89–90; name change from Blue Notes, 75, 79

"Blue Saturday" (Bowen), 132–33

blues scene, 206, 237

Bobby Stevens and the Checkmates (band), 165

Bobby Taylor and the Vancouvers (band), 235

Bobrow, Norm, 67

Bogle, Bob, 103, 105–7

Boles, Joe, 38, 75, 83, 90–91, 218; and the Amazing Aztecs, 136; and the Checkers, 130–32; and the Continentals, 108–9; and the Dave Lewis Trio, 175; death of, 165; and the Dynamics, 160; and Etiquette Records, 117; and the Fleetwoods, 68; and the Frantics, 70; and Little Bill and the Blue Notes, 73–75; and Big Jay McNeely, 38; and the Ventures, 104–5; and the Wailers, 166

Bolo Records, 39, 108, 171, 241, 245; and the Chanteurs, 139; and the Continentals, 110; and the Dynamics, 160; and the Living End, 208; and the Statics, 165; and the Viceroys, 210, 231

Bonow, Dan, 236

Booker, Sonny, 7

Bootmen (band), 167, 210, 211, 227

Bop City Records (Portland), 40, 185

Borg, Pete, 110, 156

Boss Four (band), 155, 208, 236

"bottle clubs," 8

Bown, Patti, 8

Brashear, Gerald, 7, 18

brawls, 49, 104, 155, 161–62

Breeseman's Resort (pavilion), 60, 104

Bremerton (Washington), 25, 215, 217, 220

Briem, Ray, 70

British Invasion, 202, 203–4, 234, 241, 244

Brittania Tavern (Tacoma), 104

Broadway Record Shop (Tacoma), 35, 40, 45, 51, 52, 88

Broadway Street (Tacoma), 2, 45

Brown, Bud, 34, 148

Brown, James, 24, 31, 52–55, 100, 119, 211, 218

Brown, Vernon, 20

Bucket of Blood (nightclub), 141

Buck Owens and His Bar K Gang (band), 104

Buck Owens' Bar K Jamboree (TV show), 135

Bumbershoot Festival, 243

Bumps Blackwell Junior Band, 8, 10, 11, 15, 20, 55

Bumps Blackwell's Orchestra, 15

Bundy, Evelyn, 7

Bungalow (Cannon Beach teen club), 181

Burger Bowl (Tacoma), 88

Burk, Mike, 58, 81, 116, 118, 119, 134, 154, 157, 216, 242

Burlington (Washington), 94

Burnette, Johnny, 128, 130–32

Burns, Billy, 208

"Busybody" (Dynamics), 207

Butler, Eldon, 108–9, 154–55

Calloway, Cab, 4, 9–10

Camelot Records and Studios, 108, 208, 241, 245

Cameo (band), 238

C&C Distributing Company, 65, 84, 175

Carpenters Union Hall, 150

Cascade Club (Springfield, teen club), 181

Cash, Johnny, 52

Cash Box (magazine), 39, 68–69, 78, 84, 119, 197, 229

Casuals (band), 114, 210

Catholic Youth Organization (CYO) dances, 108, 216

Celestial Records, 37, 42

Central District, Seattle (CD), 4, 8, 25, 44, 111, 144, 159, 162, 207

Paul Bearer and the Hearsemen (band), 227

Paul Revere and the Raiders (album), 193

Paul Revere and the Raiders (band), xiv, 125–27, 136, 181–82, 187, 192, 195–96, 203–4, 205, 209, 229, 243; and Dick Clark, 198–99, 203, 228; corporate influence, 227–30; costume of, 194–95; and dance steps, 138; and "Louie—Go Home," 203, 214, 223; and "Louie Louie," 190–91, 193–94, 196–97, 223; and the Northwest Sound, 225, 226, 231, 240; rivalry with the Kingsmen, 178, 190–91, 202–3; and stage show, 198–99, 209, 212, 224–25, 227–28; and Vietnam, 228–29; and the Wailers, 187

payola, 195

Penguin Records, 108–10, 137

Penthouse (Seattle nightclub), 164, 209

Peppermint Lounge (Seattle), 164–65

Perkins, Lee, 168

Perkins, Wayne, 24

Perl's Ballroom (Bremerton), 217, 220

"Peter Gunn Rock" (Kingsmen), 180

Peter Gunn theme, 143, 180

Peterson, Dick, 197, 206

Peterson, Ron, 42, 103, 155, 175

Pike Place Market, 142, 206

Pink Pussycat (nightclub), 164

Pipkin, Jimmy, 40, 99, 102, 170, 208

Playboys (band), 40–41, 44, 63, 70, 96, 108, 137, 145, 155, 170; and Jimi Hendrix, 150; and "Louie Louie," 43; and the Northwest Sound, 55, 206–7; and recordings, 98–99

Polish Hall (Seattle), 27

Portland (Oregon), 2, 40, 76, 88, 130, 206; Battle of Two Louies, 193; high school rock 'n' roll bands, 180–81; and R&B scene, xi, xii, 178. *See also* Bop City Records; Kingsmen; KISN radio

Portland Bandstand (TV show), 76, 94, 178

Portland Journal, 178

Presley, Elvis, 94, 150, 178, 238

Prohibition, 2, 17

proto-punk rock, 218, 224–27, 240–41

psychedelic rock, 241

"Psycho" (Sonics), 220–21

PTA (Parent-Teacher Association) dances, 89, 172

Pulsations (band), 155, 159–62, 165

punk rock. *See* proto-punk rock

"Purple Haze" (Jimi Hendrix Experience), 235

Puyallup (Washington), 30, 104

Puyallup Indian Hospital, 46

Puyallup Indian Reservation, 49

Pypo Club (Seaside teen club), 181–83, 185–86, 209

Rabb, Luther, 146–47, 151, 154, 207, 236, 238

race relations, 59–60

Raiders. *See* Paul Revere and the Raiders

Rainier Brewery, 242

R&B (rhythm & blues): and the Dynamics, 160; influence on teens, 34; as Northwest Sound, 163; and Paul Revere and the Raiders, 195, 212, 230; and the Statics, 136; and teen clubs, 214; and teen scene, 39, 40, 41, 108–9, 114, 139, 208, 240; and the Viceroys, 170; and the Wailers, 136

Rasmussen, Fred, 39, 97, 170–71, 218

Red Carpet (Tacoma teen club), 181, 217–19

Red Hughes Band, 122–24

Reisdorff, Bob, 65, 67–68, 70, 73–77, 83–84, 98, 103–7

Revere, Paul, 122–27, 181–82, 190, 192, 228–29. *See also* Paul Revere and the Raiders

riot, teenage, 17, 32, 48–49, 62, 117, 183–84, 185, 221

Risley, Bob, 41

"Roadrunner" (Wailers), 72, 78, 125, 187

Roberts, Frank, 2, 22–24, 55, 175

Roberts, Lan, 168, 173, 176, 208

Roberts, Rockin' Robin, 48–49, 51, 76, 210–11; and the Blue Notes, 51, 73–74, 76; and Etiquette Records, 117–18, 215; and "Louie Louie," 185–86; and the Wailers, 111–13, 115–17, 119, 121, 136, 154, 166

Robertson, Doug, 128

Robinson, Ray Charles. *See* Charles, Ray

Robinson, Red, 178

rockabilly, 47, 57, 92, 95, 128, 129, 131–32, 136

"Rock and Roll Radio" (Joe Boot), 37

"Rock around the Clock" (Chuck Berry), 180

"Rockin' Chair Blues" (Maxin Trio), 13

Rocking Kings (band), 148–49, 152–55, 237

Rock 'n' Roll Party (TV show), 29

Rogers, Mike, 169–70, 209

Rolling Stone (magazine), 235, 237

Rolling Stones (band), 204, 211, 228

Rollins, Fred, 148

Romero, Chan, 95, 240

Ron Buford Band, 155

Roosevelt High School, 169

Roslie, Gerry, 217–18, 220

Rotary Boys Club dances, 147

Rouse, Ernie, 99, 102